THE SALEM WITCH TRIALS

THE SALEM WITCH TRIALS

A Reference Guide

K. David Goss

GREENWOOD PRESS
Westport, Connecticut • London

Library of Congress Cataloging-in-Publication Data

Goss, K. David, 1952–
    The Salem witch trials : a reference guide / K. David Goss.
        p. cm.
    Includes bibliographical references and index.
    ISBN 978-0-313-32095-8 (alk. paper)
    1. Trials (Witchcraft)—Massachusetts—Salem—History—17th century. 2.
Witchcraft—Massachusetts—Salem—History—17th century. I. Title.
KFM2478.8.W5G67 2008
133.4′3097445—dc22   2007038695

British Library Cataloguing in Publication Data is available.

Library of Congress Catalog Card Number: 2007038695
ISBN: 978-0-313-32095-8

First published in 2008

Greenwood Press, 88 Post Road West, Westport, CT 06881
An imprint of Greenwood Publishing Group, Inc.
www.greenwood.com

Printed in the United States of America

The paper used in this book complies with the
Permanent Paper Standard issued by the National
Information Standards Organization (Z39.48-1984).

10 9 8 7 6 5 4 3 2 1

To my parents

Contents

Preface

The Salem Witch Trials of 1692 loom large on the landscape of colonial America for several reasons. They represent the largest and last outpouring of antiwitchcraft activity in the British colonies of the Atlantic seaboard. Second, they forever altered the legal process by which trials of this stature would be conducted in North America. Finally, they mark the final chapter of the Puritan oligarchy's control of public affairs in New England. Following the end of this unfortunate episode, popular confidence in religious leaders such as Reverend Cotton Mather waned, while prosperous merchants such as Boston's Thomas Brattle and Robert Calef emerge vindicated for their critical and cautionary writings in higher public esteem than ever before. The trials thus represent a major shift in the power base of Massachusetts Bay Colony, coinciding with a growing secularization of eighteenth-century society and the impact of the Age of Reason.

It is therefore not surprising that the trials have received an enormous amount of scholarly attention throughout the twentieth century. They have been analyzed demographically, theologically, anthropologically, and psychologically. Scholars have attempted to discover how it was that a handful of outspoken adolescent females were able to shake the Essex County community to its very foundations, and what combination of circumstances might have brought about this phenomenon. Academic explanations for their behavior range from economic self-interest on the part of the accusers' parents to the possibility of infection with ergot mold or encephalitis. More recently, writers have suggested such contributing factors as social anxiety concerning nearby Indian wars and the need of Puritan leaders to keep nonconforming women in a constant state of repression. Indeed, creative new interpretations are being advanced each successive year.

My interest in this study began when, as a graduate student at Tufts University, I was required to prepare a critique of Paul Boyer and Stephen Nissenbaum's groundbreaking demographic examination of the economic aspects of the episode, *Salem Possessed*. Subsequent readings and discussions suggested to me that in the final analysis there is no single, overriding answer to the Salem witchcraft episode. Rather, it came about as a consequence of many factors—both internal and external—which cumulatively created a particularly volatile situation which finally exploded in 1692.

What is evident is that those factors which contributed to the Salem episode were not especially unique to Puritanism, or to any other religious belief system or ethnic group. The virulent intolerance of Salem Village had surfaced many times before 1692 and has reappeared in many places and cultures since that time. It lies just below the veneer of our present-day enlightened society. This was the allegorical lesson taught by playwright Arthur Miller in his imaginative version of the Salem witchcraft event known as *The Crucible*, written at the height of the 1950's anticommunist scare brought about by the hearings of Republican Senator Joseph McCarthy's House Committee on Un-American Activities.

It is therefore incumbent upon students of history to learn the lessons of the past and recognize those factors which bring about social crisis if left unchecked. This is perhaps the most important lesson to be learned from the Salem witchcraft episode, that injustice may be met with moral courage to express an opposing opinion in the face of public hostility. In this respect the trials had their heroes who merit praise for their willingness to oppose mismanaged court proceedings and unjust verdicts.

Contemporaries such as Robert Calef, Thomas Brattle, John Proctor, and posthumously, Reverend John Hale, expressed their views that the trials made serious mistakes and that spectral evidence was faulty and legally inadmissible. Later observers from Governor Hutchinson and Charles Upham to John Putnam Demos have described how unfair verdicts were reached on the basis of the most circumstantial proof imaginable.

The purpose of this book is to provide the student of the Salem witchcraft episode with a broad overview of the subject, beginning with early episodes in the later Middle Ages and through the seventeenth century. There has been a concerted effort to place the Salem trials in their proper historical context as an outgrowth of belief systems common to Western Europe, and in particular, precedents that occurred both in Britain and New England in the years leading up to 1692. This text also provides a complete chronological narrative of the Salem episode beginning with the first instance of activity in early 1692 and following events through the end of May 1693 and beyond.

In addition, this book provides the student with a fairly comprehensive overview of the prevailing interpretations of the trials from the earliest historians through the end of the twentieth century. Moreover the text touches upon a selection of those more controversial studies that have added significantly to our understanding of the complexities of the event including the psychological and physiological aspects that should be considered.

It is left to the reader to evaluate the evidence of each argument and draw conclusions concerning causation and explanation. Interestingly, while some historians are in agreement concerning what occurred in Salem in 1692, there is little consensus in their analysis of why these events happened. This is what makes the study of the Salem episode especially intriguing for contemporary students.

Finally, the book features an extensive array of illustrations and photographs that supplement a study of the Salem witchcraft trials, as well as the text of over fifty court-related documents. Also included are an annotated bibliography of important primary and secondary sources that will enable the student to pursue a study of this subject further and a glossary of terms that may be unfamiliar to the novice in seventeenth-century witchcraft examinations. Perhaps most importantly, I have added brief biographies of the most significant persons involved in the episode. These offer the student general background information, providing insight into motives for their actions during this turbulent and tragic event.

Acknowledgments

This book could not have been written without the encouragement and support of my entire family, especially my wife, Becky, and my daughter, Cheri Grishin, who, with her husband, Alexei Grishin, worked tirelessly in organizing endnotes, appendix details, photographs, and securing permissions from museums, libraries, and private collections. For helping with editorial changes and revisions, I want to thank Nicole Rando, teaching assistant of the Gordon College history department, and for help with indexing, Maryellen Smiley, and my daughters Jenny and Bethany.

I would also like to thank John Grimes, former-Chief Librarian, Christine Michelini, Photo Services Manager, and Irene V. Axelrod, Head Manuscript Librarian, James Duncan Phillips Library, Peabody-Essex Museum for their generosity, patience and helpfulness in securing an enormous amount of appendix material. From the New York Public Library, Office of Special Collections, a debt is owed to both Eric Frazier and Wayne Furman for their responsiveness and professional courtesy. To Roberta Zonghi of the Boston Public Library's Department of Rare Books and Manuscripts I am also indebted.

In addition, I would like to thank Danvers town archivists Richard Trask and Kay Pirello who helped to bring together a wide variety of illustrative sources and helped organize the text. For academic insights and informative discussions, I am similarly indebted to Dr. Emerson Baker of Salem State College, Dr. Thomas A. Askew, and Dr. Stephen Alter of the Gordon College history faculty, and my graduate school mentor, Dr. David D. Hall, Harvard Divinity School. My special thanks for reading and critiquing the manuscript at several stages goes to my friend and colleague, Christopher Underation and my inlaws, Dr. David L. Franz, history professor emeritus, Gordon College, and his wife, Dr. Muriel Radke-Franz of the Gordon College department of education. Lastly, for their insights, guidance, understanding, and patience, I wish to thank my editors, Mariah Gumpert of Greenwood Press and Rebecca Edwards of Cadmus.

Chronology

1688	In Boston, Mary "Goody" Glover is convicted of witch craft for tormenting the four children of John Goodwin. Reverend Cotton Mather intervenes successfully and writes a popular book describing the event. The symptoms of the Goodwin children are later mirrored by the afflicted girls of Salem Village.
Nov. 1689	Reverend Samuel Parris and his family move from Boston into the Salem Village parsonage. The family includes his wife, Elizabeth, his daughter, Elizabeth (9), his niece Abigail Williams (11), and two West Indian slaves, John and Tituba Indian.
Feb. 1692	Following several weeks of afternoon fortune-telling sessions with Tituba, Elizabeth Parris and Abigail Williams begin to exhibit strange behavior which, after an examination, is diagnosed by Dr. Griggs, a local physician, as the evil hand of witchcraft.
Feb. 29, 1692	Three accused women, Sarah Good, Sarah Osborne, and Tituba, are brought to Ingersoll's Tavern in Salem Village. Here they are subjected to the first pretrial examinations by magistrate Colonel John Hathorne.
Mar. 19, 1692	Reverend Deodat Lawson, former pastor of Salem Village, returns to observe the pretrial hearings, and watches as Abigail Williams claims to be tormented by the specter of

	Rebecca Nurse. This marks the beginning of accusations against the more respectable citizens of the village.
Mar. 24, 1692	Rebecca Nurse is arrested and brought in for questioning.
Apr. 18, 1692	Mary English, wife of Salem's wealthiest merchant, Philip English, is arrested by Sheriff George Corwin. Later, her husband would also be accused. They would escape jail in Boston and sail to New York, where they remained for a year before returning to Salem.
Apr. 19, 1692	Warrants are issued for the arrest of Giles Cory, Abigail Hobbs, Mary Warren, and Bridget Bishop. Bridget is examined by magistrates John Hathorne and Jonathan Corwin who send her to jail to await trial. She will be the first victim to be executed for witchcraft.
May 10, 1692	Sarah Osborne, one of the first three accused of witchcraft, dies in prison. On this date also, George Jacobs, a prosperous farmer, is arrested for suspicion of witchcraft. Four days later, his pretrial examination will take place.
May 14, 1692	After an absence of five years, Reverend Increase Mather returns to Massachusetts bringing with him a new governor, Sir William Phips, and a new colonial charter from King William and Queen Mary.
May 25, 1692	Governor William Phips commissions a Special Court of Oyer and Terminer to try the witchcraft cases then pending.
May 27, 1692	Governor Phips appoints seven justices to serve on the Court, and names as its Chief Justice, Deputy Governor William Stoughton.
May 31, 1692	Captain John Alden—son of the famous pilgrim father—is arrested. He is imprisoned in Boston, and escapes to New York in late July.
June 10, 1692	Bridget Bishop is hanged on Gallows Hill, Salem. This is the first of the executions to take place during the course of the Salem episode.
June 15, 1692	A report entitled "The Return of Several Ministers" is delivered to Chief Justice Stoughton containing recommendations as to how the trials should be conducted, emphasizing that spectral evidence not be used.
June 29, 1692	Rebecca Nurse is initially found innocent, but the verdict is reversed.
July 19, 1692	Execution day in Salem. The first group of victims—Sarah Good, Rebecca Nurse, Susannah Martin, Elizabeth Howe, and Sarah Wildes—is executed by hanging at Gallows Hill, Salem.

Aug. 5, 1692	George Jacobs, Sr. is brought from the Boston jail to stand trial in Salem. Among those who testify against him is his granddaughter, Margaret, a confessed witch, who later retracts her testimony against Jacobs.
Aug. 19, 1692	Execution day in Salem. The second group of victims— John and Elizabeth Proctor, John Willard, Martha Carrier, and Reverend George Burroughs—would be hanged on Gallows Hill, Salem.
Sept. 9–17	Mary Eastey writes and submits to the Court her famous petition that "no more innocent blood may be shed," and suggests the Court keep the afflicted persons apart and try some of the confessing witches whom she believed to be innocent.
Sept. 19, 1692	Giles Cory is charged with witchcraft and brought to stand trial in Salem. He refuses to enter a plea, an act that prevents his trial under English common law, and he is subjected to the torture of "pressing."
Sept. 22, 1692	Execution day in Salem. The third and final group of witchcraft victims—Martha Cory, Mary Eastey, Alice Parker, Ann Pudeater, Margaret Scott, Wilmot Redd, Samuel Wardwell, and Mary Parker—is executed on Gallows Hill.
Oct. 3, 1692	Influential Boston minister, Reverend Increase Mather, points out the Court's procedural errors in his book, *Cases of Conscience*.
Oct. 8, 1692	Boston merchant Thomas Brattle issues his challenge to the Court in "A Letter to a Reverend Gentleman." In it he questions the wisdom of accepting as reliable the testimony of "afflicted girls."
Oct. 29, 1692	Governor Phips bows to public pressure and criticism and closes the Salem Court of Oyer and Terminer.
Nov. 5, 1692	New accusations are made against three women from Gloucester. These charges are met with a different public response, according to Robert Calef in *More Wonders*: "By this time the validity of such Accusations being much questioned, they found not the encouragement they had done elsewhere, and soon withdrew."
Dec. 14, 1692	The Great and General Court of Massachusetts passes a new law permitting the widow of a condemned witch to keep her dowry and inheritance, which normally would be confiscated by the court. This law also permits a condemned witch to be allowed a Christian burial in hallowed ground and provides for punishments other than death for lesser witchcraft-related crimes.

Jan. 3, 1693   A new Superior Court, presided over by Deputy Gover-
                      nor Stoughton and created by the Massachusetts Great
                      and General Court, meets in Salem. Governor Phips for-
                      bids using spectral evidence, nullifying the testimony of
                      the "afflicted children."

Jan.–Feb. 1693   Deputy Governor Stoughton does not bow to pressure,
                      but persists in trying accused witches. He brings in three
                      more guilty verdicts to be added to those of five others
                      already awaiting execution. Governor Phips grants a stay
                      of execution for all eight prisoners.

May 1693   Governor Phips receives instructions from England to
                      discontinue the trials and put an end to all proceedings.
                      Phips immediately issues a proclamation stopping all
                      further court proceedings against accused witches, and
                      pardons all condemned who are in jail.

1694   Governor Phips is recalled to England to answer charges
                      against him for misappropriation of government funds.
                      He dies in 1695.

Dec. 17, 1696   Acting Governor William Stoughton issues a proclama-
                      tion declaring a colony-wide day of prayer and fasting
                      "so that God's people may offer up fervent supplications
                      [to God] that all iniquity may be put away which hath
                      stirred God's Holy jealousy against this land ... referring
                      to the late tragedy, raised among us by Satan ... through
                      the awful judgment of God."

1

The Origins of Puritan Belief in Witchcraft

The origins of Puritan belief in witchcraft extend back to ancient times. From the early civilization of Mesopotamia, Hammurabi's Code mentions witchcraft as a serious crime and prescribes death as the penalty for practicing it. In a related passage found in the ancient law of the Hebrews, Exodus 22:18, one reads, "Thou shalt not suffer a witch to live." Later in the Bible, the prophet Samuel admonishes King Saul of the Israelites, for seeking the aid of "the Witch of Endor." For this sin God punishes him and his sons with death, and the destruction of his army by Israel's enemy, the Philistines.[1]

In the aforementioned examples, witchcraft was defined as the act of invoking spiritual powers to accomplish a supernatural task—such as placing a curse upon a neighbor or telling the future. To the ancient Israelites, the ability to predict future events was strictly limited to the realm of God (Yahweh) who spoke only through his holy prophets. Any other type of prophesying or fortune-telling was considered a form of witchcraft since it necessitated the establishment of a relationship between a human (a witch) and unholy spiritual powers.[2]

By the time of the New Testament—32 AD to 100 AD—the disciples of Jesus Christ and later Christian theologians incorporated many of the teachings of Old Testament Judaism into Christianity. Among the many ideas adopted was a profound belief in the existence of the invisible spiritual realm of God and his angelic beings which stood in opposition to the spiritual powers of Satan and his army of fallen angels (demons). According to this doctrine, the prize over which these warring spiritual factions struggled was the control of mankind, most especially the souls of every human being.

Like their Judaic brethren, early Christians, who accepted many of the teachings of Old Testament law, continued the belief that humans had the ability to ally themselves with either side of the great spiritual struggle between God and Satan. Those who dedicated themselves to follow Christ's teachings and to further God's kingdom on Earth were regarded as Christians. Conversely, those that voluntarily associated themselves with the forces of spiritual darkness by calling upon satanic powers to harm others or predict the future were regarded as "witches" and spiritual enemies of the church. Early Christian missionaries introduced this theology of spiritual warfare to Western European culture during the first half of the first millennium AD.[3] As the expanding Christian faith encountered indigenous religious beliefs which stood in opposition to the spread of the Gospel, these ancient, pantheistic religions were identified by missionaries as responsible for unwittingly invoking Satanic spiritual power. During the Dark Ages (500–900 AD) the ideas of witchcraft held by Judeo-Christians came to be considered synonymous with non-Christian, European pagan rituals and cultural traditions.[4]

By the Middle Ages (1000–1300 AD) the Roman Catholic Church had established itself as the dominant faith from Italy in the south to Scandinavia in the north and from Ireland in the west to the Slavic states of the east. In all these regions, accusations of witchcraft against individuals and small groups occasionally took place. The medieval definition of a sorcerer or witch, as found in Jean Bodin's *De la Demonornanie des Sorciers* (1580), is as follows: "A sorcerer or witch is one who by commerce with the Devil has a full intention of attaining his own ends." This description clearly implies that witches are not "born" with magical powers, but must voluntarily enter into a personal relationship with Satan in order to be given supernatural ability to work evil.[5] Often witchcraft trials in ecclesiastical courts presided over by church-appointed justices followed these outbreaks. During medieval judicial proceedings, torture was sometimes used as a means of extracting information concerning witchcraft, and confessions of witchcraft were not uncommon.[6]

Historical evidence seems to indicate that while there may have been a few individuals who actually sought to practice what, by definition, would be considered true or malicious witchcraft (attempting to worship or invoke Satan in order to cause harm) most of the suspected witches were not guilty of any intentional wrongdoing. Some were accused because they clung to earlier vestiges of pagan traditions, frowned upon by Christian authorities, while many others were wrongfully suspected of having invoked spiritual powers to harm their neighbors when unexplainable, tragic events took place.

As the Middle Ages drew to a close there were steadily increasing incidences of individuals and occasionally groups being accused, tried, and executed for the crime of witchcraft. Often these trials and executions were public events well attended by the local populace. For example, at a French execution of witches in 1460, between six and eight thousand people were in attendance. The popularity of such tragic events only served to further ingrain the idea of "witchcraft as a real and common threat to society" in the popular culture of Western Europe.

By the late Middle Ages, both secular and church courts condemned and prosecuted all practices and teachings that might be considered threatening or suspicious. One of the primary legal weapons wielded by these courts to prosecute alleged witches was the *Malleus Maleficarum*, or *Hammer of the Witches*, written and published by Heinrich Kramer and Jacob Sprenger, two Dominican monks. Both were university professors appointed by Pope Innocent VIII as the Chief Inquisitors of the Holy Inquisition in northern German provinces. Their task was to ferret out witches and heretics. The *Hammer of the Witches* is often cited as the primary authority on providing guidelines for how such persons might be discovered, tried, and condemned. Both Cotton and Increase Mather, Boston ministers involved in the Salem episode, were very familiar with its contents and referred to it in their writings.[7]

The full extent of European witchcraft trials and executions will never be known, except it is quite clear that they were widespread and involved many thousands of people. In addition to large numbers of eyewitness accounts of executions, there were also untold numbers of accused and condemned. Although most official estimates are approximate, the toll of European witchcraft victims was undoubtedly high, perhaps in the millions. Recent studies have indicated that throughout the provinces of Germany, a total of over one hundred thousand witchcraft executions took place between 1500 and 1700. Some historians claim that the casualty rates in Italy and Spain during the same period were so incredibly high—mixed with Inquisition deaths of Jews and Protestants also condemned for heresy—that no accurate estimate of the total is possible.[8] The area around what is now known as the British Isles was also caught up in this two-hundred-year-long turmoil of anti-witchcraft sentiment. Even though King Henry VIII—by virtue of the Act of Supremacy— officially made England "Protestant," belief in witchcraft, witches, Satan, and the spiritual powers of good and evil were no less real to English Protestants than to their Roman Catholic counterparts.

Virtually everyone who lived in Europe from the earliest times to the beginning of the eighteenth century had a general belief in the existence of witchcraft. Some doubted, like seventeenth-century British philosopher Thomas Hobbes, that witchcraft actually worked, but he nonetheless knew it to exist and that it was a belief system practiced by a minority of humans. Concerning his assessment of witchcraft, Hobbes believed that those who claimed to be witches would be justly punished for their false beliefs, considering these immoral practices to be closer to a new religion rather that a craft or science.[9]

Hobbes was not alone among British skeptics who took a pragmatic view concerning witchcraft. A number of writers produced books that, while never doubting the existence of people who claimed to be witches, questioned the functional ability of witchcraft to actually achieve its evil goals. The earliest of these writers was Reginald Scot who, in *The Discovery of Witchcraft* (1584), noted that witchcraft was usually unsuccessful when attempted by its alleged practitioners. He argued that most "witches" were, in fact, frauds and that the methods employed in English courts to discover persons suspected of "witchcraft" were so unreliable that no person should be condemned to death as a result.[10] A number of English writers including Thomas Ady (1655), John Wagstaffe (1669), and John Webster (1677) also questioned the practical and literal reality of witchcraft. Despite this skepticism the actual number of cases of witchcraft accusations and executions continued to rise throughout the seventeenth century.[11]

Some scholars still believed in the efficacy of witches during the last years of Queen Elizabeth I's reign, including Reverend William Perkins, a Calvinist theologian from Cambridge University, who argued that the sin of witchcraft "ought as sharply to be punished as in former times; and all Witches ... ought, according to the Law of Moses, be put to death" for making a compact with Satan and renouncing God.[12] Perkins's *Discourse on the Damned Art of Witchcraft* eventually became "a classic on the shelves of every Puritan minister."[13]

During this time England employed the activities of "witch finders." Self-styled witch-finder General Matthew Hopkins and his colleague, John Stearne, "discovered" many who became victims of the greatest witch-hunt in England's history. Recent historical data estimates the number of witchcraft-related executions in England between the years 1640 and 1660 to be about 30,000, while in less populous Scotland estimates of witchcraft-related deaths are estimated at about 4,000 during the same time period.[14]

In England there were also many unofficial witch-finders, or people who simply believed themselves to have been bewitched, but had recovered from the curse or spell. Having met and overcome "The Evil One," these individuals were believed to be especially sensitive to the workings of Satan and his minions, and adept in the identification of witches amongst the local population. In the early days of England's witch-frenzy, such amateur witch-finders volunteered to go from parish to parish to help local officials and concerned citizens to cleanse a community. The more dangerous witch-finders were paid for their services. Some were paid per town, but occasionally, professional witch-finders were paid a fee for every "witch" they discovered.[15]

A large number of pamphlets and books describing legal cases of persons accused of witchcraft were published in England throughout the seventeenth century. The literature on the subject of witchcraft was extensive and popular among the English reading public. Because of its widespread popularity, it is quite likely that many Puritans living in New England were also familiar with the most publicized witchcraft episodes. This had a direct impact upon both how the trials would be conducted in Salem, and the credibility given to Salem's own group of witch-finders—the so-called "afflicted children."[16]

It should also be noted that, from the second decade of settlement, the residents of colonial New England not only shared a belief in witchcraft with their European counterparts, but also continued the tradition of accusing and occasionally executing suspected witches. As each colony developed its own code of laws, the treatment of witchcraft was incorporated into the colonial legal system. In Plymouth Colony in 1636, communication with the devil through witchcraft was an offense liable for death, but in Massachusetts Bay Colony in 1641 and Connecticut Colony in 1642, the statute simply stated that if any person was a witch or consulted with a familiar spirit, they were to be put to death.[17]

New England's first execution for witchcraft occurred in the Colony of Connecticut with the hanging of Alice Young of Windsor, Connecticut, at Hartford on May 26, 1647. In the following year on Boston Common, midwife Margaret Jones was the first person to be hanged for witchcraft in

Massachusetts Bay Colony.[18] What makes Margaret Jones's case of particular interest is that the young Reverend John Hale, later a colleague of Reverend Samuel Parris of Salem Village and participant in the Salem witchcraft episode, visited Margaret Jones in prison immediately prior to her execution in 1648. Her final hours must have made an indelible impression upon Hale as he included his firsthand account of the event in his book, *A Modest Inquiry into the Nature of Witchcraft*, almost fifty years later. In it he notes that she refused to confess to being a witch, and maintained until her death that she was wholly innocent of such evils.[19]

Recent scholarship has examined these non-Salem cases and discovered that the great majority of them conclude with the accused being either found innocent or escaping the hangman's noose in some other way. Only a few— recent estimates place the number of executions at about sixteen—actually resulted in public execution.[20] Among the most well-known of these New England witchcraft cases are the following: Mary and Hugh Parsons, Springfield, Massachusetts (1651); Elizabeth Godman, New Haven, Connecticut (1655); Ann Hibbins, Boston (1656); Winifred and Mary Holman, Cambridge, Massachusetts (1659–1660); The Hartford Witchcraft Trials (1662–1665); Elizabeth Knapp, Groton, Massachusetts (1672); Mary Webster, Hadley, Massachusetts (1684); and Mary Glover, Boston (1688).

Mary and Hugh Parsons (1651) were a contentious couple who were constantly at odds with each other and their neighbors. In 1649, Mary accused one of her neighbors of witchcraft, and when the accusation proved false she was whipped and fined for defamation of character. She next accused her husband, Hugh, of witchcraft involving the deaths of their two sons in 1651. Hugh was ultimately found guilty, but the Great and General Court of Massachusetts refused to accept the verdict. In May 1651, Mary herself was indicted for witchcraft and afterward for the murder of a female child. She was found innocent of witchcraft in spite of her confession, but convicted of infanticide and condemned to hang. It appears that she may have died in prison, but not before creating a furor that spread throughout the colony.[21] In Hale's *A Modest Inquiry into the Nature of Witchcraft*, the elderly witchhunter provides a detailed narrative of Mary Parsons' crime and conviction as an example of a woman who confessed to witchcraft and "was the only confessor in these times in this government."[22]

Elizabeth Godman (1655) vehemently defended herself against the charges of witchcraft that were leveled by many of her neighbors in 1653 and again in 1655. She was accused of causing the illness and deaths of innocent people and livestock, and the fact that she was not a member of the New Haven church was also likely a detriment to her case. As would later occur in the Salem trials, her accusers made a direct connection between instances when they had refused to help her and "accidents" that would strangely occur immediately thereafter. Although Elizabeth was ultimately found innocent, the court grudgingly released her from prison but warned her by saying that the grounds of suspicion against her were clear and strong, though not sufficient as of yet to take away her life.[23]

Anne Hibbins (1656) was censured by Boston church leaders for her contentious behavior in repeatedly accusing a local craftsman of overcharging for his labor. She was furthermore charged with supplanting her husband's position in dealing with this problem, violating the Puritan belief that wives should submit themselves to the leadership of their husbands. For this offense she was unrepentant. She was removed from membership in the Boston church and found guilty of witchcraft in 1654 after the death of her husband. Although the magistrates denied the initial verdict, a second trial was held before the Massachusetts Great and General Court. Anne Hibbins was convicted a second time of witchcraft and executed in 1656. In his assessment of this tragedy, Governor Thomas Hutchinson, in his *History of Massachusetts*, places the blame for this conviction upon the people of Boston who disliked Anne Hibbins' contentious nature. He wrote that the trial and condemnation of Anne Hibbins for witchcraft was a "most remarkable occurrence in the colony," for he found that it was her temper and argumentative nature that caused her neighbors to accuse her of being a witch.[24]

In 1659, John Gibson and his married daughter, Rebecca Stearns of Cambridge, Massachusetts, complained against widow Winifred Holman and her daughter, Mary. The charge that Rebecca and her young son were being afflicted by the Holmans resulted in their arrest by magistrate Thomas Danforth. In the following pretrial examination no evidence was uncovered to justify an indictment for witchcraft, and the case was dismissed. In retaliation, the Holman mother and daughter jointly filed a lawsuit in 1660 against John Gibson and his daughter for defamation of character. Rebecca Stearns was exonerated, but the jury required John Gibson to publicly apologize and pay a fine. The case underscores the legal precedent in Massachusetts Bay Colony of allowing those found innocent of the charge of witchcraft to seek reparations from their accusers.[25]

Perhaps the only New England witchcraft episode approaching Salem's in terms of intensity was the series of accusations, trials, and executions that took place in the area around Hartford, Connecticut, between 1662 and 1665. A Hartford woman named Anne Cole, with the eventual support of her neighbors, claimed that two other women, Rebecca Greensmith and Elizabeth Seager, were tormenting her by means of diabolic forces. Later, a Hartford couple attributed the death of their eight-year-old daughter to the evil hand of witchcraft, accusing another neighbor known as Goodwife Ayers. When William Ayers was questioned in conjunction with his wife, he in turn accused Rebecca Greensmith of consorting with Satan. Rebecca not only confessed to having made a compact with the devil, but also implicated her husband and six other neighbors as members of her coven of witches. The resulting morass of trials and executions created a remarkable stir throughout Connecticut and beyond. At the conclusion of this ordeal, a full report of the incident was written by Hartford's Reverend John Whiting and sent to Reverend Increase Mather of Boston. This event, which resulted in four executions, influenced the elder Mather's attitude concerning the literal dangers of witchcraft as socially deviant behavior and the use of spectral evidence in identifying suspects.[26]

Another case, which in some ways mirrors the later events of Salem Village, involved a sixteen-year-old girl named Elizabeth Knapp who lived, in 1671, as a servant in the household of Reverend Samuel Willard, the minister of Groton, Massachusetts. Elizabeth began to act in an unusual way—with violent fits, barking like a dog, and speaking in a sinister voice insulting Reverend Willard. The local physician, unable to find anything physically wrong with Elizabeth, attributed her malady to a "diabolical" distemper. Following this diagnosis, Reverend Willard questioned and observed Elizabeth in the company of witnesses and produced a lengthy essay entitled, *A Brief Account of a Strange and Unusual Providence of God Befallen to Elizabeth Knapp of Groton*—a copy of which was found among the papers of Increase and Cotton Mather. First printed in its entirety in 1883, it provides an account of Elizabeth's behavior which is strangely similar in many ways to the descriptions of the afflicted children in Salem Village twenty years later.[27]

> The next day she was in a strange frame ... sometimes weeping, sometimes laughing and [making] many foolish and apish gestures. In the evening, going into the cellar, she shrieked suddenly and being inquired of the cause, she answered, that she saw two persons in the cellar; whereupon some went down with her to search, but found none; ... afterwards (the same evening) ... she was suddenly thrown down into the midst of the floor with violence, and taken with a violent fit, whereupon the whole family was raised, and with much ado was kept out of the fire from destroying herself.[28]

As with the Salem Village afflicted children, Elizabeth followed her bizarre behavior with a statement of explanation that agreed with the physician's assessment: that the devil would oftentimes appear to her, presenting her with a book written with blood of covenants. The statement claimed that the devil would urge her with constant temptations to murder her parents, her neighbors, offering her all the things that suit a youth's fancy—money, silks, fine clothes—in exchange for her soul.[29]

Unlike the Salem outbreak, in Groton, Elizabeth Knapp was the only afflicted child to "cry out against" alleged witches, whose names were kept anonymous in Willard's narrative. Only one individual was brought in for questioning, but her name was cleared. After that day, Elizabeth was never tormented by the devil, and the outbreak came to an end.[30]

The Groton case was kept under tight control. Despite a later confession that Elizabeth had signed the Devil's Book in her own blood, the episode was brought to a quiet end without any executions because of Elizabeth's sincere repentance, and her declaration of a desire to rely on the power and mercy of God in Christ only.

Throughout the five months that the episode took place, the Groton community supported Reverend Willard in his efforts to ascertain the truth concerning Elizabeth Knapp. Pastor Willard, conversely was judicious in not allowing Elizabeth's testimony to be taken as unquestioned truth since, as he said, "Whether she have covenanted with the Devil or no; I think this is a case unanswerable, her declarations have been so contradictory, one to another, that we know not what to make of them ..." In the final analysis, no one at Groton was punished since the testimony of the "afflicted" was regarded as unreliable.[31]

In early 1683, a Hadley, Massachusetts, resident, Mary Webster, was charged with witchcraft and examined by the Hampshire County magistrates in Northampton on March 23, 1683. Her case ultimately reached the Court of Assistants in Boston which found her innocent in June. Although cleared of the charge, she appears to have been regarded by her neighbors as a potential threat to their safety. The following year, when one of Hadley's leading citizens, Philip Smith, became grievously ill under mysterious circumstances, local rumor places the blame upon Mary Webster. As a result of this suspicion, according to Governor Thomas Hutchinson, "a number of brisk lads tried an experiment upon the old woman. Having dragged her out of her house, they hung her up until she was near dead, let her down, rolled her sometime in the snow, and at last buried her in it and there left her, but it happened that she survived and the melancholy man [Smith] died." Mary Webster died of natural causes in 1696.[32]

The last case of diabolical possession to take place in Massachusetts, only four years prior to the Salem outbreak, was an episode involving an Irish laundress named Mary Glover (1688). She was accused of tormenting by witchcraft four children of Boston stonemason John Goodwin. As in other cases, when the children first exhibited behavior of an abnormal nature, their own minister, Reverend Charles Morton of Charlestown, Massachusetts, was asked to intervene, as were several other Boston area clergy including Reverend Cotton Mather.[33]

Reverend Cotton Mather (1663–1728). One of Boston's most influential ministers and son of Reverend Increase Mather, his excellent reputation as a religious leader and theological scholar was damaged by his involvement with the Salem trials, which he supported. Later in his life he would be plagued by feelings of guilt, bitterness, and self-doubt concerning his role in the witchcraft episode. Courtesy Danvers Archival Center, Danvers, Mass.

The torment of the Goodwin children was precipitated by the accusation by thirteen-year-old Martha Goodwin that the family's laundress, Mary Glover's daughter, was stealing linen. Immediately following this confrontation, the young Martha and later three of her siblings were stricken with severe fits and "exquisite pain" throughout their bodies, and for several weeks "labored under the direful effects of a stupendous witchcraft."[34]

Prior to the formal accusation of Mary Glover, the Boston clergy and neighbors gathered at the Goodwin house to pray for the children. When this did not cure their torments, charges were placed against Mary Glover, who had a reputation of being "an ignorant and a scandalous old woman." Within a short time both Mary and her daughter were arrested and jailed. Since the Goodwin children only suffered their symptoms inside their house, they were sent to live with neighboring families.

During the course of her trial, Mary Glover freely confessed to having practiced black magic by making "poppets" of her victims and harming the dolls. She also confessed to having made a bargain with the devil, claiming to have been given special malicious powers in exchange for her eternal soul. Unlike the case of Elizabeth Knapp, Glover was defiant and unrepentant, confessing to the sins of witchcraft rather than the denial of her guilt. The court produced several objects that Mary would have used in tormenting the children, such as puppets and rags stuffed with goat's hair; Glover would even confess to the courts that the way to torment the objects of her malice was to wet her finger with her spittle and stroke the little images.[35]

Reverend Mather stated that he had visited Glover in her cell after her conviction, and attempted to pray with her and turn her away from the devil and give "herself to the Lord Jesus Christ." "I asked her whether she would consent or desire to be prayed for; to that she said, if prayer would do her any good, she could pray for herself. And when it was again propounded, she said, she could not unless her spirits (or angels) would give her leave. However, against her will I prayed with her, which if it was a fault it were in excess of pity." She was hanged for witchcraft on November 16, 1688.[36]

At the conclusion of this case, Reverend Mather was left with a puzzle as yet unresolved. Glover said that upon her death the Goodwin children would not be relieved for there were others who had their hand in witchcraft as well. Thus "it came to pass accordingly, that the three children continued in their furnace as before, and it grew seven times hotter than it was."

Unlike the Salem episode, these afflicted children were unable to name those responsible for their torment. As winter turned toward spring of 1689, the Goodwin children, two of whom came to live with Reverend Mather and his family, began to show signs of improvement. The case of Boston's most notable confessed witch was closed. No further suspects were brought in for questioning, and Reverend Cotton Mather took the opportunity to write his popular book, *Memorable Providences, Relating to Witchcrafts and Possessions*, in which the Goodwin children were featured as main characters in what historian John Putnam Demos calls, "a local best-seller."[37] It would be interesting to know the names of the book titles contained in the library of Reverend Samuel Parris three years later. Even if the latest Cotton Mather publication were not present, it is quite likely that its contents had been discussed and were well known to the members of the Parris household. It was a local witchcraft episode that could not help but be remembered when Salem's outbreak began. What is of particular note is that while Mary Glover confessed when charged with witchcraft and was executed, Tituba and many others likewise confessed in 1692, all escaping with their lives and leaving those who protested their innocence to hang.

NOTES

1. *The Bible,* King James Verson, Book of Exodus: chapter 22, verse 18, Book of First Samuel: chapter 28, verses 8–20. See also: D. Winton Thomas, ed., *Documents from Old Testament Times* (New York: Harpers, 1961), 29. "If a citizen has indicted another citizen for sorcery and does not substantiate the charge, the one who is indicted for sorcery shall go to the river and throw himself in. If the river overwhelms him, his indictor shall take away his house. If the river exculpates that citizen, and he is preserved, the one who indicted him for sorcery shall die, and the one who threw himself into the river shall take away his house." Also: Montague Summers, *The History of Witchcraft and Demonology* (New York: University Books, 1956), 173. "Yet it is noteworthy that from the very earliest period the attitude of the inspired writers toward magic and related practices is almost wholly condemnatory and uncompromisingly hostile."

2. Summers, *The History of Witchcraft and Demonology*, 178–79. Gives an excellent and detailed discourse on the confrontation between King Saul and the Witch of Endor, explaining why the witch was in fear of punishment for divination and necromancy.

3. Alan C. Kors and Edward Peters, eds., *Witchcraft in Europe, 1100–1700: A Documentary History* (Philadelphia: University of PA Press, 1972), 6–7. How this transition came about is discussed in Kors and Peters's introduction: "The early Christians had inherited an eclectic unorganized theory of the power of evil in the world. Satan had appeared infrequently in the Old Testament where he was depicted occasionally as a tempter of mankind, but more usually as an obedient, accusing angel (Book of Job) in particular service to God. In the Jewish apocrypha, however, more imbued as it was with the themes of Eastern dualism, the Devil often was presented as the casual agent of all that is evil, a spirit in active rebellion against God. It is this latter concept that emerged as dominant in the New Testament—coupled with the unswerving promise of Christ's ultimate triumph over him. In this role, Satan tempted both Judas and Christ. St. Paul logically warned the Christian congregations of the powers and wiles of this archfiend in his "Epistle to the Ephesians" became the fundamental scriptural proof of diabolical character and intentions."

4. Summers, *The History of Witchcraft and Demonology*, 111–12. Illustrates the many pagan and pre-Christian traditions that were later associated with satanic witchcraft and those holidays later integrated into the Church calendar.

5. Summers, *The History of Witchcraft and Demonology*, 1.

6. Henrich Kramer and Jacob Sprenger, *Malleus Maleficarium*, trans. by Montague Summers, in *Witchcraft in Europe, 1100–1700: A Documentary History*, 113–94. This contains a detailed chronicle of how confessions of witchcraft were extracted from alleged witches including details of witchcraft ceremonies and acts of magic.

7. Kors and Peters, *Witchcraft in Europe, 1100–1700: A Documentary History*, 105–89. From selected sections of the *Hammer of the Witches*.

8. Mary Ann Hester Barry, and Gareth Roberts, eds. *Witchcraft in Early Modern Europe: Studies in Culture and Belief* (Cambridge: Cambridge University Press, 1996),

81–86. This examines particularly the witch trials and numerous executions in Switzerland and Germany. Also see: Kors and Peters, *Witchcraft in Europe, 1100–1700: A Documentary History*, 190–280. This collection of essays covers persecutions of alleged witches in Lombardy, Geneva, Trier, Scotland, England, Bonn, France, and other European locations.

   9. Thomas Hobbes, *Leviathan* (Cambridge: Cambridge University Press, 1991), 18, 300, 303–4, 422–24.

   10. Kors and Peters, *Witchcraft in Europe, 1100–1700: A Documentary History*, 314–31. Reginald Scot raised his voice in skeptical opposition to episodes like the notorious witch executions of the Assizes in Essex, England, by publishing his *Discoverie of Witchcraft* in 1584. He was a hundred years ahead of his time in calling upon educated men to rethink their views concerning witchcraft in the light of rational thought.

   11. Barry and Roberts, eds. *Witchcraft in Early Modern Europe: Studies in Culture and Belief*, 65, 168n, 260n, 282n.

   12. Ibid., 148, 187, 198n, 203.

   13. Ibid.

   14. Ibid., 194n.

   15. Christina Hole, *A Mirror of Witchcraft* (London: Chatto and Windus, Ltd., 1957), 37–38. Ms. Hole notes that as witchfinders, English towns of the Cromwellian era often used children with "spectral sight." This practice set a precedent which would soon be transferred to Puritan New England.

   16. Ibid., 163–65.

   17. George Lincoln Burr, *Narratives of the Witchcraft Cases 1648–1706* (Barnes & Noble, 1914), 381.

   18. David D. Hall, *Witch-Hunting in Seventeenth-Century New England: A Documentary History 1638–1693* (Boston: Northeastern University Press, 1991), 21–23.

   19. Reverend John Hale, *A Modest Inquiry into the Nature of Witchcraft* (Boston, 1702), 17.

   20. John Putnam Demos, *Entertaining Satan: Witchcraft and the Culture of Early New England* (London: Oxford University Press, 1982), 10, 11.

   21. Ibid., 88–89, 292–96. Also: Hall, *Witch-Hunting in Seventeenth-Century New England*, 29–60.

   22. Hale, *A Modest Inquiry into the Nature of Witchcraft*, 17.

   23. John M. Taylor, *The Witchcraft Delusion in Colonial Connecticut* (New York: The Grafton Press, 1908), 85–96. Also: *New Haven Colonial Records*, Vol. 2, 151–52.

   24. Demos, *Entertaining Satan*, 64, 75, 87–88, 91, 286.

   25. Hall, *Witch-Hunting in Seventeenth-Century New England*, 134.

   26. Ibid., 147–63.

   27. Reverend Samuel Williard, *A Brief Account of a Strange and Unusual Providence of God Befallen to Elizabeth Knapp of Groton*, in Samuel A. Green's, *Groton in the Witchcraft Times*, (Hartford, 1883).

   28. Ibid. Also: Hall, *Witch-Hunting in Seventeenth-Century New England*, 198.

   29. Williard, *A Brief Account of a Strange and Unusual Providence of God Befallen Elizabeth Knapp of Groton*, in Hall's *Witch-Hunting in Seventeenth-Century New England*, 200.

   30. Ibid., 204–5.

   31. Ibid., 206.

   32. Thomas Hutchinson, *History of the Colony and Province of Massachusetts Bay*. Quoted in: Hall, *Witch-Hunting in Seventeenth-Century New England*, 264.

   33. Demos, *Entertaining Satan*, 71, 75, 280. Also: Carol F. Karlsen, *The Devil in the Shape of a Woman*: Witchcraft in Colonial New England (New York: W. W. Norton & Co., 1987), 33–35, 51, 233, 244, 260.

34. Cotton Mather, *Memorable Providences*, quoted in Hall's, *Witch-Hunting in Seventeenth-Century New England*, 267.

35. Ibid., 270.

36. Ibid., 272.

37. Ibid., 275.

2

The Accusations

In 1626, Roger Conant and a remnant of settlers from the failed Dorchester Company fishing station on Cape Ann, Massachusetts, moved farther south along the coast and established the village of Naumkeag, a community that would soon be renamed Salem. After years of struggling to survive in a hostile environment, most of the Dorchester colonists fled to Virginia, while others returned to England. Conant and his "old planters" refused to retreat. Instead, they constructed shoreline hovels near their fish drying stages and ventured seaward in their one-masted vessels.

By 1628, the London-based Massachusetts Bay Company had acquired the property and land rights of the Dorchester Company and dispatched John Endicott to serve as resident governor. His task was to prepare Massachusetts Bay Colony for the arrival of thousands of English Puritans fleeing the repression of an unsympathetic monarchy and an antagonistic Anglican Church. In September of that year, Endicott arrived at Naumkeag and chose to remain near the village established by Conant. By 1629, the new governor had changed the name of the settlement to "Salem"—the Anglicized word for *shalom* meaning "peace."

However peace would never be a characteristic of this community. Throughout the seventeenth century, Salem was the scene of many conflicts and controversies. Endicott was soon replaced when Governor John Winthrop arrived on June 12, 1630. Winthrop, displeased with Endicott's choice of location, immediately sought and found a better locale to serve as the capital of Massachusetts Bay Colony. By August, he had established a new capital at Boston and settled the neighboring communities of Charlestown and Cambridge (New Town). From this point onward, Salem would be reduced to the role of a commercial and political rival to the port of Boston.[1]

Throughout the seventeenth century, the population of Salem expanded as thousands of Puritan immigrants arrived. Indeed by 1640 more than forty thousand English colonists had relocated to Massachusetts Bay Colony. As coastal communities became increasingly overcrowded, land became scarce, and colonists began to move inland to establish farming communities. One such inland farming community—a direct outgrowth of Salem town—was Salem Village, located only five miles from the seaport.

Salem Village, although considered a part of Salem town proper, had been granted semi-independent status when it constructed its first meetinghouse and hired its first minister in 1672. Prior to this, all residents of the village were members of the First Church in Salem, and made the long journey to Salem town every Sunday (called the Sabbath) for meeting. As with all Massachusetts towns at this time, it was the ability to support a church and a minister that was the first and most important step to attaining complete independence from the mother community.

Early Drawing of the Salem Village Meeting House (1673–1701). In this structure, which was located in Salem Village rather that directly in the town of Salem itself, the later ministers of the village congregation preached, including Reverend George Burroughs (1680), Reverend Deodat Lawson (1688), and finally, Reverend Samuel Parris (1689). Courtesy Danvers Archival Center, Danvers, Mass.

The first minister of Salem Village was Reverend James Bayley, soon followed by Reverend George Burroughs. Neither of these two ministers was
able to live on the very small salary (sixty pounds per year) offered by the
village parishioners. Both resigned their positions over financial difficulties
with their congregation.

The third minister, Reverend Deodat Lawson, came from Boston and
served as pastor from 1684 until 1688. Like his two predecessors, Lawson ran
into some problems with the Salem Village congregation, who tended to be
irritable and stingy in their dealings. The Salem Village Church was also
being torn apart by two groups, each of whom wanted control of the pulpit.
The result was that much of the congregation rejoined the First Church in
Salem rather than remain in such a contentious church.[2]

In 1689, the Salem Village Church hired its fourth pastor, Reverend Samuel
Parris. A Harvard dropout, Parris had first attempted to follow his father's
profession as a West Indies merchant, but when his maritime trading business failed he returned to Massachusetts to make use of his college training
in theology and become a minister. He began this new career by guest-
preaching at several Boston area churches, until he finally secured a pastoral
invitation from the Salem Village Church. He accepted the position for sixty-
six pounds per year (a slight raise compared to those before him) with part
of that sum to be paid in farm produce and firewood. The Salem Village congregation also gave Parris "and his heirs" the village parsonage and barn as
well as two acres of land.[3]

To the parsonage Reverend Parris brought his wife, Elizabeth, his eleven-
year-old niece, Abigail Williams, his nine-year-old daughter, Elizabeth
(called "Betty"), and a slave couple he had brought from the West Indies,
John and Tituba Indian. Recent historical studies indicate that one or both of
these slaves were likely not of African descent but were actually Carib or
Arawak Indians, original inhabitants of the Caribbean islands. Owning a
domestic servant was a major advantage for Mrs. Parris who could accompany her husband on his daily visits to local parishioners since she was not
needed for the household chores.[4]

By the winter of 1691–92, the two children of the Parris home were in need
of a diversion from the dullness of daily domestic activities and study. Thus
they began to meet with Tituba in the afternoons during Reverend and Mrs.
Parris's absence. Tituba would entertain Elizabeth and Abigail with stories
from her native Barbados, particularly with her knowledge of folk magic. In
time, the secret afternoon sessions with Tituba became increasingly popular
with a few other young women from the Salem Village parish including Ann
Putnam, Jr. (age 12), Elizabeth Hubbard (age 18), Mary Warren (age 17),
Mercy Lewis (age 19), Elizabeth Booth (age 16), Susannah Sheldon (age 18),
and Mary Walcott (age 16). It was this group of girls—along with several
other women such as Ann Putnam, Sr., Sarah Bibber, Mrs. Gertrude Pope,
and Elizabeth Churchill—who would come to be known during the witchcraft trials as "the afflicted girls." Ultimately, they would accuse or "cry out
against" nearly two hundred individuals with charges of witchcraft, providing much of the spectral evidence and testimony during the trials and pre-
trial examinations.

Portrait of Reverend Samuel Parris (c. 1685). The only known image of Reverend Samuel Parris, this miniature portrait was discovered recently by archivist Richard B. Trask while researching the Salem witchcraft trials among the collection of the Massachusetts Historical Society. It shows Parris at a time when he may well have been enjoying short-lived success as a West Indian merchant, prior to his arrival at Salem Village. Samuel Parris, c. 1685 (oil on card) by American School (seventeenth century), Massachusetts Historical Society, Boston/Bridgeman Art Library.

As to exactly what activities transpired at Tituba's sessions in the Parris parsonage, little specific information remains. According to Beverly minister Reverend John Hale a spell was cast to foretell the identity of some of the girls' future husbands. This was accomplished by suspending an egg white in a clear glass of water, then holding it up to the light of a candle to discern the face that would appear. One of the girls claimed that instead of a face, she saw the shape of a coffin. This declaration brought an immediate end to the fortune-telling gatherings and resulted in some of the girls having convulsive fits and nightmares.[5]

It should be remembered that in Judeo-Christian theology, the practice of magic—even folk magic and fortune-telling—was strictly forbidden because such information was believed to come only from Satanic spiritual powers. The girls were well aware that what they were doing was considered wrong, so it would not be surprising to them that their secret behavior resulted in evil consequences.

Eventually, the convulsions and seizures of the "afflicted girls" could not be kept from the eyes of concerned parents. Betty Parris, for example, began to stare blankly into space as if in a hypnotic trance. This trance-like state would be followed by more strange behavior such as crawling upon the floor on all fours, barking like a dog, and making choking sounds. Soon Abigail Williams began to follow the behavior pattern of her young cousin.

A vivid description of these afflictions is provided by a contemporary observer, Robert Calef, in his commentary on the episode. He writes in his *More Wonders of the Invisible World* that: "They began to act in a strange and unusual manner by getting into holes and creeping under chairs and stools, and to use sundry odd postures and antic gestures, uttering foolish, ridiculous speeches, which neither they themselves, nor any others could make sense of."[6] From late December to February 1692, these strange activities continued to cause great concern on the part of the girls' parents and the elders of the community.

Finally the local physician, Dr. William Griggs, was called and declared after a thorough examination of Betty Parris and Abigail Williams that he could find nothing physically wrong with them. His diagnosis was that the girls' behavior was the result of a spell and that they were under the force and power of the "evil hand" of witchcraft. In response to this, Reverend Parris called for a meeting of ministers from the neighboring parishes to pray for the girls' spiritual healing. They also held several private fasts and prayer meetings both publicly and at the Parris's home. In spite of these sincere efforts in appealing to God to restore the girls to normalcy, their condition only worsened. The ministers concluded that the girls were indeed bewitched, and that it would be necessary to discover *who* was tormenting them.

The girls were questioned repeatedly by the frustrated Parris as to who might be responsible for their torment. In an effort to alleviate their suffering, Tituba and John Indian followed the advice of Mary Sibley, a member of Parris's congregation, by secretly collecting some of the girls' urine, baking it into a rye cake, and feeding it to the Parris family dog in an attempt to pass the affliction of the children to the animal.[7]

When this experiment in folk magic was discovered by Reverend Parris, he was outraged and physically whipped Tituba for practicing magic in his home. He then preached a sermon about the incident the following Sunday declaring that "his Indian man" and Mary Sibley, who had suggested the urine-cake spell, were practitioners of the black arts and should be severely reprimanded.

The interrogations intensified and the girls remained silent until Parris suggested some possible suspects. Upon mentioning the name of Tituba, Betty Parris repeated the name and identified her as one of the tormentors. When Abigail Williams was questioned, she responded with the names of Sarah Good and Sarah Osborne. These were the first three persons to be "cried out against," or accused by the afflicted girls. On February 29, 1692, Salem magistrates Jonathan Corwin and Colonel John Hathorne issued warrants for the arrest of Tituba, Sarah Good, and Sarah Osborne. These three individuals were brought to Nathaniel Ingersoll's tavern in Salem Village on Tuesday, March 1, 1692, to be interrogated. The crowd of spectators at this first hearing was so large that the session had to be adjourned to the Salem Village meetinghouse.

From this point on most of the questioning and testimony from the pretrial examinations was carefully written down by a court-appointed scribe. (In

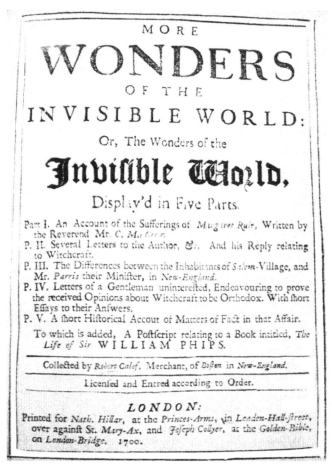

Title page of *More Wonders of the Invisible World* (1700) by Robert Calef. Printed in London, the influence of the Mathers prevented this work from being printed in Boston. This work, critical of the court proceedings and the role of Cotton Mather, helped create the somewhat undeserved negative image of Mather which has followed him down to the present time. It was burned at Harvard. Courtesy Danvers Archival Center, Danvers, Mass.

some cases that scribe was the Reverend Samuel Parris himself.) From these written records historians have been able to piece together a fairly clear picture of the episode. While hundreds of pretrial examinations, warrants, depositions, bills, and other court-related documents still exist, the actual court records of the subsequent trials have disappeared.

Another important factor, which prolonged the time between when a person was examined and when a trial date could be set, was the absence of a Massachusetts royal governor and a colonial charter. During the reign of King James II (1685–1688), both of these essential aspects of colonial government had been eliminated. Without a governor and a charter, capital court cases—such as witchcraft trials—could not be heard, and a Court of Oyer

"Witchcraft at Salem Village" by F. O. C. Darley, William L. Shepard, and Granville Perkins (1876). This illustration depicts another courtroom drama common to the trials where a girl is contorted upon the floor in a fit of affliction while an accused woman swears to the magistrate that before God she is innocent. It is taken from *Pioneers in the Settlement of America* by William A. Crafts, Volume 1, published in 1876. Courtesy Danvers Archival Center, Danvers, Mass.

and Terminer could not be created. It was not until after the arrival of the new Governor Sir William Phips and the equally new Massachusetts Charter on May 14, 1692, that the pending witchcraft cases could finally be heard in a legally convened court.[8]

Sarah Good was the first person to be formally examined during the March pretrial hearings. She was the wife of William Good, an impoverished agricultural laborer who lived a marginal existence in Salem Village by doing odd jobs. Sarah would often accompany him to the farms where he was working. Over time many of his employers had experienced mysterious accidents and misfortune which, during the hearings, were blamed upon Sarah Good. Depositions against her ranged from accusations that she bewitched cattle to death to others that she caused injury to individuals.

When Sarah was finally put on the witness stand, the questioning was handled by magistrate John Hathorne himself. He began by asking her if she was in league with an evil spirit, and if she would identify evil spirits. Sarah immediately denied ever having made a contract with the devil or of hurting any of the afflicted children. She was next asked why she muttered constantly to herself in public, to which she responded that she was reciting the Psalms from the Bible. When asked *whom* she served, she said simply

"I serve God." When asked *which God* she served, she simply replied, "The God who made heaven and earth."[9] The Court Clerk, Ezekial Cheever, who observed and recorded all of Sarah Good's testimony, was evidently not convinced of her sincerity. He added to his transcription that, "Her answers were [given] in a very wicked and spiteful manner, reflecting and retorting against the authority with base and abusive words."[10]

Unfortunately for Sarah, not only were there a number of local individuals leveling complaints against her, but her own husband, William, testified that, "she is an enemy to all good" and that he believed she "was either a witch or would become one very quickly." When Sarah Good was asked her opinion as to who might be guilty of torturing the afflicted, she suggested that it might be Sarah Osborne.[11]

On the basis of such evidence, as well as the frenzied outcries of the afflicted girls, Sarah Good, who was pregnant at the time, went to jail along with Sarah Osborne and Tituba Indian on March 7, 1692. Here she would remain until the time of her indictment by the newly appointed Court of Oyer and Terminer on June 28, 1692. Of these first three victims, Sarah Osborne would die in prison. Sarah Good would hang on July 19, 1692, and only Tituba would escape with her life.

Upon arriving in Boston, Governor William Phips discovered the colony in turmoil. Not only were there over fifty people awaiting trial for the crime of

House of witchcraft trial victim Sarah Osborne in Danvers, Massachusetts (nineteenth-century photo). One of the first three persons accused of witchcraft, Sarah Osborne had scandalized the neighborhood by marrying a young Irish indentured servant, Alexander Osborne, after the death of her first husband. The couple resided in this house, which was later moved and is a private residence today. Courtesy Danvers Archival Center, Danvers, Mass.

witchcraft in several overcrowded jails, but Massachusetts was embroiled in a war with the Indians on the Maine frontier. For Phips, the job of a colonial executive official was new. Because he lacked both legal and theological training, he appointed a committee of twelve prominent ministers from the Boston area to advise the Salem Court how they should proceed. The ministers' report, entitled "The Return of Several Ministers," was completed by early June and presented to the Court officials by Reverend Cotton Mather on June 15.[12]

The ministers recommended that the trials proceed with caution and expressed serious reservations against the use of *spectral evidence*. (Note: "Spectral evidence" is evidence presented by a witness who claimed to see the spirit or specter of an accused person committing acts of witchcraft.) Unfortunately, the magistrates of the Salem Court of Oyer and Terminer largely ignored the ministers' recommendations, since all of those executed were convicted on the basis of spectral evidence. Several historians have suggested that this judicial indifference may have been the result of a statement added to the end of the ministers' report by Reverend Cotton Mather commending the court for its handling of the trials thus far, and encouraging court officials to proceed with the same measures they had already been utilizing. Since spectral evidence was the most significant aspect of the court proceedings, Mather's words of encouragement only reaffirmed the Court's determination to make use of it. Sadly, Bridget Bishop (one of the accused) already had been found guilty of witchcraft largely upon spectral evidence and was the first to be executed.

When Reverend Parris's slave, Tituba, was questioned she denied having any contact with evil spirits or in any way harming the afflicted children. Upon being asked a second time however, she remarked, "the Devil came to me and bid me serve him." Tituba then proceeded to provide magistrates Corwin and Hathorne with an elaborate account of her activities in the realms of black magic and concluded her confession of witchcraft by accusing Sarah Good and Sarah Osborne of torturing the afflicted children.

Tituba admitted that while she had been tempted several times by the devil to torture the afflicted girls she had done so only once. She maintained that each time she refused to obey the devil's bidding she was beaten by a coven of local witches. She also claimed to have met the devil on at least four occasions, twice in human form, once as a dog, and once as a hog. She concluded by stating that in spite of being tempted by gifts and being threatened with torture, she had refused to further cooperate with Satan.[13]

As a confessed and penitent witch, Tituba had now turned "state's evidence" and provided descriptions to the magistrates of a variety of witchcraft activities. She described meetings of the Salem Village coven, flying to and from coven gatherings on "sticks." She even described the demonic "familiars" which were assigned to each of the accused witches. Tituba claimed that Sarah Good had a "yellow bird," while Sarah Osborne had a creature with a woman's head, two legs, and two wings.[14]

What is interesting about Tituba's confession is that it did not condemn her to death on the gallows as it most assuredly would have done in earlier New England witchcraft cases. In fact, a confession by an alleged witch was considered by European courts to be the most reliable proof to condemn and

"There is a flock of yellow birds around her head!" by Howard Pyle (1893). This illustration was done to accompany the published text by Mary E. Wilkins entitled: "Giles Corey, Yeoman: a Play." It appeared in *Harper's New Monthly Magazine*, December 1892–May 1893, and depicts a group of afflicted girls giving spectral evidence in the Salem Court. Courtesy Danvers Archival Center, Danvers, Mass.

execute a suspected agent of the devil. Against this long-standing legal precedent, neither Tituba nor any of the over fifty confessed witches lost their lives. On the contrary, only those who were found guilty by the jury, yet refused to confess guilt, were executed.

While Tituba provided the court with details concerning her activities as a witch, Sarah Osborne, the last of the original three victims, denied any wrongdoing and continued to uphold her claim that she was actually "a Gospel woman." During Osborne's examination she stated that she, like the afflicted girls, had actually been tortured and tempted by the devil, but had refused to give in to any of his demands. When asked why she had not attended Sabbath services in the Salem Village meetinghouse during the previous year, she replied that her poor health had prevented her. Her health was indeed in decline, since she would die while awaiting trial in prison on May 10, 1692.

Most tragic of all these early accusations was the indictment of four-year-old Dorcas Good, daughter of Sarah Good. On March 24, a warrant was issued for little Dorcas to be brought to the magistrates for questioning. Despite her young age, Dorcas was not shown any special consideration. She was held tightly by the constables to limit physical movement during her examination in order to prevent Dorcas's specter from biting the afflicted girls. The four-year-old testified that her mother had given her a demonic spirit, or "familiar," in the form of a snake which fed upon her blood from a "witch's mark" on her finger.

The child was chained and sent to jail in Salem and later moved to Boston. Here she remained imprisoned until a general amnesty of all accused persons came in May 1693. Dorcas Good never went to trial, but her life would not be a happy one. Eighteen years later, her father William Good would petition the Massachusetts Great and General Court for damages done to his daughter during her time of imprisonment.[15] He claimed that although she had been a fairly normal and well-balanced child at the time of her arrest, over a year of close confinement in Boston's jail had ruined her mental and physical health. Dorcas had been quite ill since her release, and suffered from arrested emotional development. He was ultimately awarded a settlement of thirty pounds sterling in compensation.

Rebecca Nurse's case was quite different, however, for she was not only accused by afflicted children, such as Abigail Williams, but also by several adult witnesses. The Reverend Deodat Lawson, a former minister of Salem Village, heard about the witchcraft outbreak in nearby Boston and came to his former parish to observe the episode firsthand. He testified that while visiting the home of Thomas and Ann Putnam, Sr., in early March, Mrs. Putnam was visited by the specter or spirit of Rebecca Nurse.

During his house call, Reverend Lawson observed that Mrs. Putnam was physically incapacitated, yet carried on a conversation with Nurse's apparition saying: "Goodwife Nurse! Be gone! Be gone! Are you not ashamed? A woman of your profession to afflict a poor creature so? What hurt did I ever do to you in my life? You have but two years to live, and then the devil will torment your soul. For this your name has been blotted out of God's Book, and it shall not be put in God's Book again!" On the basis of this and other similar testimony by the afflicted girls, Rebecca was arrested on Thursday, March 24, 1692, and brought in for questioning.[16]

Some historians have speculated that although she was widely known as a devout and godly woman, the afflicted girls singled out Rebecca because she had been critical of their first accusations. Nurse's skepticism and excellent reputation may have called into question their credibility. Yet whatever the reason, she was cried accused by Betty Parris, Abigail Williams, and most particularly by Ann Putnam, Jr., who confronted Rebecca at her hearing asking, "Did you not bring the black man [the devil] with you? Did you not bid me tempt God and die? How often have you ate and drank your own damnation?"[17]

At the order of the magistrates, Rebecca Nurse's body was searched by a group of women. They discovered several growths on her skin which they suspected might have been "witch's teats"—that is, places where a witch's familiar sucked blood from the witch's body. Rebecca defended herself by

House of witchcraft trial victim Rebecca Nurse in Danvers, Massachusetts (nineteenth-century photo). Rebecca lived with her husband, Francis Nurse, at the heart of a 300-acre farm. The Nurses could not have purchased such a large property had not their seven married children agreed to help pay off the mortgage. Rebecca was seventy-one years old and the mother of eight children when she was hanged on July 19, 1692. Courtesy Danvers Archival Center, Danvers, Mass.

protesting that she had nothing on her body other "than what is common in nature" or which arose "from a natural cause." However, her protests went unheeded and she was sent to the Salem jail. Following a second interview with Deputy Governor Thomas Danforth on April 11, 1692, Rebecca was removed to the Boston jail to await the arrival of Governor Phips and her trial.[18]

During her trial Rebecca's neighbors presented a petition in support of her, claiming that she was innocent of any wrongdoing. Signed by thirty-five Salem Village residents, it was a brief, eloquent, and courageous document. In the "Petition for Rebecca Nurse" her character is attested to by members of the local community who knew her for many years. Her neighbors supported her profession of the Christian faith and maintained that there were no grounds to suspect her of witchcraft.[19]

Ultimately, Rebecca was tried in Salem on June 29, 1692, and initially found innocent. When Thomas Fiske, the jury foreman, announced the verdict the afflicted children raised such an outcry that Chief Justice William Stoughton asked Fiske to reconsider. Stoughton suggested that perhaps the jury had not heard Rebecca make an incriminating statement when another prisoner was brought in to testify against her. When Fiske later questioned Rebecca as to the exact meaning of her statement, she would not reply. This lack of a response, probably due to Rebecca's partial deafness, was unexpected. Fiske waited briefly, then returned to the jury, and soon came back with a verdict of guilty. Stoughton sentenced her to be executed on July 19, 1692.[20]

Contemporary view of the Rebecca Nurse House (c. 2004). The Rebecca Nurse House, located at 149 Pine Street, in Danvers, Massachusetts, is now a historic house museum open to the public and owned by the Danvers Alarm List, a colonial-era reenactment group dedicated to the care and preservation of the Nurse homestead and its surrounding farmland. Photo by Richard B. Trask.

Interestingly, Governor Phips gave Rebecca a stay of execution in order to allow him to review her case personally. The members of the court and especially the afflicted children raised such a furor that Phips rescinded his reprieve and Rebecca's date of execution was reaffirmed. She was hanged on July 19 with Sarah Good, Susannah Martin, Elizabeth How, and Sarah Wildes.[21]

Of all the early victims the first individual to be condemned and executed for witchcraft was Bridget Bishop, an owner of an unlicensed local tavern popular with younger men in the neighborhood. She had been charged with the crime of witchcraft several years earlier, but had been acquitted. Unlike many of those individuals named only by the afflicted children, Bridget was accused by numerous adults who testified to a variety of strange experiences difficult to explain without the use of magic.[22]

During Bridget's pretrial examination Samuel and Sarah Shattuck, a Quaker couple, testified that they had had a serious disagreement with Bridget, and that another guest had warned them that Bridget would break Sarah's pride by harming their little child. A short time later their young, healthy son suddenly went insane and several physicians were consulted, but to no avail. All concurred that the boy was "under the evil hand of witchcraft." In an effort to affect a cure, the boy was brought to Bridget by a concerned friend. Bridget's angry response was "Thou rogue! What? Dost thou bring this fellow here to plague me?" while proceeding to scratch the child's face with her fingernails. The sudden deterioration of the child's mental state immediately following the bitter disagreement with Bridget, combined with her violent behavior toward their child, prompted the Shattucks to suspect Bridget of being the probable cause of their son's illness.

Another indictment was offered against Bishop by John Bly, Sr., who testified that while he was employed by her to take down the cellar wall of her old house, he and his son had found a number of "poppets" made of rags and hog bristles with pins thrust through them. These suspicious effigies had been hidden in the small spaces between the rocks of the house's foundation. More incriminating still was the testimony of William Stacey, a local farmer, who said that Bridget had paid him to do some work around her home. He claimed that shortly after carefully placing the money into his pocket, he discovered that it had entirely vanished.[23]

Stacey also claimed that once when he stopped his wagon to speak with Bridget, his wheel got stuck in a rut requiring the help of several others to remove. Having extracted the wagon wheel, he returned to look at the rut and it had reportedly disappeared. On another occasion, Stacey's horse stopped when Bridget appeared suddenly on the road. After she had passed he whipped his horse to continue pulling his wagon, but the harness snapped from the strain and the wagon rolled backwards into a tree. Stacey next testified that he had witnessed the apparition of Bridget in his bedchamber at night illuminated by a light, which radiated from her spirit. A few days later, he claimed that he had been mysteriously lifted into the air, thrown against a stone wall and violently dropped upon the ground. The following day, as he was driving past Bridget a wheel fell from the axle of his wagon. In Stacey's view, this remarkable series of events could not be coincidental, but clearly confirmed that Bridget Bishop was a practitioner of black magic.[24]

Throughout all these testimonies, Bridget steadfastly maintained her innocence claiming that she did not know what a witch was. Magistrate John Hathorne took advantage of this statement to ask Bridget: "If you do not know what a witch is, how do you know that you are not one?" Her response was terse: "If I were a witch you would certainly know it!" Bridget was reprimanded for her impudence, tried, convicted, and hanged on Gallows Hill on June 10, 1692.[25]

On the second day of executions, July 19, 1692, five more individuals were hanged including Sarah Good and Rebecca Nurse of Salem Village, Elizabeth How of Ipswich, Sarah Wildes of Topsfield, and Susannah Martin of Amesbury. By this time, the accusations had moved well beyond the boundaries of the Salem neighborhood to threaten individuals living in communities as far away as New Hampshire and Maine.

Now the afflicted children were not only accusing women, they began to single out and accuse adult males as well. By May 1692, the girls had targeted some of the more prominent males in the Salem Village community, among them George Jacobs, Sr. Jacobs was a prosperous farmer who had lived in the Salem Farms area between Salem Town and Salem Village for thirty-five years. He was arrested on May 10, 1692. Simultaneously, his son George, Jr., his daughter-in-law Rebecca, and granddaughter Margaret were also accused. Four days after his arrest, he was brought before magistrate John Hathorne for questioning.

House of witchcraft trial victim George Jacobs in Danvers, Massachusetts (nineteenth-century photo). George Jacobs resided here on his farm in Salem Village for thirty-five years. Accused by his granddaughter and by his household servant, Elizabeth Churchill, he was condemned and hanged on August 19, 1692. Courtesy Danvers Archival Center, Danvers, Mass.

Initially Jacobs took the afflicted girls and their accusations too lightly, until he was confronted by his maidservant, Elizabeth Churchill, who testified that he had tempted her to sign the Devil's Book. Mary Walcott, one of the afflicted children, also maintained that Jacobs had tempted her to sign the Devil's Book, and threatened her with physical harm if she refused. Despite Jacobs' alleged threats, both girls claimed to have resisted him.

In the face of these and other accusations, Jacobs maintained his innocence. In response to Justice Hathorne's insistent badgering, he simply responded that concerning witchcraft: "I know not of it, any more than the child that was born tonight." During his pretrial examination, Justice Corwin asked Jacobs to recite "The Lord's Prayer." It was generally believed that no witch could recite it perfectly. The old man, nervous and unlettered, omitted an entire sentence and made several other recitation errors. Knowing his mistake, and fearing the worst, he remarked bravely, "Well, burn me or hang me, I will stand in the truth of Christ."[26]

What makes the case of George Jacobs, Sr., especially tragic is that his granddaughter Margaret Jacobs, herself a confessed witch, named her grandfather as a co-conspirator along with Constable John Willard and Reverend George Burroughs. When Jacobs Sr. was finally tried for witchcraft in August 1692, Margaret Jacobs was one of nearly a dozen primary witnesses against him. Only after Jacobs's death sentence was pronounced in court did Margaret have a change of heart and write to the magistrates to retract her testimony and her own confession as a witch. The result of this reversal was that Margaret was moved from the cell of the confessed witches and back to the cell of those awaiting trials and executions. She explained to her grandfather

her feelings of regret for the part she had played in condemning him, and he forgave her.[27]

On August 19, 1692, five more victims were hanged: George Jacobs, Sr., John Proctor of Salem Village, John Willard of Salem Village, Martha Carrier of Andover, and Reverend George Burroughs of Wells, Maine. Of all of these, perhaps George Burroughs's case was the most startling to the community since he had once served as the pastor of Salem Village, and indeed was the only minister to be accused and executed.

The first accusations against Burroughs had been presented to the Court on April 23, 1692. After a warrant was issued, Burroughs was brought from his parish in Wells, Maine, to Salem, where he remained in jail until his pretrial examination on May 9, 1692. Burroughs has been described as "a small, black-haired, dark-complexioned man of quick passions and possessing great strength." He was a 1670 graduate of Harvard College, and had spent much time as minister of a small struggling parish in Casco (now Portland) Maine. He remained there until 1680 when he accepted the call to come to Salem Village for the modest salary of 60 pounds per year with only a third of this amount to be paid in cash and the rest was to be contributed by the Salem Village parishioners. Like his predecessor, Reverend James Bayley, Burroughs quickly ran into difficulties with members of his congregation when those who opposed his appointment refused to pay their share of his salary, putting him and his family in difficult financial circumstances.[28]

In spite of this situation, Burroughs continued to work with the Salem Village parishioners, initiating a capital campaign to help build a new meetinghouse and helping to draft a petition to the Great and General Court to have the village set apart from Salem as an independent community. In 1682, his wife died and he was so destitute that he was forced to borrow money against his unpaid salary in order to pay for her funeral expenses.

The following year, Burroughs left Salem Village to return to Maine and resume his pastorate there. Upon reaching Falmouth, Maine, he was met by a sheriff bearing a warrant for his arrest issued at the request of farmer John Putnam of Salem Village. The warrant claimed that Burroughs had not paid Putnam for Mrs. Burroughs's funeral expenses. The impoverished pastor was forced to return to Salem to prove that the Salem Village Church had agreed to reimburse Putnam from Burroughs's unpaid salary. Burroughs further proved that Putnam had already been paid, and the litigious farmer was forced to drop charges against him. Burroughs returned to Maine a free man.

Here he remained for ten years, first serving the church in Casco and later moving to Wells, when Indians burned Casco. He was living in Wells with his new wife in 1692 when the constable from Portsmouth, New Hampshire, arrived with a warrant accusing him of witchcraft. Shortly after his arrival in Boston on May 9, Burroughs was examined by Lieutenant Governor Stoughton, Justice Samuel Sewell, Justice John Hathorne, and Justice Jonathan Corwin as well as several Salem and Boston area ministers. No complete transcript of this private session has survived. All that remains is the commentary of pastors Cotton and Increase Mather, both of whom were present. Cotton Mather's opinion of Burroughs was that "his tergiversations

Hon. William Stoughton (1631–1701) served as Deputy Governor and Chief Justice of the Court of Oyer and Terminer which tried all of the accused, and executed the twenty victims. Courtesy Danvers Archival Center, Danvers, Mass.

(shifty and evasive answers), contradictions, and falsehoods were very sensible at his examination ..." While Increase Mather says simply that Burroughs's answers "proved him a very ill man."[29]

When Burroughs was finally brought before the open court to hear the testimony against him, the afflicted children were prepared with their spectral evidence. Susannah Shelton testified that "Burroughs's two wives appeared (to her) in their winding sheets" and said, "that [this] man had, [pointing at Burroughs] killed them." When he was asked to look upon Susannah Shelton, Burroughs turned his face upon all the afflicted children, and they all fell down, or as the court records read, "he looked back and knocked down all (or most of the afflicted) who stood behind him."[30]

Others testified that Burroughs had often demonstrated feats of supernatural strength, thus implying that such ability could only come from Satan. Thomas Greenslit deposed that he saw him "lift a gun of six foot barrel or thereabouts putting his forefinger of his right hand into the muzzell (sic) of said gun and that he held it out at arm's end only with that finger, and that ... at the same time he saw the said Burroughs take a full barrel of molasses with but two fingers of one of his hands and carry it from the stage head to the end of the stage."[31]

Upon the day of his execution, Reverend Burroughs stood upon the ladder and declared his innocence to the crowd. Following his address, he led the assembly in prayer, concluding with "The Lord's Prayer" which he—unlike George Jacobs—recited perfectly. As a result of this, some members of the

"Execution of the Rev. George Burroughs." This image represents the highly controversial execution of Reverend George Burroughs, who recited the Lord's Prayer without error immediately prior to his death. The perfect recitation of the Lord's Prayer was thought to be impossible for a true witch, causing many observers to call for his release. Courtesy Danvers Archival Center, Danvers, Mass.

crowd began to agitate for Burroughs's release. Unfortunately for Burroughs, Reverend Cotton Mather was among the audience and from his saddle addressed the crowd. He explained that Burroughs had been justly condemned and that Satan had assisted the doomed pastor in his recitation. This quelled the momentary disturbance and the August 19th execution of the five victims proceeded without further interruption.[32]

The next death to take place was not officially considered an execution. It involved a man who, along with his wife, was accused of witchcraft—Giles and Martha Cory of Salem Farms. Both of these individuals had been accused by the afflicted children—Martha in March, and Giles in April, 1692. Martha Cory, after her first examination, was confined in Salem and then moved to Boston. The elderly Giles was asked to testify at her hearing. Later he began to publicly criticize the afflicted children's influence upon the court which only served to precipitate the accusations against him.

Ultimately Giles was brought to trial in September 1692 with relatively little evidence against him. When he was asked whether he pleaded guilty or innocent to the charge of witchcraft, he "stood mute," refusing to speak. In

The Excommunication of Martha Corey by Reverend Samuel Parris (1692). Written in Reverend Parris's own hand, this document is an extract from the pastoral notebook kept by him documenting the activities of the Salem Village congregation. Courtesy Danvers Archival Center, Danvers, Mass.

response, Chief Justice Stoughton instructed Sheriff George Corwin to subject the eighty-year-old Cory to the ancient torture of *peine forte et dure*, commonly called "pressing." He was removed from the courtroom and taken to a nearby field where he was staked upon the ground, face upwards. A heavy beam was placed upon his chest, and then rocks were gradually piled on the beam in ever-increasing amounts.

The purpose of this gradual process was to force the accused to rethink his position and enter a plea since, according to English common law, no trial could take place until the accused had declared himself to be either guilty or innocent. Although Cory's exact reasoning was never recorded, it is likely that he had chosen this course as a means of preventing his property from being confiscated by the Province of Massachusetts. If no trial were to take place, Cory's innocence or guilt could not be proven, and thus his property would necessarily pass to his heirs and not the government.

Giles Cory refused to succumb to the pressure of the ever-increasing weight or to the entreaties of friends and relations, allowing himself to be crushed rather than be subjected to a trial. Judge Samuel Sewell, an eyewitness to the event, recorded his observations concerning the only case of "pressing" in American history: "Monday, September 19, 1692. About noon at Salem, Giles Cory was pressed to death for standing mute; much pains were used with him two days, one after another, by the court and Capt. Gardner of Nantucket who had been of his acquaintance, but all in vain."[33]

A long-standing tradition associated with the death of Cory suggests that, as he neared the end of his endurance, on the second day of his ordeal, he pleaded for more weight to be added to the beam speeding up his death. This request was granted by the court officers in attendance who considered Cory's death a suicide since he could have stopped the process by cooperating with the court and entering a plea to the charge of witchcraft.

The last victims were executed on September 22, 1692, just three days after Giles Cory's death. Among this final group was his wife Martha Cory, Mary Eastey of Topsfield, Alice Parker and Ann Pudeater of Salem, Margaret Scott of Rowley, Wilmot Redd of Marblehead, and Samuel Wardwell and Mary Parker of Andover. Of these persons, one of the most introspective and articulate was Mary Eastey. She was a fifty-seven-year-old mother of seven and a sister to Rebecca Nurse and Sarah Cloyce. All three sisters would be tried for witchcraft in 1692.[34]

A statement produced by Mary Eastey shortly before her execution provides insight into the mind of one who, like all Puritans, affirmed the existence of witchcraft yet strongly objected to the way the court was proceeding. In it she states:

> The Lord above knows my innocency then ... as on the great day will be known to men and angels. I petition your honours ... if it be possible, that no more innocent blood be shed, which undoubtedly cannot be avoided in the way and course you go in. I question not, but your honors do to the utmost of your powers in the discovery and detecting of witchcraft and witches, and would not be guilty of innocent blood for the world; but by my own innocency, I know you are in the wrong way. The Lord in His infinite mercy direct you in this great work, if it be his blessed will, that innocent blood be not shed ...[35]

Sadly, the Court never acted upon Eastey's petition. Robert Calef reported in his *More Wonders of the Invisible World* that immediately before her execution, "When she took her last farewell of her husband, children, and friends she was as is reported by them present, as serious, religious, distinct, and affectionate as could well be expressed, drawing tears from the eyes of all present." After Mary Eastey and the other seven victims were executed, Salem's Reverend Nicholas Noyes was heard to remark that it was "a sad thing to see eight firebrands of hell hanging there." These were the last persons to be hanged during the Salem witchcraft episode.[36]

> ## The Wonders of the Invisible World:
>
> Being an Account of the
>
> # TRYALS
>
> O F
>
> ## 𝔖𝔢𝔲𝔢𝔯𝔞𝔩 𝔚𝔦𝔱𝔠𝔥𝔢𝔰,
>
> Lately Excuted in
>
> # NEW-ENGLAND:
>
> And of several remarkable Curiofities therein Occurring.
>
> Together with,
>
> I. Obfervations upon the Nature, the Number, and the Operations of the Devils.
>
> II. A fhort Narrative of a late outrage committed by a knot of Witches in *Swede-Land*, very much refembling, and fo far explaining, that under which *New-England* has laboured.
>
> III. Some Councels directing a due Improvement of the Terrible things lately done by the unufual and amazing Range of *Evil-Spirits* in *New-England*.
>
> IV. A brief Difcourfe upon thofe *Temptations* which are the more ordinary Devices of Satan.
>
> ## By COTTON MATHER.
>
> Publifhed by the Special Command of his EXCELLENCY the Governour of the Province of the *Maffachafetts-Bay* in *New-England*.
>
> Printed firft, at *Boftun* in *New-England* ; and Reprinted at *London*, for *John Dunton*, at the *Raven* in the *Poultry*. 1693.

Title page of *The Wonders of the Invisible World: Being an Account of the Tryals of Several Witches Lately Executed in New England* (1693) by Reverend Cotton Mather. Printed both in Boston and London, this work was commissioned by Massachusetts Governor William Phips, who desired that Cotton Mather produce a sympathetic narrative justifying the increasingly controversial Salem trials. It was undertaken by Mather as a favor to a powerful member of his congregation, but ultimately did much to undermine Mather's reputation and credibility with his reading public. Courtesy Danvers Archival Center, Danvers, Mass.

By late September, public opinion had shifted and growing criticism forced both Governor Phips and Reverend Cotton Mather to defend the trials. Phips asked Mather to produce a sympathetic book that would explain the Salem trials and the reasons for the Court's handling of cases using spectral evidence. On September 20, 1692, Mather, in writing to Court Clerk Stephen Sewell, stated that he was "continually beset with all sorts of Objections and Objectors against the work now doing at Salem," and was requesting Court Records of the "principal witches" in order to write a book to justify the Court's proceedings.[37]

Mather's book, *Wonders of the Invisible World*, was finished in October 1692, but not published until 1693, because by mid-October Governor Phips had issued a ban on the publication of any books relating to the witchcraft trials. This ban did not in any way hinder the circulation of multiple copies of Thomas Brattle's handwritten letter severely criticizing the Salem court magistrates and the scandalous way in which the cases had been handled. By November 25, the Massachusetts legislature had set up the colony's new judicial system including a new Superior Court of Judicature, which was handed the responsibility of trying all future witchcraft cases. The trials were then adjourned until January.

When the witchcraft trials were finally reconvened on January 3, 1693, they were relocated to Boston and involved a different lineup of justices and jury men—except that William Stoughton, John Richards, Wait Winthrop, and Samuel Sewell were still presiding justices. Significantly, spectral evidence was no longer admissible evidence, bringing the trials into compliance with the report from the committee of twelve ministers issued on June 15, 1692. Of the final fifty-two accused persons tried under these new guidelines, only three would be convicted. With spectral evidence gone, the visions and testimony of the afflicted children were of little further use and gradually tensions began to subside.[38]

In May 1693 a long-awaited reply from the English home government came to Phips authorizing him to close down the trials. In response,

Hon. Samuel Sewell (1652–1730) kept a famous diary of the court proceedings and in 1696, stood before the congregation of Boston's South Church to apologize for his involvement as a member of the Court. Courtesy Danvers Archival Center, Danvers, Mass.

Drawing of the "Great House" of Philip and Mary English (c. 1674). Both Philip and Mary were accused by the afflicted girls in April 1692 and sent to the Boston jail. Upon their return to Salem in 1693 they discovered that Sheriff Corwin had confiscated nearly 1500 pounds sterling worth of personal belongings. They were never reimbursed. Courtesy Danvers Archival Center, Danvers, Mass.

Governor Phips issued a proclamation declaring that all accused persons were pardoned, and those awaiting trial were granted amnesty. All remaining prisoners were to pay their jailer's bill, which included costs for food and lodging during the time of imprisonment. Those unable to pay the jailer's bill were kept imprisoned for nonpayment of debt. For this reason Tituba, Reverend Parris's West Indian slave, remained in jail after May 1692 and was sold by Parris to a Southern gentleman in order to pay her jailer's bill. She was removed from Salem to Virginia.[39]

The Salem witchcraft trials drew to a close in the courts but the tremors and aftershocks from the event were to be felt for years to come. Many people continued to live with the pangs of conscience and deep regret for the wrongs committed upon the lives and families of so many victims. Natural disasters, poor harvests, attacks by Indians and the French, sickness, and general misfortune in the several years that followed convinced many people throughout Massachusetts that God was punishing the colony for its sin of falsely accusing and executing righteous people.

For this reason the once virulent prosecutor, Justice William Stoughton, as Acting Governor of the Colony of Massachusetts after the English government recalled Phips, issued a proclamation on December 17, 1696, proclaiming:

> ... A day of prayer and fasting [is to be called upon so] ... that all God's people may offer up fervent supplications ... [so] that all iniquity may be put away

which hath stirred God's holy jealousy against this land; That He ... would help us wherein we have done amiss to do so no more; and especially that wherever mistakes have been fallen into ... referring to the late tragedy, raised among us by Satan and his instruments ... [may] He ... pardon all the errors of his servants and people that desire to love his name ...[40]

As a final gesture of regret and penitence, the colony provided monetary compensation to the families of twenty-three persons who were either executed, imprisoned, or had lost property as a result of the episode. For New England, it was the last major outbreak of witchcraft.

NOTES

1. K. David Goss, *Salem: Cornerstones of a Historic City* (Beverly, MA: Commonwealth Editions, 1999), 5–6.

2. Paul Boyer and Stephen Nissenbaum, *Salem Possessed: The Social Origins of Witchcraft* (Cambridge: Harvard University Press, 1974), 45–59.

3. Ibid., 61. Although the vote to grant the parsonage to Parris was entered into the Village Records on October 10, 1689, the agreement did specify that if Parris or his heirs should decide to sell the property, the village would have the first right of refusal.

4. Frances Hill, *The Salem Witch Trials Reader* (New York: Da Capo Press, 1984), 302.

5. Boyer and Nissenbaum, *Salem Possessed*, 1.

6. Robert Calef, *More Wonders of the Invisible World*; also called *The Wonders of the Invisible World Displayed in Five Parts* (London: 1700).

7. Boyer and Nissenbaum, *Salem Possessed*, 2–3.

8. Ibid., 6–7.

9. David Levin, *What Happened in Salem*, 2nd Edition (New York: Harcourt, Bruce and World, Inc., 1960), 4–5. From a verbatim transcript of Sarah Good's testimony from *Records of Salem Witchcraft, Copied from the Original Documents*, ed., William E. Woodward, 2 vol. (Roxbury, MA: 1864), 4–5.

10. Woodward, *Records of Salem Witchcraft, Copied from the Original Documents*, 4–5; Mary Beth Norton, *In the Devil's Snare: The Salem Witchcraft Crisis of 1692* (New York: Vintage Books, 2002), 26.

11. Ibid.

12. Boyer and Nissenbaum, *Salem Possessed*, 6–7. Hill, *The Salem Witch Trials Reader*, 162–65. This contains a transcript of "The Return of Several Ministers."

13. Levin, *What Happened in Salem*, 6–7.

14. Ibid.

15. Deodat Lawson, *A Brief and True Narrative of Some Remarkable Passages Relating to Sundry Persons Afflicted by Witchcraft, at Salem Village Which Happened from the Nineteenth of March to the Fifth of April, 1692* (Boston, 1692) reprinted in: George Lincoln Burr, ed., *Narratives of the Witchcraft Cases, 1648–1706* (Barnes & Noble, 1914).

16. Lawson, *A Brief and True Narrative of Witchcraft at Salem Village*, in Hill, *The Salem Witch Trials: A Reader*, 61–64.

17. Hill, *The Salem Witch Trials Reader*, 64; Norton, *In the Devil's Snare*, 63.

18. Norton, *In the Devil's Snare*, 63, 223.

19. Claudia Durst Johnson and Vernon E. Johnson, *Understanding the Crucible* (Westport, CT: Greenwood Press, 1998), 102–3, petition taken from: Charles Upham, *Salem Witchcraft*, vol. 1 (Boston: Wiggin and Lunt, 1867), 91.

20. Hill, *The Salem Witch Trials Reader*, 75–76. The incident involving Rebecca Nurse's reluctance to respond to a question posed during her examination was attributable to her inability to hear. As she herself stated in her petition: "And I being something hard of hearing, and full of grief, none informing me how the court took up my words and therefore had not opportunity to declare what I intended, when I said they were of our company."

21. Ibid., 99–101.

22. Bernard Rosenthal, *Salem Story: Reading the Salem Witch Trials of 1692* (Cambridge: Cambridge University Press, 1993), 75–80.

23. Ibid., 57, 75.

24. Ibid., 57.

25. Hill, *The Salem Witch Trials Reader*, 233–38. Chadwick Hansen, in his book, *Witchcraft at Salem* (New York: George Braziller, 1969), asserts his belief that based upon the non-spectral nature of evidence against Bridget Bishop, she was, in all likelihood, a practicing witch. Hansen's controversial anthropological study of the Salem trials suggests that in cultures where belief in magic is ingrained in the social consciousness, witchcraft is possible.

26. Boyer and Nissenbaum, *Salem-Village Witchcraft: A Documentary Record of Local Conflict in Colonial New England* (Belmont CA: Wadsworth Publishing Company, Inc., 1972), 107–8.

27. Norton, *In the Devil's Snare*, 161–62. One of two famous nineteenth-century paintings by artist T. H. Mattson depicts Margaret Jacobs accusing her elderly grandfather, George Jacobs, Sr. Entitled "The Trial of George Jacobs," it reflects a romantic and sensational image evoked by this tragic episode in the mind of Victorian America.

28. Hill, *The Salem Witch Trials Reader*, 177–86. The story of Reverend George Burroughs is the most unusual and atypical of the Salem episode since, as a minister, a person of Burroughs's status should have been above suspicion. Interestingly, Reverend Burroughs was the only condemned witch whose execution was endorsed by Increase Mather, who was quoted: "I was not myself present at any of the trials, excepting one, viz., that of George Burroughs; had I been one of the judges, I could not have acquitted him."—Increase Mather, *Cases of Conscience Concerning Evil Spirits Personating Men* (Boston, 1693), 59, 65–66.

29. Rosenthal, *Salem Story*, 129–50.

30. Hill, *The Salem Witch Trials Reader*, 192.

31. Ibid.

32. Norton, *In the Devil's Snare*, 256–57. Norton's narrative provides a sympathetic image of Reverend George Burroughs's execution, but also reminds the reader that to many observers Burroughs was regarded as the infamous "leader of the witches," and his death did little to change that image.

33. Hansen, *Witchcraft at Salem*, 154. Hansen notes that in his opinion, "Giles Corey ... was pressed to death because he would not agree to be tried by the Special Court of Oyer and Terminer. His death was a protest—the most dramatic protest of all—against the methods of the court."

34. Ibid., 150.

35. Ibid., 151–52. This petition of Mary Eastey had very little effect upon the magistrates to whom it was directed. Nevertheless, it underscores the deeply rooted belief of even the victims themselves in the reality of *maleficarum* magic and the need to discover and destroy it wherever found.

36. Ibid., 151–52. Of the "firebrands of hell" hanged on September 22, 1692—only Wilmot "Mammy" Redd had a notorious reputation for placing curses upon her neighbors in Marblehead. She had made herself infamous as "the witch of Marblehead" but steadfastly held to her innocence when accused during the trials.

37. Norton, *In the Devil's Snare*, 278–79.

38. Ibid., 282–92.

39. Ibid., 292.

40. Robert Calef, *More Wonders of the Invisible World* (Boston, 1697), in Johnson and Johnson's, *Understanding the Crucible*, 112–13.

3

Early Interpretations of the Salem Witch Trials

Since the 1690s, contemporary observers and later historians have debated and attempted to explain what happened at Salem Village and why. Beginning with participants such as Cotton Mather and John Hale, and contemporary critics such as Thomas Brattle and Robert Calif, the episode sparked controversy and differing opinions as to why events took place and upon whom blame should rest.

The earliest published narratives were written primarily to apologize for, or accuse, the participants. For example, skeptical merchant Thomas Brattle of Boston in his "Letter to a Reverend Gentleman" expressed his conviction that the "afflicted girls" were deceiving the court and that none of the alleged accusations had any basis in fact.[1] Conversely, Reverend John Hale in his 1697 book, *A Modest Inquiry into the Nature of Witchcraft*, expressed regret for what had taken place admitting that errors in procedure and judgment had occurred, but reaffirmed that according to scripture and historical precedent, witchcraft was a real threat to a godly society.[2]

The later generations of observers were less ambivalent in their assessment, and tended to place blame upon the court for giving credence to the testimony of children whose credibility as witnesses should have been called into question and not readily accepted. Most notable in this view was mid-nineteenth-century antiquarian Rev. Charles Upham whose two-volume study, *Salem Witchcraft*, places much of the responsibility upon the afflicted children, attributing their behavior to an adolescent desire for adult attention and the need for amusement.[3]

This chapter will explore the opinions and interpretations of the trials suggested by early writers from 1692 to the early twentieth century. Some share

> # A Modeft Enquiry
> Into the Nature of
> # Witchcraft,
> AND
> How Perfons Guilty of that Crime
> may be *Convicted* : And the means
> ufed for their Difcovery Difcuffed,
> both *Negatively* and *Affirmatively*,
> according to *SCRIPTURE* and
> *EXPERIENCE.*
>
> ## By John Hale,
> Paftor of the Church of Chrift in *Beverley*,
> *Anno Domini.* 1 6 9 7.
>
> *When they fay unto you, feek unto them that have*
> *Familiar Spirits and unto Wizzards, that peep,&c.*
> *To the Law and to the Teftimony ; if they fpeak*
> *not according to this word, it is becaufe there is no*
> *light in them,* Ifaiah VIII. 19, 20.
> *That which I fee not teach thou me,* Job 34 32.
>
> BOSTON in N. E.
> Printed by *B. Green,* and *J. Allen,* for
> *Benjamin Eliot* under the Town Houfe. 1702

Title page of *A Modest Inquiry into the Nature of Witchcraft* (written: 1697 and printed: 1702) by Reverend John Hale. This work is an affirmation of the existence of the "invisible world" and its evil powers. Hale draws upon historical precedents to give examples of instances of genuine witchcraft, then critiques the Salem Court for having failed to follow the clear guidelines which should have been used in ferreting out genuine witches. The work was not published until after the author's death. Courtesy Danvers Archival Center, Danvers, Mass.

similar viewpoints, while others stand apart with differing explanations of the event.

Closest to the event itself were several Boston area ministers who sought to wrestle with the supernatural based upon their understanding of Christian faith. Most prominent among these clerical participants in the events of 1692 were a father and son team, Reverend Increase and Reverend Cotton Mather. Both of these notable personages played a significant role in the witchcraft event and each left a clear statement of opinion as to what it represented.

Reverend Increase Mather (1639–1723). Unlike his son, Cotton Mather, Increase kept himself at a distance from the trials themselves. He is best remembered for contributing advice to the Salem justices in the lengthy document "The Return of Several Ministers" warning them against using spectral evidence. Courtesy Danvers Archival Center, Danvers, Mass.

For Reverend Increase Mather, the trials were not conducted in a manner calculated to protect the rights and liberties of the accused.

In his book, *Cases of Conscience*, published in October 1692, Increase Mather severely criticizes the witch-finding methods of the Court and calls into question the Court's use of spectral evidence. His most famous statement from this essay evokes what later historian Bernard Rosenthal would call an endorsement of "civil-libertarian principles."[4] The senior Mather asserted that "It were better that ten suspected witches should escape, than that one Innocent Person should be Condemned," and later that, "It is better that a Guilty Person should be absolved, than that he should without sufficient ground of Conviction be condemned."[5]

To the mind of Increase Mather, the danger of the Salem Court was its tendency to view its victims as guilty until proven innocent—a position which resulted in a surprisingly high percentage of convictions prior to September 1692. What is more surprising is that Mather challenges the activities of the Court without directly criticizing the judiciary, the testimony of the witnesses, or by implication, his own son, Cotton Mather, who supported the Court's activities in his own book, *Wonders of the Invisible World*.[6]

It is Reverend Cotton Mather, a Harvard graduate and pastor of Boston's Second Church, who—of all Boston's clerics—has come to be most closely associated with the trials. Undeservedly, he has also gained a notorious reputation for his role in the episode. In June 1692, Cotton had served with

CASES of CONSCIENCE

Concerning

Evil Spirits

Perfonating MEN;

WITCHCRAFTS,

Infallible Proofs of Guilt in fuch as are
Accufed with that CRIME.

All Confidered according to the Scriptures, Hiftory,
Experience, and the Judgment of many Learned
MEN.

By *Increafe Mather*, Prefident of *Harvard* Colledge at *Cambridge*, and Teacher of a Church at *Bofton* in *New England*

PROV. xxii. xxi.
——*That thou mighteft Anfwer the Words of Truth, to them
that fend unto thee.*

*Efficiunt Dæmones, ut quæ non funt, fic tamen, quafi funt, confpicienda homini-
bus exhibeant. Lactantius Lib.2. Inftit. Cap.15. Diabolus Confulitur, cum iis
mediis utimur aliquid Cognofcendi, quæ a Diabolo funt introducta. Ames
Caf.Conf. L. 4. Cap. 23.*

Printed at *Bofton*, and Re-printed at *London*, for **John
Dunton**, at the *Raven* in the *Poultrey*. 1693.

Title page of *Cases of Conscience Concerning Evil Spirits Personating Men; Witchcrafts,
Infallible Proofs of Guilt in such as are Accused of that Crime* (1693) by Reverend Increase
Mather. Printed both in Boston and London, this work attempted to provide sound
reasons and historical precedents for the trial and conviction of genuine practitioners
of witchcraft. It placed little confidence in the use of spectral evidence in attempting
to discover witches. Courtesy Danvers Archival Center, Danvers, Mass.

his father, Increase, as a member of the Governor's Council of Ministers to
prepare a list of recommendations as to how the Salem trials should proceed.
This report entitled "The Return of Several Ministers" produced by June 15,
1692, encourages the Court in its work, but warns the justices to avoid the
use of "witch tests" and "spectral evidence"—both of which were regarded
as unreliable proofs for crimes of a capital nature.[7]

Had this report and the opinions of the Boston ministers been closely followed and taken seriously by the Salem Court, the horrors of the Salem trials
could have been entirely averted. Unfortunately, this was not the case.

Cotton Mather, perhaps because he genuinely believed the Court was engaged in a godly and righteous crusade against Satan and his minions, added to the Boston ministers' report his personal codicil. This postscript by the younger Mather encouraged the magistrates to continue the "good work" of the Court in the manner they were already going. In effect, and perhaps without realizing it, Cotton Mather actually negated the impact of the ministers' warning against using spectral evidence, and in effect, gave them approval for the controversial methods employed up to that point.[8]

That is not to imply that Cotton Mather approved the use of spectral evidence at all. He, like his father, agreed that it was inherently unreliable and that no one should be convicted solely upon such proof. He does, however, open the door for spectral evidence by stating that it can sometimes be helpful in identifying potential suspects—who should be subsequently convicted by more easily verifiable testimony. On this key issue, his father was very clear. In the senior Mather's view, such trials must never even take such a chance when human life is at stake:

> This then I declare and testify, that to take away the life of any one, merely because a Spectre or Devil, in a Bewitched or Possessed person does accuse them, will bring the Guilt of Innocent Blood on the Laud where such a thing shall be done. Mercy forbid that it should, in New England.[9]

Both Mathers oppose the exclusive use of spectral evidence, yet only the senior Mather is unswervingly convinced of its utter untrustworthiness at all times. Had both been equally vehement in their condemnation of the Court's use of such proof, no convictions would have been reached. That even Cotton Mather finally has second thoughts about the episode is evident from a diary entry dated January 1698, where he speculates that God might have just cause to visit his family with divine retribution for "My not appearing with vigor enough to stop the proceedings of the Judges when the Inextricable storm from the Invisible World assaulted the country . . ."[10] This view is the key to understanding Cotton Mather. To him, the outbreak of witchcraft in Salem was a very real and serious threat to the Commonwealth by forces of Satan which had infiltrated the godly community and were being allowed by God to have free reign. It was, in his mind, God's judgment upon New England's people for having rejected the original vision of a "City Set on a Hill," a godly commonwealth, in favor of the pursuit of worldly goals.

Cotton Mather's previous experience with the Goodwin children and Mary Glover in 1688 had convinced him of the realities of witchcraft and the danger it presented to innocent individuals. Both he and his father had researched, collected, and published firsthand accounts of hundreds of incidents of witchcraft from around the world. They were both unshakably certain of its existence and drew upon numerous biblical references which not only confirmed this belief, but gave clear guidelines as to how it should be punished when discovered.[11]

Standing in relative opposition to the Mathers on their position concerning the Salem episode were contemporary observers, Thomas Brattle and fellow Bostonian merchant-scholar, Robert Calef. Both of these gentlemen were outspoken critics of the Mathers—especially Cotton Mather—and the judicial process followed by the Court of Oyer and Terminer in Salem.

Brattle, a Harvard graduate, mathematician, member of the prestigious Royal Academy, and an influential businessman of Boston, was a keen observer of the activities which took place in Salem through the spring and summer of 1692, and decided to take action to oppose them. In October 1692, he produced a letter addressed to an anonymous clergyman entitled "Letter to a Reverend Gentleman" and circulated copies among his friends, members of the Boston business community, and the provincial government.

Brattle's letter severely criticized the Court proceedings which had already resulted in the deaths of twenty individuals—in large part as a direct result of spectral evidence which Brattle regarded with contempt and skepticism. In his view, too much credibility had been placed upon the antics of the "afflicted girls." He also takes exception to judges' superstitious use of the "touch test," encouraging "witchcraft" victims to touch an alleged witch proving the guilt of the accused by their returning to a normal state upon contact.[12]

Brattle's timing was excellent since the "Letter to a Reverend Gentleman" was released immediately after the governor's declaration of a Court hiatus. The letter lent weight to the wisdom of the governor's decision in light of the executions' extent and the growing number of accusations. Governor Phips was clearly frustrated with the Salem situation spiraling out of control and wished a period of calm reflection. That Phips desired stability and resolution is evident in his proclamation:

> The Salem Court of Oyer and Terminer will be adjourned until the first Tuesday in November; between this and then will be [a meeting of the] great assembly [of the Great and General Court] and this matter will be a peculiar matter of their agitation. I think it is a matter of earnest supplication and prayer to Almighty God, that He would afford His presence to the said Assembly, and direct them aright in this weighty matter.[13]

With this letter, it was Brattle's hope to influence the Massachusetts Great and General Court during their October session, inducing them to permanently shut down the Salem Court and bring the trials to an abrupt end.

Thomas Brattle attacks the testimony of the afflicted persons who were regarded as credible witnesses by the Court against its victims, asserting that, in his regard, "reason" was rejected and replaced by "superstition." Beyond merely discounting the "touch test" and "spectral evidence" as outmoded and superstitious methods of inquiry incompatible with the Age of Reason, he argues logically that neither makes sense. Why, he reasoned, should the testimony of those who admit to being under the power of evil spirits be taken as credible proof against accused persons? Using scripture to support his reasoning, Brattle points out that according to the Bible, Satan is "the father of lies" and "the Great Deceiver." He concludes:

> If I believe the afflicted persons as informed by the devil, and act thereupon [their testimony] this, in my act, may properly be said to be grounded upon the

testimony or information of the devil. If things are thus, I think it ought to be for a lamentation to you and me, and all such as would be accounted good Christians.[14]

In a direct attack upon the veracity and sincerity of the afflicted children, Brattle observed that they claimed to do things which were—by the laws of nature—*physically impossible.* "These afflicted persons ... often have declared it, that they can see specters when their eyes are shut, as well as when their eyes are open. I am sure they lie, or at the least speak falsely, if they say so; for the thing in nature is an utter impossibility." He reasons that the only plausible explanation for their behavior might be self-deception. "It is true, they may strongly fancy, or have things represented to their imagination, when their eyes are shut, and I think this is all that should be allowed to these blind, nonsensical girls ..."[15]

In contrast to Cotton Mather, who generally accepted their testimony as valid and creditable, Brattle views the afflicted children as utterly unreliable as witnesses. For this reason, it puzzled him that people of both the uneducated and "better sort" not only believed their testimony, but also sought their advice on things supernatural. He reasoned that "this consulting of these afflicted children," is "a very gross evil, and real abomination" since their advice—just like their testimony—could be influenced by Satanic powers.[16]

What is interesting is that Increase Mather, an avowed opponent to Brattle on most issues, agreed with him on this point. Charles Upham, in the second volume of *Salem Witchcraft*, relates a fascinating Increase Mather anecdote:

> ... Increase Mather sometimes was unguarded enough to express himself with severity against those who gave countenance to the proceedings. "A person from Boston, of no small note, carried up his child to Salem, near twenty miles, on purpose that he might consult the afflicted about his child, which accordingly he did, and the afflicted told him that his child was afflicted by Mrs. Carey and Mrs. Obinson." The afflicted in this and some other instances had struck too high. The magistrates in Boston were unwilling to issue a warrant against Mrs. Obinson and Mrs. Carey had fled. All the man got for his pains was a hearty scolding from Increase Mather, who asked him, "whether there was not a God in Boston, that he should have to go to the Devil in Salem for advice."[17]

In his powerful letter, Brattle concludes by stating that of the fifty-five persons who had already confessed, many were "distracted, crazed women," while others had "denied their guilt and maintained their innocence ... after most violent, distracting, and dragooning methods had been used with them to make them confess." His sentiment was that it was unfair to use these self-confessed witches as witnesses against the accused for the same reason that the testimony of the afflicted children was unreliable.[18]

He reasoned that if the confessed witches also claimed to have signed the Devil's Book, and devoted themselves briefly to Satan's service, how could their testimony be deemed trustworthy and reliable? Brattle's greatest fear was that, in view of the twenty innocent deaths which had already taken place, New England would suffer not merely the judgment of God but also the judgment of history. He concludes with a prophetic warning to his readers:

> What will be the issue of these troubles? God only knows. I am afraid that ages will not wear off that reproach and those stains which these things will leave behind upon our land. I pray God pity us, forgive us and appear mercifully for us in this our mount of distress . . .[19]

What is interesting is that Thomas Brattle seems to have achieved his objective. On October 12, 1692, just three days after the release of Brattle's letter, Governor Phips announced that he had forbidden further imprisonments for witchcraft. By October 26, the Great and General Court of Massachusetts declared a day of fasting and prayer to seek God's guidance as to how to best proceed "as to the witchcrafts." And finally, on October 29, the governor formally dissolved the Salem Court of Oyer and Terminer and banned the future use of spectral evidence. All trial activities were then relocated to Boston where no more executions took place.[20]

Following closely in Brattle's intellectual footsteps is Robert Calef, a Boston merchant who made himself notorious to the Mathers with the publication of a scathing critique of the Salem trials called *More Wonders of the Invisible World*, an ironic title chosen to mock Cotton Mather's recently published, sympathetic analysis of the trials, *Wonders of the Invisible World* (1693). It is worth noting that, even by 1700—seven years after the end of the trials, such was the Mather influence upon Boston and New England in general, that Calef found London to be the closest city which would publish his book.

Calef's view of the trials is uncompromisingly negative and places all trial participants—except the accused—in a highly controversial light, leveling blunt accusations at the Puritan leadership of Massachusetts colony, both political and religious. His first target is Cotton Mather, whom he describes as the one who believed that the community was "beset by devils and torn by the unseen power of Satanic forces." If, Calef argues, Mather's view of Massachusetts as a colony under Satanic siege is accurate, then "it is very deplorable and beyond all other outward calamities." But Calef is *not* convinced that such is, in fact, the case. He heavily implies that many others— "the sensible citizens"—of the colony, share his disbelief. To Calef, the Mathers—especially Cotton—stand apart from the sensible citizens and are instead regarded as among those who are easily deluded, naïve, and lacking in good judgment:

> But if, on the other side, the matter be, as others do understand it, that the devil has been too hard for us by his temptations, signs, and lying wonders; together with the accusations of a parcel of possessed, distracted, or lying wenches, accusing their innocent neighbors, pretending they see their specters; and that God in righteous judgment may have given them over to strong delusions to believe lies, etc., and to let loose the devils of envy, hatred, pride, cruelty, and malice against each other, yet still disguised under the mark of zeal for God, and left them to the branding of one another with the odious name of witch . . .[21]

This is a good summation of Calef's viewpoint. To him the Salem episode is attributable to "lying wenches" accusing "innocent neighbors" driven by "the devils" of "envy, hatred, pride, cruelty, and malice."[22]

Not surprisingly, Calef's book sold extensively throughout the colonies and helped shape public opinion concerning the Salem episode for many generations. It should be added that his opinions have not entirely vanished from the minds of many who currently study the trials, and are often given much weight in contemporary analyses of the event.

Like Cotton Mather in his later days, Reverend John Hale of Beverly lived to regret the part he had played during the Salem trials. Beverly was a small seaport town neighboring Salem Village and, because of its proximity, Hale had been involved with Reverend Parris from the beginning. Like Mather, too, he had been a virulent leader in the prosecution of the trials, but became less aggressive following the accusation of his wife, Sarah. Like most ministers of his generation John Hale never doubted the existence of witchcraft as a real and present threat to the community, but only expressed sincere regret for the improper and unjust way the trials had been handled and the inappropriate use of spectral evidence. His conscience was so troubled over the deaths of the innocent victims that in 1697 Hale produced a book, *A Modest Inquiry into the Nature of Witchcraft*, examining the Salem trials and other witchcraft incidences through history. Written in 1697, printed in 1702, the book was not published until two years after Hale's death.

In this very important study of Puritan thinking about the essential nature of witchcraft, Hale goes on to explain how it was that otherwise educated and rational community leaders could have allowed such a tragedy to occur. In a particularly insightful passage, he observes:

> But I would come nearer to our own times and bewail the errors and mistakes that have been made in the year 1692. In apprehending too many we may believe were innocent and executing some.... I am abundantly satisfied that those who were most concerned to act and judge in these matters, did not willingly depart from the rules of righteousness. But such was the darkness of the day, the tortures and lamentations of the afflicted, that we walked in the clouds and could not see our way.[23]

In short, Hale had been an observer and participant in the episode, and admitted that the public outcry and sense of community crisis clouded the vision and impaired the good judgment of the people in general and the justices in particular. This, in Hale's view was what went wrong with the Salem trials.[24] Upon reflection he takes exception to the Court's credulity concerning the testimony of the afflicted girls as well as its acceptance of spectral evidence, but stops short of implying that the witnesses were deliberately lying or that the threat of witchcraft was not real.

Following the publication of Hale's book, the next attempt to provide an objective historical analysis of the trials was that of Thomas Hutchinson, who served as royal governor of Massachusetts from 1771 to 1774. In 1765, he published a well-written, multivolume *History of the Commonwealth of Massachusetts* in which he analyzed the Salem witchcraft episode. Hutchinson was a gentleman-scholar influenced by the ideas of the Enlightenment and highly skeptical of explanations which rested upon unverifiable, nonscientific evidence.[25]

In his summary of the Salem witchcraft outbreak, he took a critical position concerning the opinions of the religious leaders of the colony—especially Reverend Cotton Mather—and was deeply sympathetic with the victims. He concluded by asserting that for many years after this tragedy, the people of Massachusetts colony believed "that there was something preturnatural [supernatural] in it, and that it was not all the effect of fraud and imposture . . ." He adds that by the mid-eighteenth century, there were "a great number of persons who are willing to suppose the accusers to have been under bodily disorders which affected their imaginations."[26]

While some contemporary historians, such as Linda Caporeal, might agree with this assessment, Hutchinson did not. He suggests that while such an interpretation of events may appear ". . . kind and charitable," in actuality it "seems to be winking the truth out of sight." Rather Hutchinson, like Robert Calef, maintained the conviction that "the whole was a scene of fraud and imposture, begun by young girls, who at first perhaps thought of nothing more than being pitied and indulged, and continued by adult persons, who were afraid of being accused themselves."[27]

Both these groups, he asserts, "rather than confess their fraud, suffered the lives of so many innocents to be taken away, through the credulity of judges and juries."[28] This belief that the afflicted girls were aware of their actions, and brought about the community crisis through the conscious and deliberate use of lies and deceitful dramatic performances in court, is a view that will be revisited in the mid-nineteenth century in the multivolume classic work of Reverend Charles Upham.

In 1842, prior to the publication of Upham's *History of the Witchcraft Trials*, one of his colleagues and contemporaries, Joseph B. Felt, released an exhaustive compendium of Salem history entitled *Annals of Salem*. A sizeable portion of volume two was devoted to his ideas and understanding of the episode. Like Upham, Felt is a native of Salem, and not surprisingly exhibits a native bias towards the participants. He, like Upham, reminds his readers that belief in witchcraft for the people of colonial Salem had been transferred from Western Europe and in no way reflected more than a generally held view, "Such a belief was no more indicative of their mental weakness, than of that justly attributable to all civilized Europe." [29] Felt is the first writer to emphasize the relatively few executions when compared to the sizeable number of accusations. In addition to a brief summary of the sequence of events, Felt provides details of the expenses of victims kept at the jail in Boston. This is the first known use of jailer's records in the study of the trials. Felt also attributes the decline in the power of the afflicted children's testimony to the tactical mistake of having accused Sarah Hale, wife of Reverend John Hale, the beloved pastor of Beverly, Massachusetts.[30] "A great means of counteracting the delusion, is that the wife of Rev. Mr. Hale, of Beverly, is accused. Her character forbid reliance on the [spectral] testimony." He also credits Increase and Cotton Mather with encouraging leniency in Court proceedings following the final executions in September, pointing out that none of those tried and convicted were executed. His opinion of the event as a whole was that it was "one of the most surprising and sorrowful events ever recorded in the chronicles of our country." He exonerates the members of the Court for its treatment of the victims by emphasizing that "their great and deplorable error was the misapplication of insufficient, though to some extent, remarkable testimony."[31] These justices, in Felt's view, should only "be judged by the same principle; that if any are charitably excused as influenced by honest, but mistaken views, all the rest should be alike tolerated." Concerning his assessment of the twenty victims, Felt concludes that they simply "fell guiltless victims of well-intended but ill directed zeal." He qualifies this statement with the observation that when people "think on their sufferings" they must be perceived as "wrongly accused and condemned" wishing that they "might have been spared" and lived "long to manifest their dying integrity."[32]

NOTES

1. Thomas Brattle, *Letter of Thomas Brattle* (Boston, 1692), in David Levin, *What Happened in Salem?* (New York: Harcourt, Brace and World, Inc., 1960), 127.

2. Reverend John Hale, *A Modest Inquiry into the Nature of Witchcraft* (Boston, 1702), in George Lincoln Burr, ed., *Narratives of the Witchcraft Cases* (New York: Scribner and Sons, 1914), 426–27.

3. Ibid.

4. Bernard Rosenthal, *Salem Story: Reading the Witch Trials of 1692* (Cambridge. Cambridge University Press, 1993), 135–36.

5. Increase Mather, *Cases of Conscience* (Boston, 1692), in Rosenthal, *Salem Story*, 66–67.

6. Ibid.

7. Cotton Mather, *Return of Several Ministers Consulted* (Boston, 1692), in Levin, *What Happened in Salem?*, 110.

8. Ibid.

9. Ibid., 62.

10. Cotton Mather, *Memorable Providences* (Boston, 1689), in Rosenthal, *Salem Story*, 202.

11. Ibid., 1–18.

12. Brattle, *Letter of Thomas Brattle*, in Levin, *What Happened in Salem?*, 127.

13. Ibid., 127–35.

14. Ibid., 132–33.

15. Ibid., 134.

16. Ibid., 135.

17. C. W. Upham, *Salem Witchcraft*, vol. 2 (reprinted by Williamstown, MA: Corner House Publishers, 1971), 456.

18. Brattle, *Letter of Thomas Brattle*, in Levin, *What Happened in Salem?*, 127.

19. Ibid., 135.

20. Mary Beth Norton, *In the Devil's Snare: The Salem Witchcraft Crisis of 1692* (New York: Random House, 2002), 289.

21. Robert Calef, *More Wonders of the Invisible World* (London, 1700), in Samuel P. Fowler, ed., *Salem Witchcraft* (Boston: H. P. Ives and A. A. Smith, 1860).

22. Ibid.

23. Hale, *A Modest Inquiry into the Nature of Witchcraft.*

24. Deodat Lawson, *A Brief and True Narrative of Some Remarkable Passages Relating to Sundry Persons Afflicted by Witchcraft, at Salem Village Which Happened from the Nineteenth of March to the Fifth of Arpil, 1692* (Boston, 1692), reprinted in Burr, ed., *Narratives of the Witchcraft Cases*, 323–24.

25. Lawson, *A Brief and True Narrative of Witchcraft, at Salem Village*, in Francis Hill, *The Salem Witch Trials: A Reader*, 61–64.

26. Ibid.

27. Ibid.

28. Ibid.

29. Joseph B. Felt, *Annals of Salem*, vol. 2, (Salem, MA: S. B. Ives & Co., 1849), 475.

30. Ibid., 480.

31. Ibid.

32. Ibid., 483–84.

4

Contemporary Interpretations of the Salem Witchcraft Episode

The era immediately following the Holocaust and World War II witnessed a tremendous increase in the interest of the general public and the academic world in the study of the Salem witchcraft episode. Particular focus among scholars in the field of social and intellectual history was placed upon what factors may have played a part in initiating and sustaining the trials. Far from the naïve narratives and interpretations of the antiquarians of the Victorian era, this new generation of scholars explored a wide range of possible causes from deep-seated, psychological fears of Indian attacks to the possible outbreak of diseases such as encephalitis. These academic studies, built upon the recent scholarship of some of the twentieth century's leading experts in the area of Puritan social and intellectual history, greatly expanded our knowledge of New England Puritan society, its beliefs, its laws, and its interrelationships.

The first important modern interpretation makes its appearance in 1949 in a work by historian Marion Starkey entitled *The Devil in Massachusetts*. Considered by several noted historians to be "the best researched and certainly the most dramatic account of the events of 1692," this book incorporates a significant amount of psychoanalysis in its attempt to understand the minds of the "afflicted children" and their associates. Here, for the first time, a writer provides a cogent narrative utilizing many primary sources allowing the girls to speak for themselves. While this study falls primarily under the heading of the "Freudian school" of historical analysis, Starkey makes no claim to be a psychohistorian. Rather she explores the events as they unfold and sees that "childish fantasies of some little girls" were picked up and carried to a "deadly climax by a pack of 'bobby-soxers' (teenagers)."[1]

What makes the approach of *The Devil in Massachusetts* so fascinating especially to nonacademic readers is Starkey's unique method of interpretation
by means of "story-telling." From beginning to end the narrative, testimony,
disputes, and dramatic events are interwoven with the flair of a historical
novel. Starkey at one point characterizes the Salem event as "Greek
tragedy."[2] She attributes the actions of the afflicted to a form of psychoneu-
rosis directly resulting from the emotionally stressful events preceding the
outbreak. This release of irrational, emotional tension Starkey characterizes
as hysteria. Indeed, she traces the history of numerous outbreaks which
"had occurred repeatedly in the Middle Ages ... in the wake of stress and
social disorganization." Of importance to this study is the psychological conditioning of the adolescent Puritan female. To Starkey, they responded to a
perceived supernatural threat in a manner entirely in keeping with their
belief system and religious training. She does not attach any more significance to their fits and frenzied behavior than she would to a group of contemporary adolescent girls responding emotionally to a concert by their
favorite musical group.[3]

What, in this interpretation, is most unexpected about the girls' fits, was
"the way the community received them." Under normal circumstances, Starkey argues, such behavior should have been regarded by the community for
what it truly was—the antics of a small group of hysterical female adoles-
cents. Starkey does not accept the idea that Puritan society's universal belief
in devils and witches was enough to overturn their rational understanding
of adolescent behavior under stress. In her view, there had to be another
rationale for the local adult community lending credence to the girls' testimony and responding with an emotional tumult leading to the accusation of
hundreds and the deaths of twenty individuals. Without the support of the
larger community, she argues, the trials would not have taken place.

The interpretation suggests that what made the difference was the general
public's sense of imminent danger, a perception which had grown during
the preceding twenty-five years. Starkey argues that the Massachusetts colonists had suffered successive incidences of social crises from King Philip's
War in 1675 to the ongoing frontier war between themselves and French-
supported Indians on their northern frontier. The revocation of the Massachusetts Bay Charter by the Stuarts and the subsequent appointment of the
tyrannical Sir Edmund Andros as royal governor all contributed to the community's sense of "anxiety and terror ... longer than could be borne" and
"demanded a catharsis." This psychological pressure manifested itself in an
overwhelming desire on the part of the colonial community to purge their
society of besetting Satanic powers and destroy the Devil's minions in the
process. To Starkey's view, the victims of the trials were scapegoats—sacrificial
lambs—whose deaths helped to release Puritan society's mounting social
tension, frustration, and anxiety.[4]

Written shortly following the Nuremberg war crime trials and during the
rise of the Cold War, Starkey's analysis presages the McCarthy Era writings
of playwright Arthur Miller by four years. She prophetically points out that
"witch-hunts" could become commonplace occurrences in the twentieth
century as well, intimating that "although this particular type of delusion

has vanished from the Western world, the urge to hunt 'witches' has done nothing of the kind." Her theory about a public catharsis being resorted to by society has been only slightly altered in contemporary culture "by replacing the medieval idea of malefic witchcraft with pseudoscientific concepts like 'race' and 'nationality' and by substituting for theological dissension a whole complex of warring ideologies." It is an "allegory for our times."[5]

It would be remiss to overlook the ideas of one of America's greatest historians concerning the trials. Samuel Eliot Morison released in 1956 a revised edition of his classic study, *The Intellectual Life of Colonial New England*, which contributed his personal assessment of the Salem episode within the context of Puritan intellectual history. This pragmatic narrative historian suggests that the origin of the Salem episode lay in the 1689 publication of Cotton Mather's *Memorable Providences Relating to Witchcrafts*, which became a widely read, best-selling book. Its account of the behavior of the Goodwin children and their fits, Morison asserts, provided the paradigm for the afflicted children to follow in their own incidence of possession. He attributed the episode as having "arose, as witchcraft epidemics had usually arisen in Europe, during a troubled period ... of New England history when the people were uneasy with rebellions, changes of government, and Indian attacks; and in a community which for several years had been torn by factions." He reverts to the theory akin to the traditional view advanced by Upham that the "afflicted children" found themselves the object of unusual attention, and "with the exhibitionism natural to young girls, persisted in their accusations for fear of being found out." The continuance of the episode he attributes to "a state of neurosis ... similar to that of the shell-shocked soldier torn between fear of death and fear of disgrace." He is particularly critical of the Court magistrates who "... declined to follow the best rules for detecting witches laid down by professional English witch-hunters and urged on them, ... by the ministers." Both they and the "intellectual class" who kept a "cowardly silence" are the persons Morison holds responsible for the continuance of the tragedy. Concerning the two Mathers, Morison praises the efforts of Increase to caution the Court against the use of spectral evidence, and criticizes Cotton for his timidity in not taking a stronger public stand in keeping with his true beliefs.[6]

Another theory, like Starkey, which relies heavily upon the psychological conditioning of society is the anthropological interpretation of Chadwick Hansen. This is presented in his revisionist publication, *Witchcraft at Salem*, which asserts that what happened in Salem was the result of the Puritan community's deeply ingrained belief in the reality of witchcraft and its undoubted ability to cause harm.[7] In this regard he likens seventeenth-century Salem to those primitive societies of the twentieth century where an internalized belief in witchcraft gives actual power to the community's practitioners of magic. To support this, he supplies numerous documented cases in the contemporary third world where people who believed themselves bewitched reacted to their belief by exhibiting the appropriate physiological evidence of a magical curse.

This theory contends that just as in the voodoo culture of the West Indies where many individuals have been known to suffer, and in some cases die, when convinced they were the target of a practitioner of black magic, this reaction may have occurred among many in seventeenth-century Salem. Apart from the community's affirmation of the realities of the supernatural, Hansen goes on to suggest that Anglo-American culture actually had its practitioners of malefic magic who were often known and feared by the local community. If the afflicted children and others actually believed themselves to be the object of such a dangerous member of the community, it seems likely that they would respond in an appropriate emotional and physical manner.[8] Beginning with this idea, Hansen explores the logical consequence of a community responding appropriately to a perceived threat. To him, the afflicted children are not performing for sportive purposes or public attention. Neither are they knowingly providing misinformation or perjured testimony, but they actually believed themselves bewitched. Their bizarre behavior was exactly what their psychological conditioning told them they should do.

Hansen carefully traces the origin of the episode directly to Tituba's winter afternoon sessions with Elizabeth Parris and Abigail Williams which initiated the girls' bout of clinical mass hysteria. When Dr. Griggs declared them under the power of the "evil hand" of witchcraft, and subsequently when Tituba confessed to having made a pact with Satan, a psychological dam broke, releasing a torrent of emotion and hostility on the part of the girls and shortly thereafter on the part of the entire local community.[9]

The most controversial element of this theory is Hansen's assertion that there were actually practicing witches within the Salem community. He identifies several likely suspects including Tituba and a woman who operated an unlicensed tavern, Bridget Bishop. Hansen examines the nonspectral evidence presented in the case against Bishop and concludes that "Bridget was in all probability a practicing witch." He does not find it at all surprising that she is the first person to be tried, condemned, and executed, since there was considerable nonspectral proof presented against her, none of which she was able to refute. According to this theory, Bridget Bishop's conviction and execution in June 1692 fanned the flames to further intensify feelings of community paranoia. With Bishop's case serving as the only precedent, later cases were met with less rationality and sympathetic understanding by the Salem Court.[10]

Hansen goes on to identify other cases which provided evidence of the accused having dabbled in the black arts. Among the more controversial suspects were Wilmot "Mammy" Redd, a professional fortune-teller, Dorcas Hoar, and a West Indian slave called Candy who presented the court with several rag puppets she claimed to have used in performing acts of witchcraft. Ironically, the Salem Court actually attempted to test the genuine nature of these effigies by pricking them with pins, burning them, and submersing them in water. When the afflicted girls reacted to these "witchcraft experiments" by screaming, choking, and coughing, the magistrates were convinced of the effigies' reliability as witchcraft paraphernalia.[11] Professor Hansen points out the inconsistency of a group of magistrates attempting to convict an individual of the crime of witchcraft attempting to perform acts of witchcraft as part of their investigation. The reaction of the afflicted to the burning and drowning of the dolls is, in Hansen's view, another of many examples of these witnesses exhibiting symptoms and behavior emanating from their own internalized beliefs in the efficacy of black magic.[12]

It should not be surprising that Hansen's ideas are generally considered controversial by most scholars. Yet his theory has held up well under academic criticism, and remains one of the most widely read and popular interpretations of the episode. What lends further credence to his assertions is his mastery of the subject matter and his understanding of the degree of belief of Puritans concerning the certainty and pervasive nature of the "unseen world." Moreover, as difficult as the afflicted testimony is to believe, it is doubtful that so many Puritans would consciously commit perjury or knowingly contribute to the deaths of so many innocent neighbors unless under the influence of some form of "clinical mass hysteria." In short, he would assert, their behavior was not "fraudulent" but "pathological."

A groundbreaking demographic study which examines the possible economic motivation for the Salem trials was released in 1974 by Paul Boyer and Stephen Nissenbaum in the aptly titled *Salem Possessed*. This interpretation examines the interfactional conflicts which divided Salem Village community into distinct and conflicting groups consisting of those whose fortunes were in decline and those whose fortunes were rising. To a greater extent than any previous study, *Salem Possessed* outlines the land-based and economic disputes which played a significant role in tearing apart the social fabric of Salem Village and contributing to the accusations which followed in 1692. This study is strongly supported by exhaustive analysis of primary source materials which establish the patterns of economic and social life of ordinary people and the way they related to each other.[13]

Essentially, the theory maintains that Salem Village was, at the time of the arrival of Reverend Samuel Parris, a community divided into two distinct, competing economic factions. One faction, the anti-Parris group under the leadership of the Porter Family, sought closer ties with the nearby, economically thriving port of Salem. Conversely, the pro-Parris faction, led by the Putnam Family, resented the entrepreneurial success of Salem and wished to establish an autonomous farming community. To Boyer and Nissenbaum, the Salem witchcraft trials were in reality an outward manifestation of the social conflict which existed between these two groups. Their demographic data supports the proposition that the leaders of the witchcraft hunt were members of the group whose economic fortunes were in decline, while their victims were often those whose economic fortunes were on the rise. In this theory, the trials represent a "last ditch effort" by the economically disenfranchised to "drive back the insistent forces of economic change."[14]

Boyer and Nissenbaum's idea—that there might have been an economic motivation for some of the accusations—is not entirely new. Nathaniel Hawthorne, in his romance novel, *The House of the Seven Gables*, uses this as the underlying pretext for the witchcraft accusation of Matthew Maule by Judge Pynchon. What is new is the reversal of roles as discovered by the supporting data of the study: "All our reading about the events of 1692 had prepared us to view the witch-hunters as a dominant and ruthless group that had taken the offensive against a set of weak and powerless outcasts.

What we actually found, as the trials fell into a longer historical perspective, was something quite different: the witch-hunters may have been on the offensive in 1692, but it was a fleeting offensive—counteroffensive really—in the midst of a general and sustained retreat."[15]

The key elements in this theory are the residents of the village themselves and particularly the dissention which divided them. Reverend Parris is seen as a man beset by a faction that "may have lived *in* the Village, but were not *of* the Village." His opponents were primarily prosperous farmers and merchants who inhabited the village, but saw their economic interests in close association with the rising tide of commerce in nearby Salem proper. Reverend Parris and his supporters were dedicated to resisting the economic domination of this faction and used the witchcraft episode as a convenient means of damaging the influence of the opposition.[16]

The outbreak of witchcraft and most especially the virulent witch-hunt which followed was, in the authors' view, a conscious and premeditated attempt by the pro-Parris faction to reestablish their former control over the village by attacking those who had supplanted them as the economic leadership. The degree of alienation and even the geographic pattern established by the landholdings of each rival faction is thoroughly substantiated by numerous graphs, tables, and property maps which clearly illustrate the interrelationship patterns between rival households and factions. As a study of community experience, this theory focuses heavily upon the commonplace factors which play a part in daily life. It examines divided families, disinherited children, anxious farmers, jealous neighbors, and most important, an embattled minister. It does this and also weaves a pattern that creates a convincing case that economics played a part in the Salem episode in some significant way.[17]

Yet another demographic study which examines the communities of Salem and beyond is the important work *Entertaining Satan, Witchcraft and the Culture of Early New England* by John Putnam Demos. In this interpretation the author examines witchcraft cases as an outgrowth of New England's culture in the seventeenth century. In the process he integrates huge amounts of biographical information and compares it with court documents which detail what evidence was presented in most cases of witchcraft. His focus is not primarily upon the Salem episode, rather he views it as only a part of a larger pattern of social behavior. What he discovers is that witchcraft belonged to the regular business of life in the seventeenth century. It was, in the author's view, "integral to the belief system, the value structure, and the predominant psychology of those times."[18]

Beginning in the 1630s and concluding at the time of the Salem trials, Demos explores the multitude of witchcraft cases which took place in New England. He especially examines the outbreaks of witchcraft in Connecticut and Hampton, Massachusetts, examining surviving court records, vital records, correspondence, diaries, and other firsthand accounts. The result of this work is a thorough narrative history integrated with statistical data which supports the author's thesis that witchcraft was not regarded as particularly unusual in Puritan society. What he finds is that Salem falls within a predictable pattern of social behavior common to most New England communities afflicted by episodes of witchcraft. Demos, in creating a profile of the typical witch, posits that most individuals were female, of middle age, of English ancestry, married but with few children, frequently involved in contentious disputes with family and neighbors, frequently charged with other crimes, more likely to have practiced a medical vocation like healer or midwife, and occupied a low social standing in the community.[19]

Closely paralleling the example of Reverend Parris, Demos discovers that most village ministers used outbreaks of witchcraft as moral examples to their parishioners, confirming the reality of the existence of the "invisible world," and the silent spiritual warfare being waged all around them. These instances further served as opportunities for ministers to instill and confirm the general moral values of a community, empowering them to resist the devil and his deceptions at all times.[20]

Demos discovers that the pattern of symptoms and behavior by afflicted witnesses is uniform in almost all cases. The presence of convulsive fits, biting, physical contortions, and other such complaints similar to those of Salem's afflicted children are commonly identified as belonging to all supernatural forms of affliction, and experienced by all alleged victims. Other commonly expressed forms of malefic affliction included spectral visitations, physical illness such as measles or smallpox, and damage to livestock or personal property.[21]

Demos discovered the sequence established in Salem for accusations was a standard pattern of behavior in other New England communities at different times. He identifies three specific steps: (1) witch and victim contend over some matter of mutual concern; (2) victim perceives anger in witch and fears harm; and (3) victim suffers hurt of one sort or another and accuses a witch. He also notes that, when studying most communities beset by witchcraft episodes, the initial stages of suspicion and accusation begin at the lower level of the social scale, and only involve more prominent members of society as cases evolve. As with the Salem episode, as more and more notable personages become involved, there is a greater likelihood of court proceedings.[22]

In answer to the question as to why the Salem witchcraft episode achieved such massive proportions and involved so many people, Demos suggests that the 1690s were an especially stressful and volatile decade. Like Starkey, he points to natural disasters, Indian wars, epidemics, and Constitutional changes which made the Puritan population believe that a crisis was at hand. To Demos, the triggering mechanism was pulled by "a culmination of many years of chronic factionalism and discord." He concludes his theory with the observation that the Salem episode most likely was the result of two key elements: (1) concern with witchcraft was directly tied to internal factionalism, thus one accusation immediately suggested others by guilt through association; and (2) the social climate of late-seventeenth-century New England as a whole was ambivalent, anxious, and strained. For these reasons, he contends, the "infection" of witchcraft spread well beyond Salem and adjacent communities, which produced accusations of their own.[23]

Perhaps the theory which has garnered the greatest amount of media attention is the so-called "ergot theory." This explanation suggests that the afflicted children might have ingested significant quantities of ergot mold, fostering a physiological condition known as ergotism, a disease whose symptoms are similar to those exhibited by the afflicted girls throughout the episode. The first scholar to introduce this theory to the scientific world was Linnda R. Caporeal in her 1976 article: "Ergotism: The Satan Loosed in Salem?"[24]

Rather than suggest that the girls' aberrant behavior was the product of overworked adolescent imaginations or a deliberate attempt to deceive the Court, Caporeal posits that the basis for much of the incredible testimony might in fact be the result of a serious medical condition stemming from the ingestion of ergot mold. As evidence, Caporeal points to contemporary descriptions of the girls' activities which mention choking, disorderly speech, odd postures and gestures, convulsive fits, and complaints of biting, pinching, and pricking. These characteristics, she asserts, are in keeping with traits exhibited by persons suffering from ergot mold poisoning.[25]

While acknowledging that numerous explanations have already been offered, Caporeal suggests that none of these provide an absolutely clear justification for the convulsive fits and visions which the afflicted girls claimed to experience. She also calls into question why girls raised in a "soul-searching Puritan tradition" would consciously lie and slander their neighbors unless they actually believed what they were saying was, in fact, true. To her mind, the social and spiritual pressures of Puritan New England, not to mention the threat of eternal damnation, should have been sufficient to minimize any possibility of a deliberate joint conspiracy to commit perjury and thus condemn innocent persons.[26]

She also rejects the traditional interpretation of Tituba as the prime mover of the witchcraft episode, and points to the amazing lack of proof tying Tituba to the practice of magic. In Caporeal's view, the only evidence tying anyone to an act of magic is Reverend John Hale's testimony describing a fortune-telling experiment performed by the afflicted girls involving a glass of water and an egg white to determine the future husband of one of the girls. Since Hale never actually identifies Tituba as the originator of this act of divination, Caporeal asserts, all traditional assumptions labeling her as a "voodoo priestess" are without foundation. She asserts that all activities linking Tituba and the afflicted girls together—such as in the concocting of a "witch's cake"—are not West Indian forms of magic, but actually traditional English in origin. Tituba, she maintains, has been wrongfully depicted as a practitioner of voodoo, a scapegoat for many who have made assumptions without justification.[27]

Caporeal next narrows down the field of possible interpretations. If real magic (divination) was not practiced by Tituba, were the girls simply acting out a fantasy—perpetrating a "fraud" upon the local populace to avoid punishment, gain public attention, or amuse themselves? She also rejects this theory because of the incredible skill necessary in order to convincingly duplicate all the physical symptoms they exhibited. She similarly rejects the possibility of "mass hysteria" as an explanation, since "if the girls were not practicing divination, and if they did indeed develop true hysteria, then they must have developed hysteria simultaneously, hardly a credible supposition." Finally, she suggests that the only plausible explanation must be that the girls were actually suffering from a physical malady, which forced them against their wills to behave in an aberrant manner.[28]

Ergot mold is a parasitic fungus which infests cereal grains—especially rye. It tends to infect crops of rye during warm, damp, and rainy springs and summers. Such conditions, Caporeal asserts, existed during the spring and summer of 1691. It also tends to affect females more than males and children and pregnant women even more than the rest of the population. Convulsive ergotism is characterized by "crawling sensations in the skin, hallucinations, painful muscular contractions, epileptic-type convulsions, vomiting, and diarrhea." Victims also exhibit "mental disturbances such as mania, melancholia, psychosis, and delirium." Since all of these symptoms were present and noted at different times during the testimony of the afflicted girls, Caporeal makes the diagnosis that it is possible that they had, over time, ingested bread which had been infected with ergot mold and were reacting accordingly.[29]

How was it possible that only a select few girls from several different households might have been affected, but many others who had consumed the same bread were not? This question suggests a weakness in Caporeal's argument. She identifies the most likely farm to produce infected grain as being that of the Putnam family, who distributed their grain to many of the households whose girls were involved in the testimony. The possibility that an irresistible physiological condition forced the "afflicted children" to make their wild accusations is certainly an idea which sheds a more positive light upon the accusers. Were there others not infected whose involvement was motivated by other means? Caporeal would agree: "of course there was fraud and mental illness at Salem. The records clearly indicate both." Thus the ergot mold theory, even if proven true, only explains a portion of the Salem story.[30]

It should also be noted that a similar physiological theory concerning the Salem episode has been advanced by Professor Laurie Winn Carlson in her book, *A Fever in Salem: A New Interpretation of the New England Witchcraft Trials*. In this study, the author offers the medical hypothesis that mosquitoes carried *encephalitis lethargica* from birds to horses, cows, and humans living in communities where the witchcraft outbreaks occurred. Like Caporeal, she asserts that the physical symptoms of the afflicted children, as described by contemporary observers, parallel those of encephalitis victims.[31]

Professor Carol F. Karlsen's groundbreaking, feminist study, *The Devil in the Shape of a Woman*, has been recognized by many notable historians as a formative work which uncovers and examines the basic assumptions that governed the everyday lives of people in seventeenth-century New England. Karlsen believes that despite the numbers of men executed in Europe and New England for the crime of witchcraft, the story of witchcraft is "primarily the story of women." She points out that the history of witchcraft, both in England as well as New England, tells the story of thousands of women who paid for their nonconformity with their lives. She asserts that "perhaps the strongest link between witchcraft in England and New England was the special association of this crime with women and womanhood. This fact is supported by the sheer weight of statistical evidence which confirms that, throughout the period of witchcraft persecutions in Europe and New England, the preponderance of individuals convicted and executed for witchcraft were females."[32]

Karlsen, like demographic historian John Putnam Demos, attempts to draw a profile of what constituted a typical witch in New England, and identify what characteristics were common to most of those accused of the crime of witchcraft. She points out that "the single most salient characteristic of witches was their sex," noting that of the 342 persons who were accused of witchcraft in colonial New England whose sex can be identified, 267, or 78% were female. She provides substantial demographic data to illustrate this point by identifying that more females than males were not only accused, but also tried, convicted, and executed in both individual cases as well as general massive outbreaks of witchcraft. The total number of female executions for witchcraft in colonial New England was twenty-eight as compared to only seven male executions. This fact, Karlsen believes, is illustrative of a tendency on the part of New England's Puritan male hierarchy to use the threat of witchcraft as a means of enforcing female conformity to a subservient and subordinate role in society.[33]

Karlsen maintains that in Massachusetts colony, Puritan women who were outside the conventional profile of the typical "good-wife"—or handmaiden of the Lord—were viewed by the male ruling elite as threats to the divinely appointed social hierarchy, which maintained that only men should be in positions of political, religious, and economic authority. She acknowledges that most Puritan women supported this prevalent belief, and actually helped reinforce it by bringing female peer pressure to bear upon other women who in one way or the other had violated this unwritten code of behavior. It was these nonconforming women—or, handmaidens of the devil—who were most likely to find themselves accused of witchcraft.[34]

To Karlsen, there was, among Puritan leadership, an inherent fear of women's sexual power and tendency to exercise independent judgment when liberated from the control of fathers and husbands. This, in the author's view, is one of the reasons why virtuous Puritan women were expected to marry as soon as they had an opportunity. Puritans, following the teachings of Judaic Law as outlined in the Old Testament, demanded a systematic and orderly society. To them, the most fundamental social unit, which exemplified order, was the family. In the family unit, women, children, and servants were expected to submit to adult male authority, and subordinate all feelings of individuality and independence. Fathers and husbands were regarded as occupying, to their families, the same relationship that God occupied in relationship to his Church. God loves and honors his Church, and expects respect, obedience, and love in return. Rebellion against adult male leadership was tantamount to rebellion against God's divine order. For this reason, women who stepped outside of this acceptable framework were challenging male authority, God's system of order, and inviting suspicion of witchcraft.[35]

The well-known Puritan hatred of the Quakers is, in Karlsen's view, only another example of this mistrust of unconventional women, since the Quakers adhered to the New Testament teaching of a "priesthood of all believers" allowing women to occupy roles of leadership in their societies.

This made them a dangerous threat to the established, male-dominated religious order, especially because Quakers sought to proselytize and convert Puritans to the Society of Friends. For this reason, Quaker women teachers were given the same treatment in Boston as Ann Hutchinson, and immediately subjected to repression, imprisonment, and banishment from Massachusetts Bay Colony. Karlsen illustrates: "when the first Quaker preachers arrived in Boston Harbor in 1656, the authorities were prepared. Ann Austin and Mary Fisher were arrested as witches before they even reached shore." Without the benefit of trial, they were quickly imprisoned and their books "containing corrupt, heretical, and blasphemous doctrines" were confiscated and burned. The windows of their cells were boarded up until, after five weeks of incarceration, "they were thrown out of the colony." As with the capital crime of witchcraft, if the banished Quaker persisted in her sin, and returned to the Massachusetts Bay Colony, she would be hanged. Heresy in Puritan New England was regarded as witchcraft, and visa-versa.[36]

What happened in Salem, in Karlsen's view, was a situation which, like many similar outbreaks, began on a very small scale and would have ultimately served the ends of the community leaders had it remained relatively obscure. Unexpectedly, under the rapidly growing influence of the large number of afflicted children, the episode lasted too long, spread to too many communities, and generally went far beyond what the Puritan elite would allow, necessitating their intervention in order to bring matters under control. Ironically, in the process of discrediting the afflicted children and their testimony, while admitting that some innocent persons had been accused and executed, the ministers and political leadership forever changed traditional beliefs about witchcraft in New England.[37]

Thus does Professor Karlsen help to define the previously undefined boundaries that existed between men and women in pre-1692 Massachusetts, and the unwritten code of behavior, which enforced the role of good-wives in Puritan society. Her study indicates that this code changed slightly after 1692, but it is not able to demonstrate why. She disagrees with historians who assert that the Enlightenment contributed to the decline in the popular belief in witchcraft in the Massachusetts Bay Colony. What is not clear is why this rapid change in popular belief in Massachusetts was similarly mirrored by a nearly concurrent shift in popular beliefs about witchcraft in the British Isles and continental Europe as well. An equally important question would be to ask if, when the repressive, male-dominated Puritan experiment had collapsed, the role of women improved in any way in a more secular New England society.

More recently, another feminist historian, Professor Elizabeth Reis, published a study entitled *Damned Women: Sinners and Witches in Puritan New England*, where she concerns herself principally with the issue of why so many women were accused in witchcraft episodes in seventeenth-century New England. Like Karlsen, she believes that the threat of witchcraft accusations was a means of keeping women in conformity with expected modes of behavior established by a repressive male hierarchy. As a means of justifying this repression, she points to numerous instances of women described by Puritan clergy as being more closely connected to evil than men. For this reason, women needed constant oversight in order that they might not succumb to the temptations of the devil. On the positive side, Reis indicates that the Salem episode helped to change the public opinion about women, the devil, and sin in general.[38]

In 1984, a completely new theory was advanced which placed a great deal of significance upon the role of fear of New England Indian attacks during the latter half of the seventeenth century. Such terror fostered a deep-seated paranoia concerning the threat of Indian attacks, as well as a belief in God's willingness to allow Satan's minions—the Indians and French—to punish Puritan settlements along the frontier. Professor James E. Kences, in his thought-provoking essay, "Some Unexplored Relationships of Essex County Witchcraft to the Indian Wars of 1675 and 1687," examines the possibility that the longstanding threat of Indian attacks psychologically conditioned the minds of the people of Essex County in general, and Salem in particular, to expect a social disaster of terrifying proportions in 1692.[39]

Kences calls this malady *invasion neurosis*, which is "the extreme tension of anticipating an attack which does not materialize." In Kences's theory, it may well have been the January 1692 massacre of York, Maine, which pushed the fearful and vulnerable "afflicted children" and some of their elders over the edge in their need to locate and destroy the potential threats to the community—be they Indians or witches.

Kences discovered multiple links between many Salem Village residents and recent Indian attacks on the Province of Maine. A surprising number of the "afflicted children" had recently experienced the terror of violent deaths in their families, or the need to flee for their lives from earlier homes "down eastward." Many of the "afflicted children" had come to Salem Village in search of sanctuary from these Indian attacks in Maine. Among them was Susannah Sheldon, a member of the Maine family whose brother had been killed by Indians in 1691. There was also Mary Walcott, a girl who cried out against Indian trader John Alden because he sold ". . . powder and shot to the Indians and French, and [lay] with Indian squaws and had Indian papooses." Ann Putnam, Jr., one of the foremost accusers, testified against former Salem Village minister, Reverend George Burroughs, who had miraculously escaped two Indian attacks in the area around York, Maine.[40]

Another aspect of this "invasion neurosis" is manifested by testimony in the witchcraft courtroom concerning the mysterious appearance in 1692 of "men which looked like Frenchmen," in a swamp near present-day Gloucester, Massachusetts. These "Frenchmen" vanished without a trace after they had been fired upon by Ebenezer Babson. The episode was quickly reinterpreted by Essex County residents as a manifestation of satanic forces in their midst, only accentuating feelings of paranoia and anxiety. This sentiment was further heightened by recent decisions by the Massachusetts Great and General Court that, in the opinion of Essex County residents, greatly compromised their ability to meet and combat an invasion by the French and Indians, should one take place. Salem Village residents complained to the selectmen of Salem Town that their houses were spread too far apart to adequately protect them from attack.[41]

This feeling of helplessness was exacerbated by the decision to remove the Boxford militia from the Upper Regiment of Essex County, which guarded the northwest corner of the region. This would have been the unit most likely to face the onslaught from the north. The Andover militia sent a petition of protest to Boston's Great and General Court to prevent the split from happening. Incidentally, Andover, next to Salem Village, was one of the primary communities to experience multiple cases of alleged witchcraft in 1692, and Kences believes their high level of anxiety was directly attributable to the Indian crisis. To Kences, the 1692 witch-hunt, which began in Salem Village, was very much the product of the ongoing struggles with New England's hostile Indian tribes, particularly the Abenaki. His assessment concludes by saying, "New England Puritanism transformed the anxieties of children in wartime into a witch panic, because Puritans regarded the relationship of Indian and witch as fundamental to a perception of Indian war ..."[42]

More recently, Professor Mary Beth Norton, published a major study entitled *In the Devil's Snare: The Salem Witchcraft Crisis of 1692*, which further examines the theory that the fear of Indian attacks might have played a significant role in the psychological conditioning of the people of Salem Village, and particularly the afflicted children. She underscores the commonly held Puritan belief that the Native American people were minions of Satan and served the powers of darkness. Puritans would regard an attack by Indians upon York, Maine, as having Satanic overtones.[43]

In 1991, Enders A. Robinson published *The Devil Discovered: Salem Witchcraft, 1692*, which introduces to the Salem episode a conspiracy theory on a far grander scale than previously suggested by any scholar. According to Robinson, Thomas Putnam and Samuel Parris formed a circle of local men who decided to take advantage of the testimony of the afflicted children and eliminate the opposition faction in the Salem Village Church. Among the leaders of this conspiracy who were responsible for instigating the witchcraft accusations he lists Reverend Samuel Parris, Sergeant Thomas Putnam, Dr. William Griggs, Deacon Edward Putnam, Captain Jonathan Walcott, Constable Jonathan Putnam, and Lieutenant Nathaniel Ingersoll. These ringleaders were assisted by an outer circle of co-conspirators including Thomas Putnam's two uncles, John Putnam, Sr., and Nathaniel Putnam, his cousin Edward Putnam, Joseph Houlton, Thomas Preston, and Joseph Hutchinson. These men were less involved yet helpful when accusations and testimony were needed.[44]

Robinson alleges that what tied these conspirators together were bonds of kinship and friendship. Their goal was merely to reassert power over the families and forces that had gradually assumed control of Salem Village, seeking vengeance against those suspected of wrongdoing or what they deemed to be undesirable elements. In this task, they were ably assisted by their female children, servants, and relatives, including Mary Walcott, Sarah Churchill, Ann Putnam, Jr., Ann Putnam, Sr., Mary Warren, Susannah Sheldon, and Elizabeth Booth—in short, the majority of the "afflicted girls."[45]

The author has identified the key members of this conspiracy through their high level of participation in making court appearances, formal accusations, and the sheer number of times their names appear on depositions and complaints. Like Kences and Mary Beth Norton, Robinson acknowledges the motivational importance of the fear of Indians on the part of many of the afflicted girls who were victims of the recent King William's War in Maine, especially Sarah Churchill and Susannah Sheldon.[46]

What guaranteed the conspiracy's success was the unwitting support of the Salem Court of Oyer and Terminer. As Robinson asserts: "... the nascent conspiracy never could have guessed the extremes to which they would be allowed to go ... that the highest level of government, the ruling old-guard Puritans, would not only act in collusion to support their cause of destroying the enemies of the Salem Village Church, but would give them a free hand in determining who those enemies were." In this manner, Robinson envisions the Salem witchcraft episode as the result of a premeditated and carefully crafted plot, which literally went well beyond the hopes, and even the goals, of its creators. Robinson agrees with many historians when he concludes that only when Governor Phips recognized the inherent danger of the trials to himself and his career, did the government intervene to bring matters under control by October 1692.[47]

While every historical controversy is open to a conspiracy theory, Salem is particularly susceptible since the Salem Village community was so small and was already fragmented into rival factions before the arrival of Reverend Parris. Having said this, one cannot discount that certain individuals, like Thomas Putnam, had much to gain by encouraging the afflicted girls to direct their accusations at those who had been responsible for past injuries, or who were displacing the Putnams within the social hierarchy of the Salem Village community. One of the advantages of this study is the author's ability to show the interrelationships of so many of the key characters in the Salem episode.

NOTES

1. Marion Starkey, *The Devil in Massachusetts: A Modern Inquiry into the Salem Witch Trials* (New York: Alfred Knopf, 1949), viii.

2. Ibid., 17.

3. Ibid., 46.

4. Ibid., 46–47.

5. Ibid., 15.

6. Samuel Eliot Morison, *The Intellectual History of New England* (New York: New York University Press, 1956), 258–62.

7. Chadwick Hansen, *Witchcraft at Salem* (New York: George Braziller, 1969), 225.

8. Ibid., 1–11.

9. Ibid., 11.

10. Ibid., 65.

11. Ibid., 70–74.

12. Ibid., 71.

13. Paul Boyer and Stephen Nissenbaum, *Salem Possessed: The Social Origins of Witchcraft* (Cambridge: Harvard University Press, 1974), preface, xi–xii.

14. Ibid., 110–32.

15. Ibid., preface, xiii.

16. Ibid., 106.

17. Ibid., 216n.

18. John Putnam Demos, *Entertaining Satan: Witchcraft and the Culture of Early New England* (London: Oxford University Press, 1982), vii.

19. Ibid., 12, 93.

20. Ibid., 310–11.

21. Ibid., 382–86.

22. Ibid., 195.

23. Ibid., 385.

24. Linnda R. Caporeal, "Ergotism: The Satan Loosed in Salem?" *Science* (April 2, 1976), 21–26. In Frances Hill, *The Salem Witch Trials Reader* (New York: Da Capo Press, 1984), 257.

25. Ibid., 267.

26. Ibid., 260.

27. Ibid., 261.

28. Ibid., 262.

29. Ibid., 263–64.

30. Ibid., 262

31. Laurie Winn Carlson, *A Fever in Salem: A New Interpretation of the New England Witchcraft Trials* (Chicago: Ivan R. Dee, 1999).

32. Carol F. Karlsen, *The Devil in the Shape of a Woman: Witchcraft in Colonial New England* (New York: W. W. Norton & Co., 1987), xii.

33. Ibid., 47.

34. Ibid., 117–19.

35. Ibid., 120, 163–65

36. Ibid., 125.

37. Ibid., 248.

38. Elizabeth Reis, *Damned Women: Sinners and Witches in Puritan New England* (Ithaca, NY: Cornell University Press, 1999).

39. James E. Kences, "Some Unexplored Relationships of Essex County Witchcraft to the Indian Wars of 1675 and 1687." Essex Institute Historical Collections (EIHC) (July 1984), in Hill, *The Salem Witch Trials Reader*, 270–86.

40. Ibid., 271–72, 274.

41. Ibid., 274.

42. Ibid. To Kences, the visions or hallucinations of the afflicted children could be directly attributed to their "neurosis"—brought about by an extreme fear of attack by Indians and their French allies.

43. Mary Beth Norton, *In the Devil's Snare: The Salem Witchcraft Crisis of 1692* (New York: Vintage Books, 2002). Professor Norton has built upon the foundation laid by Kences and his theory of invasion neurosis.

44. Enders A. Robinson, *The Devil Discovered: Salem Witchcraft, 1692* (New York: Hippocrene Books, 1991), in Hill, *The Salem Witch Trials Reader*, 289–90.

45. Ibid., 286–88.

46. Ibid., 288, 291–92.

47. Ibid., 293.

The Impact of the Salem Witch Trials on Later Generations

The Salem Witch Trials had an effect upon American life and society following the spring of 1693 carrying all the way through to present day. Probably the single most important result of the episode was its direct effect upon the Salem Village community itself. Reverend Samuel Parris remained on in the village church as pastor until after the birth of his son, Noyes, and the death of his wife, Elizabeth, in 1695. The hostile Nurse family censured Parris, demanding his resignation and persuading many attendees to stop paying their tithes of money to the Salem Village Church. This policy made it impossible for the already stressed pastor to collect his salary and placed him in a severe economic crisis, for he received his salary through voluntary contributions from 1691 to 1694, and was paid only a partial salary from 1694 to 1696. The Salem Village congregation sued him for occupying the parsonage nine months after his dismissal; he in turn countersued for unpaid salary. The villagers lost their suit, were compelled to pay court costs, and in 1697 finally paid Parris a settlement of 79 pounds in back salary.[1]

Immediately prior to the resolution of Parris's suit, twelve of the men who had served as witchcraft trial jurors signed a petition asking the "forgiveness of you all, whom we have justly offended ..."[2] In an effort to defuse the situation, Parris publicly admitted that he had been unwittingly deceived by Satan in the accusation of innocent persons. He even apologized for his role in the episode, but this attempt at reconciliation proved to be too late to save his position, and popular opposition to Parris continued to grow. The contending factions within Salem Village Church were never able to reconcile their differences during Parris's tenure. In the tense post-witchcraft climate, the pro-Parris faction finally lost control of the majority of the village

The gravestone of Elizabeth Parris, wife of Reverend Samuel Parris (1696). Located in the Wadsworth Cemetery in Danvers, Massachusetts, the gray, slate headstone of Elizabeth Parris bears an inscription composed by Reverend Samuel Parris. Photo by Richard B. Trask.

parishioners, and the Salem Village congregation dismissed the reverend in 1697.[3]

The now-unemployed clergyman returned to Boston and to his West Indian merchant business yet again. Again not successful in this venture, he decided to revive his pastoral ministry holding brief appointments at churches in Stow, Concord, and Dunstable, Massachusetts, until Parris finally settled at the First Church in Sudbury where he remained until his death in 1720.[4]

As far as those who remained in Salem Village, the impact of the episode was both divisive and devastating. Hostilities between Rebecca Nurse's family and the family of Thomas Putnam were nearly irreconcilable until the influence of Parris's gentle successor, Reverend Joseph Green, began to have an ameliorating effect. In 1699, Green welcomed the Nurse family back into communion and restructured the seating arrangements in the meetinghouse, placing the Nurse family and the Putnams on the same bench. In 1703, he requested that the congregation repeal their excommunication of Martha Corey, wife of Giles Corey.[5]

In August 1706, Anne Putnam, Jr., one of the most influential of the "afflicted girls" in accusing Rebecca Nurse, rose in a Sabbath meeting amid the Salem Village congregation while Reverend Green read her statement of apology to those assembled. In this remarkable document, Anne Putnam stated that she desired "... to be humbled before God for [that] sad and humbling providence that befell my father's family in the year about '92, [that] I ... by such a providence of God be made an instrument for [that] accusing of several persons, of a grievous crime whereby their lives were taken away from them, whom now I have just grounds and good reason to believe they were innocent persons ..."[6] Anne Putnam's expressions of

Memorial to Rebecca Nurse in the Nurse family graveyard. A granite monument erected by the Nurse family in memory of Rebecca Nurse on the Nurse farm in Danvers, Massachusetts. The inscription is from the poem, "Christian Martyr" by John Greenleaf Whittier. Courtesy Danvers Archival Center, Danvers, Mass.

regret were considered so heartfelt that she was restored to full fellowship with the church and, at least superficially, was reconciled to the Nurse family.

In Salem Town proper, the impact of the trials was strongly felt for years afterward. Although Judge John Hathorne died in 1717 and was buried in Salem's Charter Street cemetery, he never at any time publicly expressed regret concerning the role that he played. His legacy of guilt would be passed on to subsequent generations of the Hathorne family, in particular his great-great-grandson, the famous writer Nathaniel Hawthorne, who would revisit the subject of the Salem witchcraft trials in his fictional writings, portraying the event and the actions of the Puritan leadership in a very negative light.[7]

Other Massachusetts magistrates and participants almost immediately began to reflect upon their involvement in the trials and concluded that they had been either mistaken or expressed regret for the manner in which the trials were conducted. Others began to experience what was interpreted then as God's judgment for mishandling the crisis. The newly appointed Governor Sir William Phips, who had let the trials and executions continue through September in Salem—yet had moved the court to Boston and granted amnesty to all survivors by 1693, was ordered back to England in 1694 to answer charges of embezzlement of government funds. Within weeks of his arrival in England, Phips mysteriously died thus leaving Lt. Governor

William Stoughton in the role of acting governor of Massachusetts colony until 1698.[8]

It was William Stoughton, who as Chief Justice of both the 1692 and 1693 Court of Oyer and Terminer had pushed for convictions and executions, while Governor Phips encouraged leniency. Now, after three more years of crop failure, drought, smallpox outbreaks, French and Indian attacks on land and sea, and general misfortune, Governor Stoughton issued a Proclamation on December 17, 1696, in hopes of alleviating God's displeasure. In this statement, even the harsh magistrate begged the people of the Commonwealth that there should be "... observed a Day of Prayer with Fasting throughout the Province, ... so that all God's people may put away that which hath stirred God's Holy jealousy against this land; that He would ... help us wherein we have done amiss to do so no more; and especially that whatever mistakes on either hand have been fallen into ... referring to the Late Tragedy, raised among us by Satan and his instruments, through the awful judgment of God, he would humble us therefore and pardon all the errors and people that desire to love his name ..."[9]

On this appointed day, the Honorable Captain Samuel Sewell, a former Associate Justice of the Courts, attended worship services at Boston's South Church. As he stood facing the congregation, the pastor Reverend Samuel Willard read a document Sewell had written. In it Sewell declared that he "... was sensible of the reiterated strokes of God upon himself and his family ... that he desires to take the blame and shame of it, asking pardon of men, and especially desiring prayers that God ... would pardon that sin and all other of his sins ..." It was a public demonstration of acknowledged guilt and the need for repentance.[10]

During that same year in Beverly, Reverend John Hale, once an enthusiastic witch-hunter, now joined the growing number of introspective men of conscience who would express regret for their role in the witchcraft episode. In his book *A Modest Inquiry into the Nature of Witchcraft*, not published until after Hale's death in 1700, the eminent pastor would discuss how the Court had failed in its duty to provide a fair and impartial trial according to the rule of law and the scriptures.

Hale felt inclined to "... bewail the errors and mistakes that have been in the year 1692. In the apprehending too many we may believe were innocent, and executing some, I fear, not to have been condemned ..." He attributed the lack of clear legal thinking and poor judgment upon the extenuating circumstances which surrounded the trials themselves, but doubted that any action was deliberately taken to falsely accuse the innocent victims. He was in fact "... abundantly satisfied that those who were most concerned to act and judge in those matters did not willingly depart from the rules of righteousness. Yet such was the darkness of that day, the tortures and lamentations of the afflicted, and the power of former presidents (sic), that we walked in the clouds and could not see our way."[11]

At the same time, even the members of the First Church in Salem stated collectively "we are, through God's mercy to us, convinced that we were on that dark day, under the powers of those errors which then prevailed in the land." While on July 8, 1703, the Congregational ministers of Essex County,

Massachusetts, produced a collective petition which stated that they believed there was "great reason to fear that innocent persons then suffered, and that God may have a controversy with the land upon that account."[12]

On October 11, 1711, the Province of Massachusetts enacted an act of legislation called a "Reversal of Attainder" whereby twenty-two convicted witches were pardoned and their reputations officially restored. In the same year, a more tangible form of compensation for damages suffered by the victims' families came in the form of a cash payment of 578 pounds and 12 shillings to be divided among the heirs of the witchcraft trial victims and others who had been wrongfully accused.[13] As a result, the people of Salem, and Massachusetts in general, attempted to put the event behind them, expunge their collective guilt, and return to the more mundane aspects of life in colonial New England.[14]

However New England would never again be the same for the legacy of the witch trials continued to haunt the memories of future generations. Beginning with contemporary critics of the trials, such as Robert Calef and Thomas Brattle, a number of books—particularly Calef's scathing *More Wonders of the Invisible World* (London, 1700)—began to widely circulate. Reverend Cotton Mather is vilified in these accounts as a man of intolerance with a fanatic zeal to condemn innocent persons in the face of reason and common sense. Conversely, Cotton's father, Reverend Increase Mather, President of Harvard College, is shown as having supported a more moderated position and strongly opposing the use of spectral evidence throughout the trials in his 1692 book, *Cases of Conscience*. As a result, the senior Mather has retained the characterization of a man of moderation who never positioned himself in the camp of the chief prosecutors of the witchcraft trials.[15]

Early explanations of the episode, apart from Hale and Mather, were reluctant to place the blame upon real satanic activity. As the Age of the Enlightenment began to dawn in America, skeptics were less inclined to excuse the religious leaders of Salem and Boston and more inclined to blame them. This does not imply a sudden rejection of religious faith or a complete reversal of a belief in witchcraft. It does imply that the role of community leadership, which once was thoroughly dominated by the Puritan clergy, was—shortly after the witchcraft hysteria—undermined by a growing lack of public confidence in the authority of Puritan ministers.

As the clergy's influence gradually lessened, the political power of the New England merchants continued to rise, and public confidence increased toward those whose skills had proved monetarily successful in the secular world. Royal governors too, anxious to avoid the pitfalls of leaders like Phips and Stoughton, turned to secular businessmen for advice, and eschewed relying upon the advice of New England's theologians. This secular shift in Massachusetts's political power partly accounts for the fact that in such mid-eighteenth century upheavals as the Seven Years War and the American Revolution, the merchants of Boston and Salem wielded great influence over popular opinion with little direct input from ecclesiastical leadership.[16]

From a legal perspective, one of the more positive results of the Salem episode in colonial New England was the reluctance of courts to tolerate accusations and trials of witchcraft after 1693. It should also be noted that a

Regni *ANNÆ* Reginæ Decimo.

Province of the
Massachusetts-Bay.

AN ACT,

Made and Passed by the Great and General Court or Assembly of Her Majesty's Province of the Massachusetts-Bay in *New-England*, Held at **Boston** the 17th Day of **October**, 1711.

Nal Lambert Sales

Jan 28ᵗʰ 1808

An Act to Reverse the Attainders of *George Burroughs* and others for Witchcraft.

FOR AS MUCH *as in the Year of our Lord One Thousand Six Hundred Ninety Two, Several Towns within this Province were Infested with a horrible Witchcraft or Possession of Devils ; And at a Special Court of Oyer and Terminer holden at Salem, in the County of* Essex *in the same Year One Thousand Six Hundred Ninety Two,* George Burroughs *of Wells,* John Procter, George Jacob, John Willard, Giles Core, *and his Wife,* Rebecca Nurse, *and* Sarah Good, *all of Salem aforesaid :* Elizabeth How, *of Ipswich,* Mary Eastey, Sarah Wild *and* Abigail Hobbs *all of Topsfield :* Samuel Wardell, Mary Parker, Martha Carrier, Abigail Falkner, Anne Foster, Rebecca Eames, Mary Post, *and* Mary Lacey, *all of Andover :* Mary Bradbury *of Salisbury : and* Dorcas Hoar *of Beverly ; Were severally Indicted, Convicted and Attained of Witchcraft, and some of them put to Death, Others lying still under the like Sentence of the said Court, and liable to have the same Executed upon them.*

A   The

Reversal of Attainder (verdict) of Reverend George Burroughs and others for witchcraft (1711). The first page of a 1713 printed version of an act passed by the Great and General Court of the Province of Massachusetts in 1711 declaring the colony's regret for the "Prosecution . . . of persons of known and good Reputation, . . ." and its desire to reverse convictions and judgments against the accused. Courtesy Danvers Archival Center, Danvers, Mass.

Anno Regni. ANNÆ Reginæ Decimo·

The Influence and Energy of the Evil Spirits fo great at that time acting in and upon thofe who were the Principal Accufers and Witneffes, proceeding fo far as to caufe a Profecution to be had of Perfons of known and good Reputation, which caufed a great Diffatisfaction and a ftop to be put thereunto, until Their Majefties Pleafure fhould be known therein.

And upon a Reprefentation thereof accordingly made, Her late Majefty Queen M A R Y the Second, of bleffed Memory, by Her Royal Letter given at Her Court at Whitehall the Fifteenth of April 1 6 9 3. was Gracioufly Pleas'd to approve the Care and Circumfpection therein ; and to Will and Require that in all proceedings againft Perfons Accufed for Witchcraft, or being Poffeffed by the Devil, the greateft Moderation, and all due Circumfpection be Ufed, fo far as the fame may be without Impediment, to the ordinary Courfe of Juftice.

And fome of the Principal Accufers and Witneffes in thofe dark and fevere Profecutions have fince difcovered themfelves to be Perfons of Profligate and Vicious Converfation.

Upon the humble Petition and Suit of feveral of the faid Perfons, and of the Children of others of them whofe Parents were Executed.

Be it Declared and Enacted by His Excellency the Governour, Council and Reprefentatives, in General Court Affembled and by the Authority of the fame, That the feveral Convictions, Judgments and Attainders againft the faid *George Burroughs, John Proctor, George Jacob, John Willard, Giles Core,* and *Core, Rebecca Nurfe, Sarah Good, Elizabeth How, Mary Eaftey, Sarah Wild, Abigail Hobbs, Samuel Wardell, Mary Parker, Martha Carrier, Abigail Falkner, Anne Fofter, Rebecca Eames, Mary Poft, Mary Lacey, Mary Bradbury* and *Dorcas Hoar,* and every of them, Be and hereby are Reverfed, Made and Declared to be Null and Void to all Intents, Conftructions and Purpofes whatfoever, as if no fuch Convictions, Judgments or Attainders had ever been had or given. And that no Penalties or Forfeitures of Goods or Chattels be by the faid Judgments and Attainders, or either of them had or incurr'd.

Any Law, Ufage or Cuftom to the contrary notwithftanding.

And that no Sheriff, Conftable, Goaler, or other Officer fhall be liable to any Profecution in the Law for any thing they then Legally did in the Execution of their refpective Offices.

B O S T O N : Printed by B. Green, Printer to His Excellency the GOVERNOUR and COUNCIL. 1 7 1 3.

The second page of the Reversal of Attainder (verdict) of Reverend George Burroughs and others for witchcraft (1711). Courtesy Danvers Archival Center, Danvers, Mass.

lesser-known, contemporaneous witch trial episode that took place in Fairfield, Stratford, and Wallingford, Connecticut, during the 1692–93 period resulted in five complaints, one formal accusation, one conviction, but no executions.[17]

American colonial legal procedures from 1693 onward demanded a change in the process by which suspected capital offenders might be charged and brought to trial. Most important was the complete rejection of the superstitious methods of discovery used in the Salem court—such as the "test of touch," the search for witch's marks, "pressing," and the use of spectral evidence in cases involving witchcraft. Since the Salem trials were largely conducted by men who lacked formal legal training, there were numerous violations of British court procedure. These judicial errors clearly embarrassed the colonial government and were carefully avoided in later capital trials in New England. For example, in all later cases the accused would be offered the right of a defense counsel. Sadly, this benefit was not offered to those accused in Salem in 1692. Similarly, court justices would no longer act as both judge and inquisitor—interrogating the accused in the manner of an attorney for the prosecution. Also, persons accused of a crime would now be presumed innocent by the court, placing the burden for proof of guilt upon the state. Not surprisingly, there would be no further convictions for the crime of witchcraft in New England. Recent research has, however, uncovered four other incidences of alleged witchcraft in post-1693 New England. Of these cases, none resulted in a condemnation.[18]

In the British Isles, the crime of witchcraft would resurface only twice after the Salem incident ended. In 1716, the last episode in England occurred in Huntingdon, Cambridgeshire, when a woman and her nine-year-old daughter were convicted and hanged for raising a storm to endanger shipping and causing harm to their neighbors. The last documented execution in Scotland took place in 1722 when a woman was burned at the stake. The statute making witchcraft a capital offense in England was finally repealed in 1736.[19]

However, public sentiment concerning the Salem trials continued to take shape as public attitudes changed with the weakening of Puritan religion in New England and the skepticism of the Age of Reason began to take full effect. As aforementioned, Governor Thomas Hutchinson in his mid-eighteenth-century *History of the Commonwealth of Massachusetts Bay* balked at the notion that those involved may have actually been disturbed by either spiritual or mental disorders, rather attributing the activities of the afflicted children to those of frivolous seekers of attention in which "the whole was a scene of fraud and imposture, begun by young girls." This was the prevailing opinion throughout the latter eighteenth and nineteenth centuries.[20]

Without question, the general public's imagination and attitude concerning the Salem witchcraft episode was stimulated and shaped most dramatically by the writings of Nathaniel Hawthorne (1804–1864). More than any other American writer, Hawthorne—in stories such as *The House of the Seven Gables* and *Young Goodman Brown*—popularized the view that the Salem witchcraft trials were the result of Puritan prejudice and social repression. Hawthorne, as noted earlier, wrestled throughout his life with the awareness that he was the great-great-grandson of Justice John Hathorne, a notable actor in the most virulent stage of the trials. Most important in the author's mind, Justice Hathorne was a magistrate who never expressed feelings of guilt or regret for the notorious part he had played in the unjust deaths of twenty fellow citizens. Consequently Nathaniel Hawthorne—ever the sentimental and enlightened Victorian intellectual—took every opportunity to cast literary shadows over his Puritan forbearers who had showed little mercy and liberality in the treatment of innocent victims.[21]

As a result, nearly all of Hawthorne's numerous fictional Puritan authority figures are characterized in his prose as evil men imbued with a fanatic religious zeal to persecute and condemn. In addition, Hawthorne held the view that the religious faith of his Puritan ancestors was rarely sincere. He often depicted Puritan divines, magistrates, and prosperous merchants as hypocritical community leaders using their religious, political, or economic power as a means to accomplish religious, political, or economic objectives. For example, in *The House of the Seven Gables* the villainous Judge Pyncheon (a character loosely based upon Judge Hathorne) falsely accused Matthew Maule of witchcraft and executes him in order to acquire Maule's land as the location for his new mansion. Thus, from the 1840s onward, Nathaniel Hawthorne's best-selling Gothic fiction negatively shaped the reading public's imagination concerning not only the Salem witchcraft event itself, but Puritans in general.[22]

This image of the Salem trials would not be helped or altered in any significant way by other authors of the nineteenth century. Noted New England poets John Greenleaf Whittier and Henry Wadsworth Longfellow both come down hard upon the likes of Reverend Cotton Mather and Justice John Hathorne. Whittier's poem "Calef in Boston," written and published in 1849, depicts Reverend Cotton Mather as a self-righteous teacher of spiritual lies, while "simple tradesman" Robert Calef speaks the honest and simple truth against Mather in words "frank and bold." Similarly H. W. Longfellow, a friend of Hawthorne's, produced a play in 1868 entitled "Giles Corey of the Salem Farms" in which he explores the superstitions and spectral evidence accepted as truth by Mather and Hathorne in their faulty efforts to ferret out

Site of the Reverend Samuel Parris parsonage (nineteenth-century photo). By the mid-1800s the Salem Village parsonage occupied by the family of Reverend Samuel Parris was gone. The land upon which it stood was returned to agriculture with the original location only identified by a small granite marker. Courtesy Danvers Archival Center, Danvers, Mass.

Contemporary view of the site of the Reverend Samuel Parris parsonage (c. 2004). Visitors to Danvers, Massachusetts, today may view the original location of the Reverend Parris's parsonage excavated in the 1970s by local historian and archivist Richard B. Trask. Artifacts removed from this archeological site are currently exhibited at the nearby Danvers Town Archives located in the Peabody Institute Library. Photo by Richard B. Trask.

those responsible for witchcraft in Salem Village. As with Hawthorne, these two literary giants had a profound impact upon their own readership. Their published works served to further erode the reputation of the Puritan leadership of Massachusetts in the late seventeenth century and elevate the status of those who were victimized by the witchcraft trials. In this way, the public became increasingly more critical of the Puritans in general, while the subject of witchcraft in Salem grew ever more popular.[23]

A direct result of this general public skepticism and popularization of the subject of the witchcraft trials was the rise of tourism in Salem. No longer was the subject of witchcraft considered a serious topic of discussion reserved for historians and theologians. By the 1890s, it had already begun to take on a P. T. Barnum-esque quality. A local pharmacy occupied the downstairs floor of the Justice Jonathan Corwin House—already a tourist attraction—and produced a brand of cosmetics known simply as "Salem Witch Cream." Local Victorian artist Tomkins Mattson produced two powerful and idealized romantic paintings entitled "The Examination of a Witch" and "The Trial of George Jacobs." The former of these depicts a romantic Victorian heroine modestly attempting to cover her nakedness as she is examined for a "witch's mark" by a clutch of evil-looking crones, while Judge Hathorne and a gathering of other interested male observers look on. The latter painting is the artist's image of alleged witch George Jacobs on his knees pleading for leniency from the merciless Judge Hathorne as his

Site of the 1692 Salem Village meetinghouse (nineteenth-century photo). Like the nearby parsonage, by the mid-1800s nothing remained of the original 1692 meeting-house. Other meetinghouses were built, lost, and rebuilt down to the present. What is interesting to note in this view is the proximity of a pine forest along the crest of the hill in the distance. Courtesy Danvers Archival Center, Danvers, Mass.

granddaughter Margaret Jacobs testifies against him. Both of these late Victorian images are more imaginative than accurate, yet they are the two most influential depictions of the Salem Witch Trials in existence, and have shaped public opinion for the past century.

By the turn of the twentieth century, far from wishing to avoid the subject, the City of Salem had named its high school sports teams the "Salem Witches." A prominent local jewelry store, Daniel Low's Inc., produced a line of engraved sterling silver Salem witch spoons with a witch motif for discriminating tourists. For less prosperous visitors, Salem shops were selling tourist guidebooks, postcards, and custom-made Staffordshire plates with witch trial themes. Even the city and its citizens took pride in referring to Salem as "The Witch City" and began a long and profitable association with the Salem Witch Trials, one which has only expanded with the passage of time. The poetic irony of this trend is that "Salem Village"—the hometown of Tituba, the Parris family, the Putnams, the Proctors, the location of the original hearings, the Salem Village Church, Reverend Samuel Parris's parsonage site, Rebecca Nurse's house and farm, and many other original locations—is now known as Danvers, Massachusetts. Danvers attracts very little attention from the millions of tourists that now annually flock to the city of Salem in search of the witchcraft trial experience.[24]

From the mid-twentieth century to the present, the public has been nearly overwhelmed with a variety of mass media productions—films, plays, and

The gravestone of George Jacobs (c. 1992). Located in Danvers in the Nurse family cemetery at the Rebecca Nurse House site, this slate gravestone is a recent reproduction done in the seventeenth-century style. Like Rebecca Nurse's body, George Jacobs's body was secretly removed by his family from the mass grave on Gallows Hill and buried on the family farm. During the 1992 tercentennial, the remains of George Jacobs were exhumed and relocated to the Rebecca Nurse House site and reburied in the Nurse family graveyard. Photo by Richard B. Trask.

television documentaries—all of which purport to provide the viewer with a glimpse of the Salem Witch Trials. Undoubtedly, the most significant of these was Arthur Miller's 1953 play "The Crucible," which is generally regarded as one of the greatest plays of the twentieth century. In the 1950s and '60s, it played to millions of Americans as a morality play, warning theatergoers of the dangers of mass hysteria in hunting "witches" in the same way that Congressman Joseph McCarthy and his House Committee on Un-American Activities hunted alleged "Communists." By 1996, it was transformed into a film directed by Nick Hytner, featuring the acting talents of Daniel Day Lewis, Winona Ryder, Joan Allen, and Paul Scofield.

While "The Crucible" is an excellent play, it must be regarded as an unfortunate distortion of history. Playwright Arthur Miller conceived of this work in the early 1950s as a means of striking back at those whose power, prejudices, and fanatic zeal against the perceived "Communist threat" had blacklisted many of his colleagues and threatened his own career. In his attempt to write a good play, Miller took liberties with the facts, for example identifying one of the leading causes of the episode as a romantic liaison between

The Salem Village Witchcraft Victims' Memorial (c. 1992). Located in Danvers, Massachusetts, at 176 Hobart Street, this monument was designed and erected by the Salem Village Witchcraft Tercentennial Committee. The land upon which it stands was donated to the Town of Danvers. It is open to the general public from dawn to dusk. Photo by Richard B. Trask.

Abigail Williams and John Proctor. In actuality, Williams was eleven years old and Proctor nearly sixty, an unlikely pair—even by seventeenth-century standards.[25]

In 1992, the City of Salem, and the nearby town of Danvers (Salem Village) commemorated the three hundredth anniversary of the Salem Witch Trials with a yearlong schedule of events, including a conference where scholarly papers on the subject of the Salem episode were presented. Both communities commissioned and created monuments to honor the memory of the victims of the trials. Salem also established an annual award to honor that person who during his/her lifetime had done the most to further the cause of human rights.

A Commonwealth was humbled, prayers of forgiveness offered, laws were changed, payments were made, histories were written, Gothic tales, documentaries, plays, and films have been produced, millions of lives have been affected because of the events of 1692. In spite of it all, however, the full impact of the Salem Witch Trials has yet to be fully realized or comprehended.[26]

NOTES

1. Paul Boyer and Stephen Nissenbaum, *Salem Possessed: The Social Origins of Witchcraft* (Cambridge: Harvard University Press, 1974), 78.

2. Charles W. Upham, *Salem Witchcraft*, vol. 2 (Williamstown, MA: Corner House Publishers, 1971), 439.

3. Leo Bonfanti, *The Witchcraft Hysteria of 1692* (Burlington, MA: Pride Publications, 1979), New England Historical Series, 47–48.

4. Boyer and Nissenbaum, *Salem Possessed*, 78–79.

5. Ibid., 219. Also Chadwick Hansen, *Witchcraft at Salem* (New York: George Braziller, 1969), 214.

6. Danvers Church Records, August 25, 1706, in *The New England Historical and Genealogical Register*, vol. 12, July 1858, 246.

7. Frances Hill, *The Salem Witch Trials Reader* (New York: Da Capo Press, 1984), 302.

8. Ibid., 226.

9. "Gov. Wm. Stoughton's Proclamation, Dec. 17, 1696," in Hansen, *Witchcraft at Salem*, 207–8.

10. Ibid., "Hon. Samuel Sewell's Confession," 209–10.

11. Reverend John Hale, *A Modest Inquiry into the Nature of Witchcraft* (Boston, MA, 1702), 109–10.

12. Winfield Nevins, *Witchcraft in Salem Village in 1692*, 249.

13. David Levin, *What Happened in Salem?* (New York: Harcourt, Brace and World, Inc., 1960), "Reversal of Attainder," 140.

14. Ibid., 139.

15. Hansen, *Witchcraft at Salem*, 186–87.

16. John Putnam Demos, *Entertaining Satan: Witchcraft and the Culture of Early New England* (London: Oxford University Press, 1982), 393–94. The decline of witchcraft did not proceed evenly or equally through all the major social ranks. Persons of more than average education and wealth composed an advance guard of skeptics—in some individual cases as early as the Salem Witch Trials, and in ever larger numbers by the second half of the eighteenth century.

17. David D. Hall, *Witch-Hunting in Seventeenth-Century New England* (Boston: Northeastern University Press, 1991), 315–16.

18. Demos, *Entertaining Satan*, 408–9.

19. Nevins, *Witchcraft in Salem Village in 1692* (Boston: Lee and Shepard, 1892), 265.

20. Hon. Thos. Hutchinson, quoted in Hansen, *Witchcraft at Salem*, 26.

21. Hill, "From: Nathaniel Hawthorne, Young Goodman Brown (1835)", in *The Salem Witch Trials Reader*, 314.

22. Ibid., 325.

23. Ibid., 314, 381–82.

24. Bernard Rosenthal, *Salem Story* (Cambridge: Cambridge University Press, 1995), 204–6.

25. Ibid., 172.

26. Ibid., 206–9. Rosenthal discusses the various ways contemporary Salem has endeavored to both commemorate and capitalize on its celebrity as the site of the 1692 trials.

Biographies of Key Figures Involved in the Salem Witch Trials

The following biographical sketches are intended to provide basic background information concerning the majority of principal characters involved in the Salem witchcraft trials episode. In some instances so little information is available even a superficial biographical overview is not possible. This is true in the cases of three of the so-called "afflicted girls" Elizabeth Hubbard, Abigail Williams, and Susannah Sheldon, whose biographies have not been included below.

THE AFFLICTED GIRLS

Mercy Lewis (1673–)

A nineteen-year-old domestic servant of the Putnam Family at the time of the Salem trials, Mercy Lewis was born on the Maine frontier into the pioneer family of Philip Lewis, whose father, George Lewis, had come from England in the 1640s. When Mercy was three years old, on August 11, 1676, her community of Falmouth on Casco Bay was attacked by Wabanaki Indians. The young child escaped with her parents, but the assault claimed the lives of several relatives including Mercy's paternal grandparents. Her parents sought safety on an island in Casco Bay along with the village minister, Reverend George Burroughs. After a brief period in Salem, Massachusetts, the Lewis family returned to Maine and resettled at Casco Bay in 1683. A second Indian attack in the summer of 1689 resulted in the deaths of her parents, and Mercy was briefly placed as a servant in the home of Reverend George Burroughs, later moving to Salem Village where a married sister resided. Here she was taken in as a servant by the Putnam family, and became a confidant of Ann Putnam, Jr., joining her in corroborating her accusations of several local residents including Giles Corey, Bridget Bishop, Mary Lacey, Sr., Susannah Martin, John Willard, Nehemiah Abbot, Jr., Sarah Wildes, and her former master, Reverend George Burroughs. Little is known of her life following the end of the trials. Historians such as Mary Beth Norton in her recent book, *In the Devil's Snare*, have speculated that the traumatic effect of the Indian attacks and her subsequent life in the home of George Burroughs contributed to Mercy's aberrant and hostile behavior during the Salem witchcraft episode, motivating her to lash out at a man who managed to almost miraculously survive two attacks which virtually wiped out her own family. After the trials, Mercy married a twenty-two-year-old yeoman farmer named Allen from her hometown of Casco Bay, Maine. She bore a child in New Hampshire, and later moved with her family to Boston. Her age at the time of her death is unknown.

Elizabeth "Betty" Parris (c. 1683–1760)

In 1689, Betty Parris and her cousin Abigail Williams were brought from their hometown of Casco to live at the Salem Village parsonage by Reverend Samuel Parris. Betty was most likely born in Boston in 1683 and lived there with her family as her father, Samuel Parris, attempted to earn a living as a merchant and later as a minister. She and her cousin Abigail were the first two "afflicted children" who began to exhibit signs of demonic torment during the winter of 1691–92. They allegedly initiated the episode by attempting to foretell the identity of their future husbands through the use of a clear glass containing a suspended egg white held up to a lit candle. Such "fortune-telling" experiments were strictly forbidden in Puritan households. These activities were followed by hysterical behavior including barking, screaming, crying, and violent fits which prompted Betty's father to call for a local physician, Dr. Griggs, to examine her. His diagnosis was that Betty and her cousin were under the power of "the Evil Hand" of witchcraft. This began the questioning which led ultimately to the accusation, trial, and deaths of twenty persons.

By March 1692, in an effort to remove her from the spotlight of witch-finding and isolate her from the other girls, Betty Parris was sent by her parents to Salem Town to reside in the home of Major Samuel Sewell (1657–1725), a member of the Essex County militia and clerk of the Governor's Special Court of Oyer and Terminer then trying the witchcraft cases. Her role after this relocation diminished greatly. After the dismissal of her father as minister from the Salem Village Church she traveled with her family to her father's new parish in Sudbury, Massachusetts, where Betty continued to live until adulthood.

In 1710, Elizabeth Parris married Benjamin Baron, a shoemaker residing in Sudbury who fathered her four children, Thomas, Elizabeth, Catherine, and Susanna. She died at her home in Concord, Massachusetts, on March 21, 1760.

Ann Putnam, Jr. (1680–1716)

Ann Putnam, Jr., was born in 1680 to Thomas and Ann Putnam of Salem Village. She was twelve years old at the time of the Salem witchcraft episode.

Her closest friends were Mary Walcott and Mercy Lewis, both of whom were seventeen years old. Ann Jr., Mary, and Mercy were the first girls outside the home of Reverend Samuel Parris to be afflicted and testify during the pretrial hearings.

Ann was one of the original group of eight young girls who gathered at the Parris parsonage to listen to Tituba's stories and attempt to engage in fortune-telling activities to predict the identities of their future husbands. According to Reverend John Hale, Ann Putnam, Jr., in the company of Betty Parris and Abigail Williams, while studying the white of an egg suspended in a glass of water, claimed to have seen a coffin. As a result of this frightening apparition, Ann Putnam, Jr., Abigail Williams (Reverend Parris's niece), and Betty Parris (Reverend Parris's daughter) all began to exhibit irrational behavior, including contortions, fits of hysteria, involuntary muscle spasms, and violent behavior.

Following the removal of Betty Parris from Salem Village, Ann and Abigail became the most active and aggressive of the so-called afflicted children. Ann Jr. "cried out against" sixty-two people during the course of the trials. Ann's father, Thomas Putnam, was one of the primary instigators of complaints against alleged witches in Salem Village. For this reason he has been identified by several key historians (including Paul Boyer and Stephen Nissenbaum) as a chief agitator and manipulator of the testimonies of both his daughter and his wife, Ann Putnam, Sr. Evidence indicates that many of those who were afflicted or gave testimony against the accused were connected to the Putnam family either by ties of kinship or faction.

Both of Ann Putnam, Jr.'s parents died in 1699, leaving her at the age of nineteen to raise her nine younger brothers and sisters. Never marrying, she dedicated the remainder of her life to the care of her family. In 1706, she asked to be reconciled to the family of Rebecca Nurse, seeking their forgiveness as well as that of the other members of the Salem Village congregation.

On that occasion, she stood in the village church as the Reverend Joseph Green read her confession declaring that she desired "to be humbled before God for that sad and humbling Providence that befell my father's family in the year about '92; that I, then being in my childhood, should by such a Providence of God be made an instrument for the accusing of several persons of a grievous crime, whereby their lives were taken away from them, whom now I have just grounds and good reason to believe they were innocent persons; and that it was a great delusion of Satan that deceived me in that sad time. I did not do it out of anger, malice, or ill-will to any person, for I had no such thing against any of them; but what I did was ignorantly [done], being deluded by Satan."

Ann Putnam, Jr. died in 1716 in Salem Village at the age of thirty-seven. She was the only member of the group of "afflicted children" to apologize for her actions.

Mary Walcott (1675–after 1729)

Mary Walcott was the daughter of Captain Jonathan Walcott (1639–1699) and Mary Sibley Walcott (1644–1683). She was born and raised in Salem,

Massachusetts, and was about seventeen years old at the time of the Salem episode. Because her mother died at an early age, her father remarried a Salem Village girl, Deliverance Putnam, sister of Thomas Putnam. This family connection with the Putnam household placed Mary among the most outspoken and dangerous of the young accusers, Ann Putnam, Jr. and the Putnam domestic servant, Mercy Lewis. Not surprisingly, she was therefore among the first to accuse others and support the accusations of the "afflicted girls."

Bernard Rosenthal in his study, *Salem Story*, refers to Mary as "an old standby" supporter of the afflicted but not one of the most virulent accusers. In some respects she appeared almost passive by comparison. She was observed on several occasions calmly knitting during the testimony while her companions were engaged in violent convulsions. Although not one of the most virulent of the afflicted, when needed, she would become involved and participate usually by exhibiting physical symptoms of witchcraft. On one occasion she showed Reverend Deodat Lawson a strange set of teeth marks upon her arm which she claimed had been the result of a specter biting her.

After the trials ended in 1693, Mary fell back into obscurity. In 1696, at the age of twenty-one, she married Isaac Farrar, the son of John Farrar of Woburn, Massachusetts. They had several children and moved to the remote town of Townsend, Massachusetts. Following her first husband's death she married David Harwood in 1701 and moved to Sutton, Massachusetts. With David Harwood she had nine children, the last of whom was born in 1725. She was known to be alive in Sutton in 1729.

Mary Warren (1672–c. 1697)

Genealogical evidence indicates that Mary Warren was the daughter of Abraham and Isabel Warren of Salem, Massachusetts. Her mother died shortly after Mary's birth in 1672 and her father died intestate in 1689. At the time of the Salem witchcraft episode, Mary was employed as a domestic servant in the household of John and Elizabeth Proctor. This was a common practice as a means of enabling unmarried girls without family to support themselves until marriage. During the trials, Mary was among the initial group of "afflicted girls," but her master, John Proctor—displeased with her behavior—brought her home and "kept her close to the [spinning] wheel & threatened to thresh her, & she had no more fits 'til the next day. . . ." She is known for the role she played as a confessed witch in providing testimony against Alice Parker, whom she accused of murdering her mother and father by witchcraft, and against her masters, John and Elizabeth Proctor. She was one of the first of some fifty individuals to save their lives by confessing guilt and turning state's evidence by providing the Court of Oyer and Terminer with the names of other alleged witches.

Nearly nothing conclusive is known about Mary's later life. It does not appear that Mary married following the death of John Proctor, but perhaps suffered mental illness and depression for several years prior to a premature death. The possible suggestion of this is provided by Reverend John Hale in his book, *A Modest Inquiry into the Nature of Witchcraft*, which was written in 1697. In it Hale indicates that an anonymous member of the afflicted girls "was followed by diabolical manifestations to her death and so died a single woman." Since only three members of the "afflicted girls" group—Mary Warren, Elizabeth Hubbard, and Abigail Williams—are not known to have lived beyond 1693, there is the remote possibility that Mary is the "single woman" who died prior to 1697.

Tituba (no dates available)

Tituba was purchased by Reverend Samuel Parris in Barbados during his residence there in the early 1680s. She was most probably Native American, not an African American, probably of Arawak or Carib Indian extraction. As a slave, she accompanied Reverend Parris on his journey to Boston from Barbados in 1680, along with Parris's other slave, John Indian.

Tituba and John Indian were married in 1689 and joined Parris and his family in living at the Salem Village parsonage that year. Prior to the outbreak of witchcraft activity, Tituba was given traditional housekeeping duties, including the care and supervision of Betty Parris and her cousin, Abigail Williams. During the winter of 1691–92, Tituba allegedly entertained the girls with fortune-telling activities that served to trigger their aberrant behavior.

When questioned as to her role in the episode, Tituba confessed to having baked a "witch's cake" made from oatmeal and the afflicted girls' urine and feeding it to the Parris's dog in an attempt to cure the children of their malady. The girls accused her as being their tormenter, and when interrogated, she confessed to having made a pact with the devil and other acts of witchcraft.

Following this, Tituba was held in custody and served as a witness for the court until her release in May 1693, when she was sold to a gentleman from Virginia for seven pounds to pay the cost of her jailer's bill. Nothing is known of Tituba's life following her release from jail. It is assumed that she traveled to Virginia with her new master.

THE VICTIMS

Bridget Bishop (1632–June 10, 1692)

Bridget Bishop was born sometime between 1632 and 1635, putting her in her late fifties at the time of the Salem witchcraft episode. Her first husband was a man known as Goodman Wasselbe, who left Bridget widowed and childless by July 26, 1666, when she married her second husband, Thomas Oliver. Thomas Oliver had three children by his previous wife, two of whom had been born in England prior to 1637. Bridget and Thomas had one daughter, Christian, born in Salem on May 8, 1667. There are no extant records of Bridget having any other children.

Bridget's union with Thomas Oliver is well documented in local court records due to the contentious nature of their marriage. In January 1670, both Bridget and Thomas were sentenced to be whipped and fined for fighting. In the testimony of the hearing, a witness observed that Bridget's face had been bloodied on at least one occasion and was black and blue on several others. Thomas testified in his defense that Bridget had struck him "several blows."

In 1678 they appeared in court again for defaming the Sabbath by engaging in public name-calling. Being found guilty, both Bridget and Thomas were sentenced to stand before the public in the Salem Town marketplace on market day tied and gagged with a sign announcing their offense. One of Thomas's daughters voluntarily paid a fine releasing her father from this humiliating punishment. No record of a similar reprieve for Bridget exists. In 1679, Thomas Oliver died without leaving a will, and Bridget was granted administration of his estate on November 28, 1679.

In February 1680, Bridget was accused of witchcraft by a man described as "Wonn [Juan?], John Ingerson's Negro." In this first witchcraft case, she was accused of frightening horses, then vanishing into thin air. Other accusations included the mysterious appearance of an unknown cat and the experience of physical pain by the accuser. Corroborating testimony came from several other Salem youths including John Lambert and Jonathan Pickering, who concluded that the "horses were bewitched." The final outcome of this case is inconclusive. Bridget appears to have paid her bail bond, but was not tried or convicted of witchcraft at this time.

On December 14, 1687, Bridget was arrested on a charge by Thomas Stacey for stealing brass objects from him. She was brought before Salem magistrate John Hathorne, who would later interrogate her for witchcraft. She was allowed to post bail, and apparently was never convicted of the crime. She did not appear again before the court until April 19, 1692.

Before 1692, Bridget remarried a third time to Edward Bishop, a wood sawer of Salem. In addition to her somewhat independent and free-thinking lifestyle, the fact that Bishop "was in the habit of dressing more artistically than women of the village" also contributed to making her a primary suspect. Trial testimony described her as wearing, "a black cap, and a black hat, and a red paragon bodice bordered and looped with different colors." This was considered an ensemble reflecting personal vanity and pride, two characteristics not considered appropriate for a godly person in Puritan New England.

On April 18, 1692, a warrant was issued for Bishop's arrest for suspected acts of witchcraft. She boldly faced her accusers, denying any wrongdoing. When asked by one of her jailers if she were not moved by the sufferings of the afflicted children, Bishop claimed that she was not troubled to see them tormented. She frankly observed that she could not tell what to think of them and did not concern herself about them at all. These statements weighed heavily against her since witches were thought to be devoid of sympathy for their victims.

The afflicted girls were not Bishop's only accusers, however. Her sister's husband claimed that "she sat up all night conversing with the Devil" and that "the Devil came bodily into her." Besides this, two laborers, John Bly and his son, claimed that they had found several "poppets" made of rags and hog bristles with headless pins stuck through them embedded in the cellar wall of Bridget's house foundation. Perhaps most damning of all was the testimony of a Quaker couple, Samuel and Sarah Shattuck, stating that immediately after having "a falling out" with Bridget, their previously normal son had gone insane and now required constant care. On the basis of this circumstantial evidence, as well as a great deal of spectral evidence, Bridget was found guilty. She was hanged alone on Gallows Hill in Salem on June 10, 1692, the first victim of the Salem witchcraft episode.

Reverend George Burroughs (1652–August 19, 1692)

George Burroughs was born in Suffolk, England, in 1652. At a young age, he immigrated with his family to Boston and settled with his mother at Roxbury, Massachusetts. He graduated from Harvard College in 1670 and traveled to Falmouth, Maine, where he hoped to establish a ministry. He served as pastor of the Falmouth Congregational Church until the town was attacked by Indians in 1676, forcing him to retreat south to Salisbury. At Salisbury, he again served as a minister until he received a call from the congregation of the Salem Village Church in 1680. He remained at Salem Village for two years.

By 1683, he had alienated the members of the village church and returned to Maine. He served a new parish in Wells, Maine, until a warrant was issued following his accusation for "sundry acts of witchcraft" by Thomas Putnam and Jonathan Walcott. On May 4, 1692, Reverend Burroughs was arrested and brought to Salem for questioning. At this time, he was interrogated privately by Reverends Cotton and Increase Mather, both of whom declared him to be suspect. Increase Mather was especially suspicious of Burroughs, to the extent that in his post-trial book, *Cases of Conscience*, he stated that "had I been one of the judges, I could not have acquitted him." In fact, Burroughs's trial was the only one of over fifty which Increase Mather attended. Burroughs was brought to trial in August 1692 and hanged along with three other men and one woman on Friday, August 19, 1692.

Martha Carrier (165?–August 19, 1692)

Martha was the daughter of Andrew Allen, Sr., one of the original settlers of Andover, Massachusetts, and a prosperous landowner. Although her exact date of birth is unknown, it is likely she was born in the mid-1650s. She scandalized her community when, in 1674, she married a Welsh indentured servant, Thomas Carrier, the father of her illegitimate child. After living fifteen years in nearby, Billerica, Massachusetts, she and her husband returned with their impoverished family of five children to her hometown of Andover in early 1690.

By November 1690, a minor smallpox epidemic swept Andover devastating the community and killing seven of Martha's relatives, but none of her immediate family. This was the first recorded incidence of smallpox in Andover, a situation rare for most New England towns which regularly experienced outbreaks of the disease. Altogether the community suffered thirteen smallpox deaths that year. Unfortunately, since the outbreak occurred immediately following Martha Carrier's return to Andover, she was generally regarded as the source of the plague, a fact that did not enhance her popularity in the community. Suspicion as to her motive for these deaths was based on the public awareness that she stood to inherit property from some of the relations who succumbed to the disease.

This incident would return to haunt Martha in 1692 when several of the afflicted girls—Ann Putnam, Jr., Elizabeth Hubbard, Mary Walcott, and Susannah Sheldon—said they could see thirteen ghosts of Andover whose deaths were the result of Martha's witchcraft. She was accused of bringing deadly smallpox upon these victims by malefic magic. She was arrested under suspicion of witchcraft on May 28, and brought in for questioning on May 31, 1692.

Martha firmly denied the accusation in Court and suggested pointedly that the afflicted girls were either lying or mentally ill. In a famous response to the magistrate, she summed up what many have thought about the veracity of the girls' testimony, saying "it is a shameful thing that you should mind these folks that are out of their wits!" During the pre-trial hearing, one of the accusers, Mary Lacey, Jr., described Martha as a woman who the devil had promised would be "a Queen in Hell." Reverend Cotton Mather, in his book, *Wonders of the Invisible World*, described Martha in a similar, more elaborate manner: "This Rampant Hag, Martha Carrier, was the person of whom the Confessions of the Witches, and of her own Children among the rest, agreed, that the Devil had promised her, she should be Queen of Hell."

Four of her children were imprisoned with her and questioned. Her two older sons, eighteen-year-old Richard and fifteen-year-old Andrew, refused to cooperate with Court authorities until they were tortured by being tied neck-to-heels. By this means both young men confessed to being witches and added that their mother had "had made them so." Later, Martha's eight-year-old daughter, Sarah, and ten-year-old son, Thomas, testified against their mother, confessing themselves to be witches, too. In spite of this, Martha maintained her innocence and was convicted by the Salem Court and hanged on August 19, 1692. On September 13, 1710, her husband, Thomas, petitioned the Commonwealth of Massachusetts for financial compensation for the costs he sustained during Martha's imprisonment and the return of her good name. He demanded seven pounds, six shillings and was granted his request. The Great and General Court also reversed the verdict of guilty on Martha, clearing her of any wrongdoing.

Giles Corey (1621–September 17, 1692)

Giles Corey was born in Northampton, England in 1621. The son of Giles and Elizabeth Corey, he did not immigrate to Massachusetts Bay Colony until after he married Margaret, his first wife and mother of all his surviving children. With her he settled in Salem Town, where he lived until 1659 when he relocated to Salem Farms, an outlying agricultural community between Salem Town and Salem Village. Shortly following their settlement upon an extensive farm, Margaret died, leaving Giles with a large family. Corey married an English woman from London, Mary Brite, on April 11, 1664. Both Giles and his new wife were forty-three years old at the time of the marriage. During the next twenty years, Corey's wealth grew as did his role in the community. He became an active member of the Salem Village Church, yet also became known for behavior inconsistent with that of a devout Christian.

In 1675, in a fit of anger, Corey beat a hired field hand named Jacob Goodale to death. For this crime he was charged with unintentional manslaughter and he was forced to pay a heavy fine. As a result, Corey's reputation in the local community was forever tainted by this incident. It was a memory that would resurface during the testimony of the afflicted girls.

Mary Brite Corey died on August 27, 1684, at the age of sixty-three. In 1690, Giles Corey wed his third and final wife, Martha Panon, widow of Henry Rich. They continued to live comfortably in his house at Salem Farms and attend Salem Village Church until 1692, when on March 19, Martha was arrested for witchcraft. By April 19, 1692, Giles was also accused and arrested.

The most incriminating accusations were submitted against Giles by confessed witch Abigail Hobbs, who testified that Giles and his wife, Martha, were fellow witches, and by Court Clerk, Ezekiel Cheever, and John Putnam, Jr., on behalf of the afflicted girls—Ann Putnam, Jr., Abigail Williams, Mary Walcott, Mercy Lewis, and Elizabeth Hubbard.

On September 16, 1692, Giles was formally charged with the crime of witchcraft and pled not guilty, but refused to submit himself to the Court for a jury trial. He was keenly aware that all persons who had thus far been tried had been found guilty, and the likelihood of an impartial verdict was remote. He therefore "stood mute" before his accusers and the proceedings came to a standstill. As a result of his unwillingness to further cooperate with the Court, he was sentenced to undergo the ancient procedure according to English common law of *peine forte et dure*, otherwise known as the torture of "pressing," which was actually declared illegal in Massachusetts Bay Colony under the *1641 Body of Liberties*.

On the morning of September 17, Giles was taken to a field near the Salem jail, stripped of his clothing and laid upon his back and staked to the ground. Wooden beams were then rested across his chest upon which heavy stones were placed. Periodically, the number of stones would be increased. On the following day, September 18, 1692, Giles was excommunicated from the Salem Village Church. Friends and family were brought to him to persuade him to submit to a trial, but without success. Corey steadfastly refused to speak or cooperate with the Court except to demand "more weight." The Essex County Sheriff, George Corwin, complied with his request and Giles finally died when the weight of stones crushed his rib cage. He was seventy-one years of age at the time of his death. There is a widely circulated belief that Giles Corey refused to cooperate with the Court specifically to ensure that his substantial estate would not be confiscated by the Court.

In actuality, it appears that his course of action only guaranteed that he would never have the stigma of a guilty verdict attached to his name, since his case would never be tried in a court of law. However, he wisely took the preliminary precaution to deed all his land into the possession of his sons-in-law, William Cleeves and John Moulton, in the event that Sheriff Corwin attempted to seize the Corey estate illegally, as he had done with property of several other victims.

Martha Corey (d. September 22, 1692)

Born in England, Martha Panon was the third wife of Giles Corey and among the last group to be hanged in September 1692. She had a controversial past prior to her marriage to Corey. In 1677 she bore a mulatto son named Benjamin or Ben-Oni (named after Rachel's son in the book of Genesis 35:18, meaning "son of my trouble"). Following this event, she lived a reclusive life with her apparently illegitimate child in the home of John Clifford of Salem, who continued to help raise the boy to manhood. Benjamin (aka Ben-Oni) was upwards of twenty-two years of age in 1699, and still living in Salem.

Her fortunes improved somewhat when, in 1684, she married Henry Rich of Salem, Massachusetts, and by him produced a legitimate son, Thomas Rich. Sometime between 1684 and 1690, Henry Rich died allowing Martha to marry Giles Corey on April 27, 1690. At that time she was accepted into membership of the Salem Village Church as Martha Corey. She and Giles were among the first persons to attend the pre-trial examinations held in Salem Village. She soon openly expressed skepticism about the truthfulness of the afflicted girls' testimony. It is likely that Martha's unsympathetic opinion reached the ears of the afflicted girls, and Ann Putnam, Jr., was the first to accuse Martha of witchcraft. Martha's attitude concerning the girls' testimony hurt her case, and convinced court officers that she was indeed a witch. She was arrested on Monday, March 21, 1692, and immediately brought to the Salem Village meetinghouse where she was examined by magistrate John Hathorne. Throughout the examination, although faced with an overwhelming amount of spectral evidence and hysterical behavior on the part of Ann Putnam, Jr., Mercy Lewis, Abigail Williams, and Elizabeth Hubbard, Martha maintained that she was a "Gospel woman." In response the girls shouted that she was a "Gospel Witch!"

After the pre-trial hearing, Martha was sent to jail in Salem, and later, due to overcrowded conditions, transferred to the jail in Boston. Besides the usual witnesses and afflicted accusers, the Court called her husband, Giles, to testify against her. He unfortunately provided incriminating evidence against her during the course of his testimony indicating that she had lied to the Court concerning information she claimed to have received from him. At the conclusion of her trial, Martha stood condemned with the sentence of death for acts of witchcraft. She was excommunicated from the Salem Village Church on September 11, 1692. Twenty-two days later she was hanged on Gallows Hill. On October 17, 1711, the verdict of guilty against Martha (and Giles) Corey was removed, and on December 17 of that year the Commonwealth compensated their heirs with the sum of twenty-one pounds. The lifting of their excommunication from the Salem Village Church took somewhat longer, however; Giles and Martha were not restored to membership until 1992.

Martha's son, in 1723, petitioned the Court in Salem for damages resulting from the wrongful death of his mother. In the court petition he is identified as "Thomas Rich of Salem, only surviving child of Martha Corey, alias Martha Rich, deceased." He was awarded fifty pounds on June 29, 1723.

Mary Eastey (1636–September 22, 1692)

Mary Towne Eastey was a sister of Rebecca Towne Nurse and Sarah Towne Cloyce. Her parents, William and Joanna (Blessing) Towne had come to Salem, Massachusetts, in 1632 from Great Yarmouth, England. Mary was born in Salem in 1636, and moved with her family to a farm in Topsfield purchased by her father in 1652. Altogether, the Townes had eight children, four of whom were females. Of these, three Towne sisters—Rebecca, Mary, and Sarah—were accused of witchcraft by the afflicted girls in 1692. Only Sarah would escape with her life.

Mary became the second wife of yeoman farmer, Isaac Eastey, and lived with him on the Eastey Farm in Topsfield, Massachusetts, at the time of the Salem episode. Isaac's first wife, Elizabeth, had given birth to two children who were living with Isaac at the time of his marriage to Mary. Altogether the Isaac Eastey family of Topsfield would have nine children. Mary and her family were tied by bonds of kinship to the Nurse family, and the Townes. It is perhaps not surprising to discover that the Nurses, the Townes, and the Eastey families were frequently at odds with the Putnams of Salem Village over boundaries of parcels of land claimed by one family or the other bordering along the Topsfield–Salem Village line.

Mary Eastey was first accused by Ann Putnam, Jr. and the afflicted girls on April 21 and examined by Hon. John Hathorne on April 22, 1692. She denied the charges against her and was sent to jail. Following this was a lengthy period during which all the afflicted girls ignored Mary and refrained from crying out against her—with the single exception of Mercy Lewis. Consequently, the court authorities ordered her released from jail on May 18. On May 20, Mercy Lewis began complaining strongly against Mary, claiming that Mary's specter had threatened to kill her if she did not back off as the others had done. By this time, Mercy had the renewed support of Ann Putnam, Jr. and Abigail Williams who joined in testifying to the activities of Mary Eastey. On May 20, another warrant was issued for Mary's arrest for afflicting Mercy Lewis, Ann Putnam, Jr., Abigail Williams, and Mary Walcott. By the following day, Mary was back in jail. She would remain in jail until the time of her execution on September 22, 1692. Her trial did not take place until September 9, by the end of which she was condemned to be hanged.

Interestingly, what distinguished Mary Eastey's case was not the various testimonies and indictments against her, but rather her eloquent and important petition to the Court of Oyer and Terminer. Written between the date of her conviction (September 9) and her execution (September 22), this petition is a remarkable document in that it calls into question the veracity of the afflicted girls' testimony and the confessions of many alleged witches. Mary further suggests a course of action which, if followed by the Court, would help to bring the trials to a conclusion with minimal further loss of innocent lives. (see Appendix of Primary Documents: "Petition of Mary Eastey")

While calmly acknowledging that she must die according to the verdict of her trial by law, Mary stresses that she is totally innocent and that because of this, she suspects that others may be innocent as well. Instead, she advocates that the "Afflicted Persons" be kept apart [from each other and questioned individually], and that the "confessing wichis [witches]" be tried by the Court for the crime of witchcraft. Her rationale for this was that she was "confident there is severall of them [who] has belyed [perjured] themselves" and that a thorough examination of their claims to witchcraft would prove them to be false witnesses. This, she maintained, would remove the incentive for people to confess, and she was right. The Court began to make preparations to try confessed witches, and predictably the number of persons retracting their confessions increased. Unfortunately, this turn of events did nothing to save Mary Eastey and she was hanged on September 22, 1692.

Sarah Good (1653–July 19, 1692)

The daughter of John Solart, a prosperous owner of a public house or tavern in Wenham, Massachusetts, Sarah Good was born with excellent prospects in 1655. Unfortunately, her father committed suicide in 1672 when Sarah was only seventeen, leaving an estate of five hundred pounds and no will. As a result, Solart's estate was divided between his widow and his two sons with a small portion reserved for each of his seven daughters when they came of age. When his widow remarried, her new husband took charge of the family estate and refused to divide the remainder with the daughters. Consequently, Sarah began life with no dowry to attract a prosperous suitor and instead married an impoverished former indentured servant, Daniel Poole, who died in 1682 or shortly thereafter, leaving Sarah deeply in debt.

These debts were assumed by her second husband, William Good, who lost a portion of his property in payment to Sarah's creditors. Ultimately, Sarah and William were forced to sell their home and remaining land to settle their debts, leaving themselves virtually homeless. By 1690 William was reduced to doing odd jobs and farm labor for whoever would hire him, while Sarah would work as a hired domestic servant or follow William to the various farms in the Wenham community. Accommodations for the Goods would often take the form of a rented room, or occasionally a barn or stable provided by a family that employed their services. Added to these difficulties, by 1692, was the constant presence of their four-year-old daughter, Dorcas, who accompanied her mother. By the time of the Salem trials, the sight of this sad, impoverished little family traveling from farm to farm along the rural roads of Salem Village and Wenham was a familiar scene.

By this time, Sarah's attitude had become bitter and sullen. She developed a common habit of cursing and scolding many individuals who occasionally refused to extend charity to her and her family. Certainly on the social scale of Salem Village, Sarah Good occupied the bottom rung. It is therefore not surprising that on February 29, 1692, when Tituba, Samuel Parris's West Indian slave, was badgered for the names of her accomplices in witchcraft, she chose Sarah Good as a safe target. Good was one of the few individuals who would have been absolutely no threat to Tituba socially, and indeed was regarded as a nuisance by most local residents.

During the course of Sarah's trial, she maintained her innocence, claiming boldly that she was being "falsely accused!" However, she did not flinch at the opportunity of accusing her neighbor, Sarah Osborne, as a witch in the hope of deflecting blame elsewhere. At length, her husband was asked to bring testimony against her, which he did. His worst indictments were to simply say that in his opinion, "she is an enemy to all good" and that she either "was a witch or would be one very quickly." Even her young daughter, Dorcas, who was herself accused of witchcraft on March 24, confessed that she had been trained in the black arts by her mother, who had given her a snake as a familiar. Ultimately, Dorcas Good was confined in chains at the Boston jail from April 1692 until May 1693. Sarah was condemned to hang but was granted a temporary reprieve until she had given birth to the child she was then carrying. She was executed on July 19, 1692, shortly after her newborn child had died in prison. Perhaps her most famous statement came as she stood at the place of execution being asked by Salem pastor Reverend Nicholas Noyes to confess to witchcraft. Witnesses remembered her responding with: "You are a liar! I am no more a witch than you are a wizard, and if you take away my life, God will give you blood to drink!" Ironically, in 1717, Noyes reputedly died of a hemorrhage with blood dripping from his mouth. This incident became the basis for "Maule's Curse" in Nathaniel Hawthorne's gothic romance, *The House of the Seven Gables*. In 1710, William Good petitioned the Great and General Court for damages done to his wife, Sarah, and their daughter, Dorcas, the latter suffering from ill health and mental illness following a year of harsh confinement. He claimed Dorcas needed constant attention as a consequence of the experience and had not matured beyond the age of four. The Commonwealth awarded William Good the sum of thirty pounds sterling, one of the largest sums granted to the families of the witchcraft victims.

Elizabeth Jackson Howe (c. 1637–July 19, 1692)

Elizabeth Howe was born in May 1637, in the hamlet of Hunsley, near the town of Rowley in East Yorkshire, England. She was christened and baptized at St. Peter's Church at Rowley, East Riding, in Yorkshire and came on board the ship *John* arriving in Salem, Massachusetts, with her parents, William and Deborah (Jackson) Howe, in 1638. Having passed the first winter with friends in Boston, by 1639, they were relocated to the newly established community of Rowley near Ipswich. The Jackson family had come with their two young children and others from their old community in England to help establish a new parish with their English pastor, Reverend Ezekiel Rogers. Her father was a yeoman farmer and soon became one of the original settlers of Rowley, Massachusetts, named after their original parish in England. By 1652, Elizabeth's father owned twelve acres and was soon appointed overseer of the common ways.

At the tender age of seven, Elizabeth was listed as a "maid" in the household of Reverend Ezekiel Rogers. This was most likely a means of relieving the Jackson family of the burden and expense of caring for a child in an already overcrowded household of six persons. At about the age of twenty-one, Elizabeth married twenty-five-year-old James Howe, formerly of Hatfield, Essex, England, on April 13, 1658. Howe was also a farmer, and resided in the neighboring town of Ipswich. With James she had five children: Elizabeth, Mary, John, Abigail, and Deborah. A busy mother, Elizabeth added to her many responsibilities those of caring for the farm of her husband, who was blind.

In 1682, during a periodic fit or seizure, Hannah Perley, a ten-year-old daughter of a neighbor family, accused Elizabeth Howe of causing her illness by means of witchcraft. When later confronted by Elizabeth and Ipswich's two ministers, the young girl denied that Elizabeth had done anything wrong. Several years later the child died, but no further steps were taken against Elizabeth. During the years that followed, Elizabeth attempted to gain membership in the Ipswich Church, but was repeatedly denied. Unfortunately, it appears that the local community remembered the incident involving the Perley girl, and the afflicted girls would resurrect it in 1692.

She was accused by the afflicted children of witchcraft and arrested on May 31, 1692. The usual afflicted group was present: Mercy Lewis, Mary Walcott, Abigail Williams, Ann Putnam, Jr., Susannah Sheldon, and Mary Warren. Elizabeth was charged with afflicting these persons and others. She was also charged with witchcraft by a person from Ipswich. To these accusations, Elizabeth expressed complete innocence. Her eloquent response being: "If it were the last moment I was to live, God knows I am innocent. . . ." During the examination, several persons claimed that Howe's specter was attacking them, much to Howe's confused denial. To this was added the testimony and accusation of Hannah Perley's parents who maintained that they believed their daughter had been killed by malefic witchcraft performed by Elizabeth Howe. Several other Ipswich persons—including the brother of her husband, John Howe—claimed that their livestock had been harmed after having arguments with Elizabeth. In light of all this testimony, Elizabeth Howe was transferred to jail to await her trial. In late June, she was found guilty and sentenced to death. She was hanged in Salem at Gallows Hill on July 19, 1692.

George Jacobs, Sr. (1620–August 19, 1692)

George Jacobs, Sr. was born around the year 1620 in England. Little is known about his childhood or education. He appears to have married and settled in Salem prior to 1649. In that year, he and his first wife had the first of their three children, George, Jr. The following year, they welcomed the arrival of their first daughter, Mary, and in 1655, their last child, Ann.

The Jacobs farm was located in an outlying district of Salem called Salem Farms, near present-day Danversport, Massachusetts. He purchased this parcel in 1658 and within a short time became a prosperous yeoman farmer. After the death of his first wife, he married again in 1673. His second wife, Mary, would also be accused of witchcraft in 1692.

On May 10, 1692, George Jacobs, Sr. and his granddaughter, Margaret Jacobs, were both arrested and charged with witchcraft. On that day, chief among his accusers was his servant, Sarah Churchill, who testified that George's specter had appeared before her with the Devil's Book and tempted her to sign it. Similarly, another of the afflicted girls, Mary Walcott, claimed that he had likewise threatened her if she did not sign the book.

Initially, he took the accusations lightly, laughing at the allegations of the afflicted. He claimed that he was as innocent of the charges as a newborn infant. In response to his protestation of innocence, Sarah Churchill reminded him of his unwillingness to participate in family devotions. He agreed to this, but explained that Bible reading was difficult for him because he was illiterate.

When asked to recite the Lord's Prayer, he failed to do so correctly which confirmed the Court's suspicion of his sinfulness and lack of spirituality.

His frustration was so great at this point that he made the famous statement, "Well burn me, or hang me, I will stand in the truth of Christ!" On the following day, his granddaughter Margaret confessed to the crime and quickly followed her admission of guilt by accusing her grandfather. He was finally sent to jail in Boston until his trial in Salem on August 8, 1692.

The trial resulted in a verdict of guilty. Among those who testified against George were Sarah Bibber, Elizabeth Churchill, John Doritch, Joseph Flint, George Herrick, Elizabeth Hubbard, Mary Warren, Mercy Lewis, and Margaret Jacobs. Following the conviction of her grandfather, Margaret wrote to the magistrates of the Court of Oyer and Terminer and withdrew her confession and testimony. As a result, she was placed in jail with those awaiting execution and had an opportunity to ask forgiveness of her grandfather, which he readily granted. On August 19, 1692, George Jacobs, Sr. was executed along with Reverend George Burroughs, John Proctor, John Willard, and Martha Carrier.

Susannah North Martin (c. 1621–July 19, 1692)

Susannah Martin was baptized in Olney, Buckinghamshire, England on September 30, 1621. Her parents were Richard and Joan (Bartram) North. After his first wife's death, Richard North married Ursula (North) and relocated the family to New England in 1639, becoming one of the first settlers of Salisbury, Massachusetts.

Susannah at the age of twenty-five married blacksmith George Martin of Salisbury on August 11, 1646. It was his second marriage and her first. George Martin came from the town of Ramsey, Hampshire, England, birthplace of Susannah's father, Richard North. George also had one daughter by his previous marriage. The following year, Susannah gave birth to her first child, a son named Richard. This birth was followed the next year with that of a second son, George. Altogether, Susannah and George had eight surviving children, five sons and three daughters, all of whom were born and raised in Salisbury. Susannah's name appears twice in the court records of Essex County prior to 1692. Two years following her marriage, Susannah was fined twenty shillings for an unidentified offense. No further punishment for this mysterious offense has been uncovered.

During the Salem trials, a Salisbury resident, William Browne, testified that he remembered his wife, Elizabeth Browne, accusing Susannah Martin of witchcraft in the early 1660s. Mrs. Browne testified before a grand jury that she was frightened by Susannah Martin when she suddenly and mysteriously vanished. Later, she claimed, she was regularly tormented by Susannah's specter. Two local physicians examined Mrs. Browne and declared her to be under the evil hand of witchcraft. Interestingly, Susannah was released from jail and no further information about this case has been discovered. On April 13, 1669, Susannah was again accused of witchcraft. This time she was forced to post a sizable bond with the court to guarantee she would return to stand trial. Once again there is no surviving record of either her trial or of a conviction. The only existing record of Susannah being tried and convicted comes from the testimony transcripts of the Salem witchcraft trials themselves.

A warrant for Susannah's arrest was issued by the Salem Court on April 30, 1692. She soon made herself a memorable character by the clever manner and reasoning of her responses to the questions posed by the magistrates. She was asked if she thought the afflicted children were bewitched, and replied simply, "No, I do not think they are!" When asked why it was that a specter appeared to the afflicted in her likeness, she referenced the biblical story of Saul consulting the Witch of Endor to contact the prophet Samuel's spirit: "He [Satan] that appeared in Samuel's shape, a glorified saint, can appear in anyone's shape."

During a particularly vociferous outbreak of the afflicted children, she laughed at them causing the magistrates to wonder at this odd reaction to their torment. Her reply was to observe "Well I may [laugh] at such folly." Did she not have any sympathy for their suffering, they queried? Her response: "No, I have none!" Did she not believe they were bewitched? Susannah's blunt reply: "No, I do not think they are." When pressed as to whether she thought the afflicted children were bearing false witness against the accused, she frankly suggested that "They may lye for ought I know." If she was incredulous about their behavior, she was asked, what were her thoughts about them? She demurred, "I do not desire to spend my judgment on it ... my thoughts are my own when they are in ... but when they are out, they are another's."

Besides the usual incidences of afflicted behavior by the Salem Village accusers, a number of Susannah Martin's neighbors from the Salisbury community appeared at court to give testimony against her. Most of their tales were set in the distant past making them difficult to prove or disprove conclusively. For example, John Kemball told a twenty-three-year-old tale involving an argument with Susannah followed by the mysterious death of some head of cattle. He also related an incident when he was attacked by a young black dog that would not stop until rebuked in the name of Christ. He kept the frightening incident to himself, but strangely was met by Susannah the following day who teased him about having been frightened by puppies. He wondered how she would have known about the incident. Numerous stories of this kind involving Susannah and some remarkable or mysterious occurrence were presented to the Court. These combined with her contemptuous attitude about the court proceedings proved her undoing. Reverend Cotton Mather summed up his opinion about Susannah Martin: "This woman was one of the most impudent, scurrilous, wicked creatures of this world; and she did now throughout her whole trial discover herself to be such a one."

In the face of all such circumstantial evidence she staunchly maintained her innocence. She was subjected to a physical examination whereby a court-appointed committee of women searched her body for abnormalities called "witch's marks or teats." These were places where a witch's familiar was believed to suck upon the body of the witch to draw out blood. Nothing suspicious was found on Susannah's body. Her trial took place on June 26, 1692, after which she was found guilty and condemned to death. She was hanged on Tuesday, July 19, 1692, along with Rebecca Nurse, Sarah Wilde, Sarah Good, and Elizabeth Howe. Unlike many of the families of the victims, Susannah's children never applied for compensation in 1711, and as a result of this Susannah's name was not cleared.

Rebecca Nurse (1621–July 19, 1692)

Rebecca Nurse was born Rebecca Towne, the daughter of New England colonist William Towne, sometime in February 1621. Two of her sisters lived in the Salem Village area at the time of her indictment—Mary (Towne) Eastey and Sarah (Towne) Cloyce. All three would be accused by the afflicted children and only Sarah Cloyce would escape with her life.

Rebecca was married to a Salem Village farmer, Francis Nurse, a prosperous member of the community. A housewife, mother of eight children, and nearly seventy years old at the time of the trials, she had a spotless reputation. Despite this, she was accused by both Anne Putnam, Sr. and Ann Putnam, Jr. of visiting them in specter form and harming them by sundry acts of witchcraft. She was served with a warrant on March 23, 1692, and examined by John Hathorne at the Salem Village meetinghouse on March 24. On that occasion, her principal accusers were Abigail Williams and Ann Putnam, Jr., who claimed she had tortured them and asked them to sign the Devil's Book.

The local community rallied behind Rebecca's protestations of innocence and circulated a petition testifying to her good character. It was signed by thirty nine members of Salem Village, including the influential Israel Porter, who personally testified on Rebecca's behalf in court. She was described as "not only innocent of any crime, but a very model of Christian piety."

Despite these claims, Ann Putnam, Jr. was adamant in her accusations, claiming that Nurse had brought "the black man" with her to tempt the afflicted girls to sign the Devil's Book and provoke God's wrath. Others joined Putnam in a litany of claims against Rebecca blaming her for untimely deaths and convulsive fits. When her body was examined by a court-appointed panel of women, "witch's marks" were discovered, which Rebecca claimed were natural growths which might be found on any older person.

Ultimately, she was tried on June 29, 1692, and eventually found guilty. Her family petitioned Governor Phips to review her case. Phips did so and granted Rebecca a stay of execution until he could reach a verdict. The Court responded with such virulent protest to Phips's leniency that he rescinded his reprieve and Rebecca was hanged on July 19, 1692, along with Sarah Good, Susannah Martin, Elizabeth Howe, and Sarah Wildes.

Alice Parker (d. September 22, 1692)

The wife of John Parker of Salem, Alice Parker was arrested on May 12, 1692, along with Ann Pudeater. She was accused of various acts of witchcraft by Mary Warren, servant of John and Elizabeth Proctor, and by Margaret Jacobs, granddaughter of George Jacobs, on May 13, 1692. Mary and Margaret's testimony was supported by Salem minister Reverend Nicholas Noyes, who at Alice's September execution characterized her as one of the "firebrands of Hell." She was also accused by several others including Abigail Hobbs and a sixteen-year-old boy named John DeRich, a nephew of John and Elizabeth Proctor, who testified that the spirit of Mary Warren's mother visited him and told him she had been killed by the witchcraft of Alice Parker. The murder of Goodwife Warren by Alice Parker was reaffirmed by Mary Warren herself in her testimony in September: "Goody Parker told me she bewitched my mother & was a cause of her death; also that she bewitched my sister Eliz[abeth] that is both deaf & dumb." Warren attributed this malefic action as revenge for her father not having mowed a field when asked by Alice Parker. Even Quaker Samuel Shattuck who had accused Bridget Bishop of bewitching his son, leveled a remarkably similar accusation at Alice Parker. In early June she was physically examined along with Rebecca Nurse, Bridget Bishop, Sarah Good, Sarah Martin, and Elizabeth Proctor for "witch's teats." Nothing unusual was discovered by the search committee, but this did little to save her. Shortly following her trial and condemnation, she was hanged on September 22, 1692, along with Martha Corey, Mary Eastey, Ann Pudeater, Wilmot Redd, Margaret Scott, and Mary Parker.

Mary Ayer Parker (c. 1633–September 22, 1692)

Mary Ayer Parker was born to John and Hannah Ayer, probably in the early 1630s. The family came from England and settled in the newly established town of Haverhill, Massachusetts, in 1647. In 1652 Mary became the second wife of a prosperous Andover yeoman farmer, Nathan Parker. In 1653 she gave birth to their first son, John. Over the years of their marriage, Mary Ayer Parker would give birth to nine children: John, James, Mary, Hannah, Elizabeth, Peter, Joseph, Robert, and Sara.

Nathan Parker died in June 1685 leaving an estate worth nearly 464 pounds. Of this amount, Mary received one-third of the Parker farmhouse and one-third of the Parker farm. This legacy was valued at slightly over 154 pounds, making her a fairly well provided-for widow. On September 16, 1692, she was dragged into the Salem crisis by means of the testimony of a confessed Andover witch named William Barker, Jr., who testified that on September 1, 1692, Goody Parker "did in company with him, the said Barker, afflict Martha Sprague by witchcraft." Barker elaborated his story with details of how Mary Parker "rode upon a pole" through the air on the night in question and had been baptized into the witches' congregation in Five Mile Pond. Mary's response to this accusation was to suggest that they had apprehended the wrong Mary Parker, since there were several other women in Andover by that name. This excuse was largely ignored by the court since when she entered the courtroom and was announced, Mary Warren, Sara Churchill, Hannah Post, Sara Bridges, and Mercy Wardwell all cried out against her. Their affliction was only stopped after she was compelled to touch them, thus removing the curse. Added to this evidence was the return of William Barker, Jr., who faced Mary in court and affirmed that she was indeed the one he had consorted with on the night described in his affidavit. Sara Phelps and Hanna Bigsbee both testified that they had been tortured, afflicted, pined, consumed, wasted, and tormented by the specter of Goody Parker, and concluded by accusing her of "sundry acts of witchcraft." On September 16, Mary was condemned to death and hanged on September 22, 1692.

John Proctor (1631–August 19, 1692)

John Proctor was born in the town of Assington, Suffolk, England on October 9, 1631. He was the first son of John Proctor, Sr. and his first wife, Martha, Harper Proctor. Altogether, the couple would have nine children. He immigrated to New England with his parents sometime between 1633 and 1635 and settled in Ipswich, Massachusetts. Here his father became quite successful as a yeoman farmer with substantial property. In 1666, at the age of thirty-five, young Proctor left Ipswich and moved to Salem where he leased a 700-acre farm known as "Groton," a portion of which he later purchased.

At the time of his father's death in September 1672, Proctor inherited a one-third share of his father's estate then valued at 1,200 pounds—including houses and lands in Ipswich—and became a well-established citizen in his own right. He married his first wife, Martha, in 1651 and, after her death in 1659, he married Elizabeth Thorndike, in 1662. When she passed away on August 30, 1672, he married his third wife, Elizabeth Bassett Proctor, in April 1674, and lived with her until the time of his death.

John applied for and received a license to operate a tavern in 1668. The Proctor Tavern was located along the Ipswich Road about half a mile south of the Salem Village boundary. This enterprise proved to be very lucrative and placed John Proctor among the area's more prosperous citizens.

Initially, it was John's wife, Elizabeth who was accused of witchcraft by the afflicted children. She was charged and arrested on April 8, 1692. John was quick to defend his wife in the face of these accusations and soon found himself accused as well. As such he was the first man to be accused of witchcraft, but by no means the last. Ultimately, three of his own children, William, Benjamin, and Sarah Proctor would also be accused. It has been suggested that what prompted this anti-Proctor behavior was his and his wife's open skepticism about the actions of the afflicted children. Proctor's maidservant, Mary Warren, attended Rebecca Nurse's examination with the Proctors on March 24 and began to act in an afflicted manner also.

In response, on March 25, Proctor told his neighbor Samuel Sibley that he was able to cure his "jade" Mary by keeping her at the spinning wheel for many hours at a time and by threatening to thrash her if she went into any more fits. He went on to suggest that what needed to be done is that the fathers or guardians of the afflicted girls should drag them each to the whipping post, strip them to the waist, and whip some sense into them instead of listening to their ridiculous accusations.

On April 12, John Proctor was also arrested and both he and his wife were sent to the Boston jail to await trial. Prior to the trial, Reverend John Wise of Ipswich parish tried to stem the tide of mounting evidence against the Proctors by circulating and submitting a petition signed by thirty-two men of Ipswich "on behalf of our neighbors John Proctor and his wife" maintaining their Christian reputation. Another petition was signed by twenty Salem neighbors of the Proctor family stating that, "having several years known

John Proctor and his wife, do testify that to our apprehension they lived Christian lives in their family and were ever ready to help such as stood in need of their help." Neither of these documents had the slightest impact upon the court. Finally, out of desperation, John wrote to several ministers of Boston begging them to influence the Court to move to Boston away from Salem's prejudiced environment. He went on to justly claim that by the order of Deputy Governor Stoughton, and with the authority of Sheriff of Essex County Jonathan Corwin, physical tortures had been used to force prisoners to confess, and that private property had already been seized from victims who had not yet even been tried.

John and Elizabeth Proctor were both tried on August 5, 1692, and both were found guilty and sentenced to hang on August 19. Sarah, fortunately, was able to ask for a temporary reprieve in view of the fact that she was pregnant, and a stay of execution was granted until the child was born. John Proctor, however, was hanged on Gallows Hill on August 19, 1692. Shortly before the day of execution, Proctor asked for a small amount of additional time to prepare his soul for death. This request was denied. At the time of execution he asked Reverend Cotton Mather and Reverend Nicholas Noyes to pray for him. This request they also refused unless Proctor would confess his guilt. Proctor then said a short prayer and was hanged.

Ann Pudeator (c. 1625–September 22, 1692)

Probably English in origin, Ann Pudeator's background is one of the least known of all the witchcraft trial victims. Prior to 1674 she is identified as the wife of Thomas Greenslit, and had five children with him. She is mentioned in the records of Salem in 1674 as having presented to court a probate inventory of her late husband's estate. Some historians believe that during the years of her first marriage she and her husband were settlers in the Maine frontier settlement of Falmouth.

After Thomas Greenslit's death Ann is believed to have taken on the profession of a midwife, a person who specialized in assisting women with childbirth and often caring for women in illness. In 1675, she was given the task of caring for Isabel Pudeator, the young wife of Jacob Pudeator of Salem. Immediately following Isabel's unexplained death in 1676, she married Jacob Pudeator who was younger than Ann by nearly twenty years. It is likely these strange circumstances did not go unnoticed by the Salem community.

In 1682, Jacob Pudeator also died, leaving his property to Ann with amounts of money as a legacy for each of her five children. This last turn of events, though immediately beneficial to Ann and her family, almost certainly set her apart from the other women in the Salem community by giving her financial independence, but also by making her the focal point of local gossip. Historian Carol Karlsen in *The Devil in the Shape of a Woman* suggests that women in a Puritan community, like Ann, who defied the conventional female stereotype, invited persecution by members of that community.

On May 12, 1692, Ann was arrested and brought into court for questioning along with Alice Parker. She was cried out against by Mary Warren, one of the so-called afflicted children. However, it appears likely that following this first session of questioning Ann was released. Later in June another accusation against Ann was made by Sarah Churchill, who claimed Ann's specter appeared to her, tortured her, and asked her to sign the Devil's Book. This is quite consistent with the testimony of all the afflicted girls.

On July 2, 1692, Ann was brought back to the Salem Court. At this session Sarah Churchill was joined in her accusations by five of the afflicted girls, with Ann Putnam, Jr. and Mary Warren falling into convulsions in court. She was accused of using effigies of the afflicted children as a means of harming them, and demonstrated her magical abilities in court when she is forced to heal the afflicted children by touching them.

Other witnesses presented proof against Ann in her capacity as a midwife. Jeremiah Neal testified that he had discovered jars of suspicious ointments in her house when he came to arrest her, and that he believed she had adversely affected his sick wife for whose death he held Pudeator responsible. She was identified as a spectral visitor by numerous individuals including Elizabeth Hubbard, Mary Walcott, and Sarah Bibber, who charged Ann's specter with pinching, pressing, and choking them. Against all these claims, Ann maintained her innocence and denied her involvement in witchcraft of any kind. She even went so far as to claim that some were bearing false witness against her, reminding the Court that one of her accusers, John Best, "hath been formerly whipped and likewise is [convicted] as a Lyar." She was condemned on September 17 and hanged with Martha Corey, Mary Eastey, Alice Parker, Mary Parker, Margaret Scott, Samuel Wardwell, and Wilmot Redd on September 22, 1692. Her name was not officially cleared of wrongdoing until the Massachusetts Legislature lifted the attainder in 1957.

Wilmot Redd (c. 1635–d. September 22, 1692)

One of the last victims to be hanged, Wilmot Redd (aka Wilmet Reed), was the only resident of Marblehead, Massachusetts, to be condemned during the Salem episode. She was arrested and brought to Salem for questioning on May 31, 1692. Known locally as "Mammy" Redd, Wilmot was a colorful if somewhat eccentric character distinguished by her volatile temper and her ability to engage in lively disputations with her Marblehead neighbors. Some historians, most notably Chadwick Hansen in his *Witchcraft at Salem*, assert that there is reliable evidence based upon the testimony presented at her trial to identify Wilmot as a practicing witch. This controversial point has been disputed by other scholars, such as Bernard Rosenthal, who maintain that witches do not exist and that Wilmot was wrongfully convicted entirely upon circumstantial and spectral evidence.

Regardless of this academic disagreement about Wilmot Redd's role, during the May hearing a number of individuals presented testimony against her similar to that presented against the other accused. Predictably her specter was cried out against by the usual group of afflicted children including Mercy Lewis, Mary Walcott, Abigail Williams, Ann Putnam, Jr., and Susannah Sheldon, as well as John Indian. She was charged with afflicting Elizabeth Hubbard, one of the individuals commonly involved in the group of afflicted girls. One deponent, Elizabeth Booth—who was a mature woman—claimed that she had been knocked down by Redd's specter. Interestingly, the Court chose to reject Booth's deposition.

Throughout the summer, Wimot Redd's case was allowed to rest until she was called back on September 14, 1692. On this occasion the afflicted girls returned, particularly Elizabeth Hubbard, Mary Walcott, and Ann Putnam, Jr. Mary Warren, one of the usual members of this group, for some unexplainable reason chose not to charge Wilmot Redd with witchcraft. Perhaps the most suspicious of all the evidence presented against her on this occasion was the testimony of Charity Pitman who described an encounter in 1687 between Wilmot Redd and a Salem woman identified as Mrs. Syms.

According to Charity Pitman's testimony, Mrs. Syms confronted Wilmot Redd concerning her servant, Martha Laurence. Mrs. Syms claimed that Laurence had stolen from her some pieces of linen cloth, and demanded compensation and punishment. Wilmot Redd denied knowing anything about the theft and demanded that Mrs. Syms leave the premises. The latter responded by threatening to go to Salem and swear out a warrant for the arrest of Wilmot Redd's maid. At this point, Wilmot Redd told Mrs. Syms that she would soon find herself unable to urinate or defecate for an indeterminate amount of time. According to Charity Pitman, this condition suddenly fell upon Mrs. Syms: "Mrs. Syms was taken with the dry belly-ache and so continued many months during her stay in the Towne, and was not cured whilst she tarried in the Country." Unwilling to acknowledge her guilt, Wilmot Redd was condemned at the end of her trial on September 14 and executed on September 22, 1692.

Margaret Scott (c. 1615–September 22, 1692)

A longtime resident of Rowley, Massachusetts, Margaret had lived most of her life in poverty. She is one of the most obscure and least-known of the victims of the Salem trials. In part this is because nearly all the records pertaining to her case are missing.

She was almost certainly born in England and moved to New England with her parents at a young age. That they were not especially prosperous is inferred by her choice of husband, a struggling husbandman, Benjamin Scott, who lacked the resources to purchase his own farmland. Together Margaret and Benjamin produced seven children; only three of whom lived to adulthood. In 1664, the town of Rowley gave Benjamin a parcel of farmland. The following year, at the Essex County Court, a man named Benjamin Scott is fined and admonished for theft.

The next year, Benjamin Scott signed the Freeman's Oath in Rowley, an act which identified him as the head of a household, a property owner, a church member, and generally a pillar of the community. Five years after this accomplishment, Benjamin Scott was dead, leaving his family with an estate valued at 67 pounds and 17 shillings. Margaret was about fifty-six years of age at this time, and would never remarry. She continued to live off the remainder of her husband's meager estate for another twenty-one years. Not surprisingly she was forced, as old age set in, to beg for support from her neighbors.

Similar to Wenham's beggar, Sarah Good, Margaret Scott became an unpopular and disliked member of the Rowley community in large part because of her habit of begging neighbors and passersby for assistance. Those that denied providing Margaret with money or goods came to expect verbal abuse or, worse, a curse. Not surprisingly, several of her alienated Rowley neighbors appeared at the Salem Court to provide evidence and depositions against her.

Among these were certain members of Rowley's two most prominent families, the Nelsons and the Wicoms. At Margaret's examination on August 5, 1692, seventeen-year-old Frances Wicom testified that she had been tormented by Margaret's specter since early June. She likewise provided testimony at Margaret's trial on September 15, along with her neighbor, Mary Daniel, a servant girl in the household of Reverend Edward Payson of Rowley. These depositions were quite graphic descriptions of spectral visits by Scott during which she allegedly choked and pinched her victims. At this session, a total of six depositions were presented against Margaret Scott. From outside Rowley came another deponent, twenty-two-year-old Sarah Coleman, a Newbury resident, who also testified to nocturnal visits by Margaret's specter which resulted in the "pricking, pinching, and choaking of me!" Another piece of damaging evidence was presented by Philip and Sarah Nelson who related conversations with a Rowley resident named Robert Shilleto who in the 1680s complained to them that he believed himself to be the victim of Margaret Scott's witchcraft: "We have often heard him complaining of Margaret Scott for hurting him, and often said that she was a witch."

These complaints, the Nelsons maintained, had gone on for three years prior to Shilleto's death. The clear implication of this was that Scott was responsible for his murder by malefic witchcraft. Besides this serious accusation, other neighbors came forward to describe incidences when Margaret would be denied a request and evil consequences would befall the object of her wrath. Most often these instances took the form of harm to livestock. To all this evidence, spectral and otherwise, Scott maintained her innocence, claiming that she harmed no one in spirit or any tangible way. She was condemned on September 15, and executed on September 22, 1692.

Samuel Wardwell (1643–September 22, 1692)

Samuel Wardwell was born on May 16, 1643 in Boston to Thomas and Elizabeth (Hooper) Wardwell. The Wardwell children were Eliakim, Benjamin, Samuel, and Martha. Samuel was apprenticed to a master carpenter in Boston and finished his apprenticeship in 1664 at the age of twenty-one. During that same year he followed his brother Benjamin to Salem and began to take advantage of the wide-scale rebuilding and expansion of that town. During this formative time, he met and married a young woman in Salem and had a son, Thomas Wardwell. Shortly following this, in 1671, his young wife died.

Grief-stricken, Samuel left Salem with his little son for the newly established inland community of Andover. Here he began his life anew, meeting and falling in love with twenty-five-year-old Sarah Barker, daughter of Richard Barker, one of Andover's most prominent citizens. Because of Samuel's low status in the community, the match was not encouraged and was soon broken off.

During the 1670s and 1680s in addition to his work as a carpenter, Wardwell established a reputation as an accurate fortune-teller, in spite of clear official Puritan opposition to the practice. Although he was never charged with violating the law, this reputation for predicting the future proved a problem for Samuel during the Salem witchcraft trials episode.

Samuel's fortunes improved remarkably in 1673 when he attracted the attention of a young and well-to-do widow, Sarah Hawkes. The couple married on January 9, 1673. Within a short time they began to produce a large family: Samuel, Jr., Eliakim, William, Mercy, Elizabeth, and Rebecca. Samuel continued to work as a carpenter which, together with Sarah's inheritance, allowed the Wardwells to purchase a large farm in Andover. It was to this farm that the Essex County sheriff came to apprehend Samuel Wardwell on August 15, 1692.

At his hearing, testimony was presented from years earlier when Samuel had entertained Andover people with his ability to predict the future correctly. This was not considered a harmless pastime, but reflected possible links to the realm of the supernatural—the "invisible world." With undeniable evidence of dabbling in fortune-telling, Samuel decided to save his life by pleading guilty. He was aware that all those who had confessed were allowed to live. He held nothing back.

Samuel Wardwell, knowing that his wife and two daughters had also recently been accused and were at risk, proceeded to confess to the Court. He freely acknowledged his complicity in fortune-telling, and admitted having made a pact with Satan in order that he might live comfortably. This confession was quite detailed and elaborate, providing the Court with tales of demonic activity. What is puzzling is that after providing the Court with details about his life as a witch, Wardwell decided to deny everything and plead innocent to all charges.

The Court had no choice but to convict him on the basis of the evidence presented against him by several Andover residents as well as himself. His trial took place on September 17, and he was hanged on September 22, 1692. His wife and daughters were exonerated.

Sarah Averill Wildes (1629–September 22, 1692)

The story of Sarah Wildes went back many years prior to the outbreak in Salem. Sarah was a Topsfield resident married to a farmer, John Wildes, Sr. She had been involved in a number of disputes with her neighbors over the years, and had the tendency to be vindictive. Some of these neighbors believed that Sarah had used witchcraft as revenge for perceived wrongs done to her. This testimony was first presented at Sarah Wildes' hearing on April 22, 1692. (Magistrates John Hathorne and Jonathan Corwin had issued warrants for Sarah Wildes' arrest on April 21 based upon an April 19 complaint by Thomas Putnam and John Buxton on behalf of Ann Putnam, Mercy Lewis, and Mary Walcott.) The most significant of these tales involved Sarah Wildes and Mary Reddington.

Reverend John Hale, pastor of the Beverly congregation, testified in court on April 22, that nearly fifteen years earlier he had been visited by Mary

Reddington who "opened her griefs to him." She was the wife of John Reddington and mother-in-law to Essex County Marshall John Herrick. During this pastoral visit, Hale related that Mary Reddington had expressed to him the belief that she was being bewitched by Sarah Wildes. Hale added to this testimony additional information from Wildes' family relations which further incriminated Sarah, including that her stepson, John, believed "his mother Wildes was a witch." Others quickly began to complain about her, including Abigail Hobbs and the rest of the afflicted girls. Sarah Bibber, a newcomer to the group, claimed to see Wildes sitting overhead on a beam, to which Sarah responded: "I am not guilty, sir."

The aforementioned self-confessed witch, Deliverance Hobbs, during her own examination claimed that the specter of Sarah Wildes had almost torn her to pieces. Many other incidences were recalled at the April session. Elizabeth Symonds recollected an incident when she met Sarah Wildes on the road and argued with her briefly over a borrowed scythe. Sarah threatened Elizabeth and later that evening a dark shape appeared in her bedroom chamber which came and laid upon her in bed preventing her from moving all night.

Most intriguing of all was a charge by forty-eight-year-old Mary Gadge who claimed that she recollected that David Balch had told her two years earlier he had been bewitched by a coven of witches, one of whom was Sarah Wildes. Added to this was the reminder that Sarah Wildes had also been accused of witchcraft, but acquitted, in 1676. She was determined by the magistrates to be a likely candidate for witchcraft and was ordered to stand trial on June 29, 1692. On that day a verdict of guilty was submitted against her and she was executed along with Rebecca Nurse, Sarah Good, Susannah Martin, and Elizabeth Howe.

John Willard (d. August 19, 1692)

John Willard is another of the more obscure witchcraft trial victims. He appears to have been born and spent his youth in Lancaster, Massachusetts. Shortly following his relocation to Groton, Massachusetts, he married Margaret Wilkins, the daughter of a prominent Boston family. Finally, he moved his young family to Salem Village. By the year 1689, Willard's first connection with a Salem Village family was his role as a Putnam family retainer at the time Mrs. Thomas Putnam had just given birth to her daughter Sarah. On rare occasions, the infant was placed in his care. Sadly, within six weeks the child was dead. This incident would return to cause John Willard difficulty during 1692.

By the time of the Salem trials Willard was serving Essex County as a Deputy Constable of Salem Village. As the accusations of the afflicted girls began to increase in number and intensity, Willard began to doubt the veracity of the afflicted girls' testimony. This tendency developed gradually over the course of March and April until by May 1692, Willard refused to serve warrants on accused witches. When the afflicted girls heard rumors to this effect, John Willard became a target for their hostility. Upon being informed that he was being cried out against by Ann Putnam, Jr. and the others, he decided to seek the aid and support of his wife's influential family—particularly his wife's grandfather, Bray Wilkins. He arrived at the Wilkins house "greatly troubled," seeking Bray Wilkins' help and advice. Unfortunately, Bray was on his way to an appointment and could not remain with his grandson-in-law. He promised to return later that night, but was unable to get back and the meeting was cancelled. On May 4, the two men met again at a family gathering in Boston and on this occasion Wilkins recalled: "Willard looked after such a sort upon me [looked at me in such a way] as I never before discerned in any." Within minutes, Wilkins claimed, he began to find himself in a "strange condition." Not able to urinate, he felt in pain "like a man on a Rack." Grandfather Wilkins thought he knew immediately what the cause of his distress was. "I was afraid that Willard had done me wrong!" Later, Wilkins was examined by a wise woman in Boston who asked him "whether none of those evil persons [in Salem] had done me damage." Upon returning home, Bray Wilkins was dismayed to discover his grandson, Daniel, sick to death. Interestingly, this same young man had once complained against John Willard saying that it were well "if Willard were hanged!" On May 9, 1692, Susannah Sheldon claimed to see a vision of four dead people who turned "Red as Blood" when they identified Willard as their murderer. On May 10, magistrates Hathorne and Corwin issued a warrant for the arrest of the former court officer.

John Willard, fearing for his life, fled the Salem vicinity intending to reach New York colony and safety. Court officer John Putnam, Jr. was sent after him and caught Willard in Lancaster, Massachusetts, the place of his childhood, only about forty miles from Salem. He was arrested and then brought back to Salem to stand trial. In the meanwhile, Willard's specter was busy visiting people throughout the Salem Village vicinity. Ann Putnam, Jr. testified that his shape had admitted to her that he had whipped her newborn sister Sarah to death and that he intended to kill Daniel Wilkins, grandson of Bray Wilkins, who now was suffering. On Monday, May 16, Mary Walcott and Mercy Lewis testified that Willard was choking and pressing Daniel Wilkins, and not surprisingly, Daniel died that night. Willard was brought in for a pre-trial examination on May 18, 1692. All through May more and more testimonies, affidavits, and depositions were gathered against John Willard. He was finally indicted on June 2, 1692, and brought to trial on July 22, 1692. The trial resulted in a verdict of guilty and Willard was hanged on Gallows Hill along with Reverend George Burroughs, George Jacobs, Sr., John Proctor, and Martha Carrier.

THE MINISTERS

Reverend John Hale (1636–1700)

Reverend John Hale was born in Charlestown, Massachusetts, on June 3, 1636. The son of blacksmith, Robert Hale (1609–1659) and his wife, Joanna Cutler Hale (1612–1679), he grew up living in the Boston area. Working his way through Harvard College, he graduated with a bachelor's degree in theology in 1657. The next few years he spent serving as a tutor and teacher. In 1664, he received an invitation to preach at the newly formed congregation at the Bass River community of Salem. By September 20, 1667, his abilities and personality had so impressed the parishioners that he was invited to become their first official pastor, and he was ordained as a minister of the church. This was a post John Hale would occupy for the remainder of his life.

In 1668, he was asked by the leading members of the Bass River community to draw up a formal petition to be submitted to the Great and General Court asking for Bass River to be officially set apart from Salem and established as a new town. The petition was granted, and the town was given the name of Beverly after Beverley, Yorkshire, England.

As the community expanded and its population grew, so did the reputation and popularity of Hale. As a gesture of high esteem, the congregation deeded to him and his heirs in perpetuity the newly constructed parsonage along with 200 acres of shoreline pasturage. This structure is presently known as the Hale Farm and is located on Hale Street in Beverly, Massachusetts. Throughout the course of his life, Reverend Hale was married three times. His first wife, Rebecca Byles Hale, died in 1683 and was followed by Sarah Noyes Hale, who married John in 1684 and died in 1695. His third and last wife was Elizabeth Somerby, who married Hale in 1698 and outlived her husband by fifteen years. During the Massachusetts campaign led by William Phips to capture the French fortress of Louisburg in Canada in 1690, Reverend John Hale served as a chaplain to the militia. Shortly following his return from the war, the Salem area was torn by the infamous Salem witchcraft trials in which Hale would play a prominent part.

In February 1692, Reverend Hale was called to the home of Reverend Samuel Parris in nearby Salem Village to observe the activities of the so-called afflicted children and participate in vigils of fasting and prayer with other local ministers to achieve a miraculous cure for the girls' condition. When their behavior did not improve, Reverend Hale was among the foremost ministers intent upon seeking out and eliminating the witches responsible. As the episode expanded and intensified, Hale was called upon to testify against members of his congregation and he became more deeply involved in the proceedings. As the number of cases grew, Hale became less vocal and visibly less involved. By the fall, accusations were leveled at Hale's wife, Sarah, who was so far above reproach that she was never in serious danger. Nevertheless, Hale seems to have at some point changed his opinion concerning the way in which the trials were conducted and the advisability of using the testimony of the afflicted children.

After the end of the episode, and the subsequent death of his wife in 1695, Hale reflected upon the trials and two years later produced a book, *A Modest Inquiry into the Nature of Witchcraft*, which provides a firsthand assessment of what took place and what went wrong. While never denying the reality of witchcraft or the existence of witches, Hale took exception to the manner in which the Court proceeded against those accused. By way of explanation, he attempted to justify the actions of the officials by explaining that those in authority were so fearful of the threat of witchcraft to the community that they were unable to think clearly and rationally. For this reason, regrettably, he believed that innocent blood was shed: "Such was the darkness of the day, and so great the lamentations of the afflicted, that we walked in the clouds and could not see our way."

Hale died in his home in Beverly on May 15, 1700.

Reverend Cotton Mather (1663–1728)

Reverend Cotton Mather was born on February 11, 1663, the son of the famous Boston cleric and president of Harvard College, Rev. Increase Mather. He graduated from Harvard feeling uncertain about his abilities as a preacher due to a speech impediment. In spite of his limitations as a public speaker, he managed to excel in his calling as a minister and soon became pastor of the Second Congregational Society, also known as the Old North Church of Boston.

In 1688, while serving in this capacity, Reverend Mather was called upon to investigate a suspected case of witchcraft involving members of his own congregation, the family of John Goodwin. This incident involved four Goodwin children who exhibited symptoms resembling the effects of malefic magic, including sharp pains, paralysis, involuntary spasms, and verbal outbursts of profanity.

Mather took a leading role in tracing these afflictions to their source—the family's Irish washerwoman, known as Mary Glover. Interestingly, when confronted with the evidence, "Goody" Glover freely and frankly confessed that she had been tormenting the children and went so far as to demonstrate to Mather how such spells were cast upon her victims using a crude "poppet." Unwilling and unable to express regret or ask forgiveness for her sin, Goody Glover was hanged on Boston Common, and Mather chronicled all the details of the incident in his best-selling book, *Memorable Providences*.

Four years later, Reverend Mather was made aware of the Salem disturbances similar to the Goodwin episode and took an active interest in the proceedings. Throughout 1692, Reverend Cotton Mather became directly involved with the Court of Oyer and Terminer at Salem which was overseen by five magistrates, three of whom were members of Mather's congregation. As events intensified during the summer months, Mather expressed the opinion that the people of New England were being assaulted by "an Army of Devils," accounting for the numerous accusations and confessions of witchcraft.

By late 1692, Governor William Phips, also a member of Mather's Boston parish, asked Mather to write a text justifying the trials and the measures which, by September, had resulted in the execution of nineteen people. Subsequently, Mather produced *Wonders of the Invisible World*, a publication providing insights into the rationale for the trials and Mather's unique perspective on certain specific cases.

As public criticism grew, both Reverend Mather and Governor William Phips came under more intense scrutiny, forcing both to attempt to minimize their roles in the now highly controversial Salem episode. Despite this, the publication of *Wonders of the Invisible World* only seemed to focus more blame upon Mather, diminishing his once stellar reputation in Boston. The later published critiques of the trials by Thomas Brattle and Robert Calef only further served to tarnish Mather's image to an extent that he began to express feelings of regret, self-doubt, and despair concerning the role he had played. He died on February 13, 1728, having survived two wives and only two of his fifteen children.

Reverend Increase Mather (1639–1723)

Increase Mather was born in Massachusetts Bay Colony in the town of Dorchester on June 12, 1639. After graduating from Harvard College in 1656, he received his M.A. from Trinity College, Dublin, in 1658. After the Restoration (1660), he was forced to return to Boston and by 1664 was made pastor of the Second Congregational (Old North) Church, a position he held throughout his life. One year prior to his appointment, his son, Cotton Mather, was born. As a leader of the Boston community, Increase worked to support the Puritan establishment and oppose the anti-Puritan influence of Restoration political appointees, especially Sir Edmund Andros, who revoked the Massachusetts Bay Charter and created the Dominion of New England in 1685.

In 1688, Increase traveled to London and obtained a new charter from King William and Queen Mary which united the colonies of Massachusetts Bay and Plymouth under a new royal governor—Sir William Phips. It was during this period that he also began his tenure as president of Harvard College—a position he would hold from 1685 to 1701. A prolific writer, he wrote numerous books and pamphlets during his years as Harvard's president, among them *Cases of Conscience Concerning Evil Spirits*, which decried the use of spectral evidence during the Salem witchcraft episode. During the trials, Increase was much more critical of the trial proceedings than his son, Cotton. Increase remained detached from the episode except to serve as one of the contributors to the lengthy document entitled "The Return of Several Ministers," which cautioned justices upon the use of spectral evidence, and as an interviewer of Reverend George Burroughs when he was brought to Boston for questioning. Although the trials dimmed his reputation slightly, Increase remained an important religious leader in New England until his death on August 23, 1723.

Reverend Samuel Parris (1654–1720)

Samuel Parris was born in London in 1654, the son of merchant Thomas Parris, and was brought with his family to a newly purchased sugar plantation in Barbados in the late 1650s. At the time of his father's death in 1673, young Samuel was attending school at Harvard College in Massachusetts Bay Colony. Leaving his studies at the age of twenty, Parris moved back to Barbados to take charge of his father's estate. Establishing himself in the sugar trade as an agent at Bridgetown, Parris was unable to succeed in business, and soon found it necessary to relocate.

In 1680, Parris moved with two slaves—John and Tituba Indian—to Boston. Within a year following his arrival, he married Elizabeth Eldridge, a young woman of good family, who bore him his first child, Thomas, a year later. In 1683, a daughter, Betty Parris, was born, and five years later, Susanna. Once again, Parris attempted to establish himself in business in Boston, but soon became disenchanted with the life of a merchant. By 1686, he began serving as a guest minister and interim pastor for several Boston area churches. In 1688, Parris began formal negotiations with Salem Village to become that congregation's new preacher. In July 1689, he and his family were settled, and Parris began his ministerial duties.

Within a short time, certain members of the village congregation began to express dissatisfaction with Parris resulting in the occasional payment of his salary. By October 1691, the anti-Parris faction began to resist providing his requirement of winter fuel. At this point, Parris's sermons began to warn his parishioners of the dangers of succumbing to the satanic impulse to thwart God's work by hurting the Lord's anointed messenger. Following this initial period of confrontation, Parris's daughter, Betty, and niece Abigail Williams began to spend their afternoons in the company of Tituba, the family domestic servant. Throughout the winter, these three—and possibly other young females—engaged in fortune-telling activities considered sinful by the Christian community.

By February, Betty and Abigail began to complain of various ailments including pinching, choking sensations, and partial paralysis. Local physician Dr. William Griggs evaluated the girls' condition and declared his belief that they were under the power of the "evil hand" of witchcraft. Reverend Parris then organized a series of fasts and prayer meetings with local ministers hoping to bring about spiritual healing, but to no avail. Finally, in desperation, he summoned magistrates John Hathorne and Jonathan Corwin to Salem Village to conduct inquiries as to the source of the girls' afflictions. This marked the beginning of the Salem episode which would continue until spring 1693.

The disastrous effects of the Salem trials ruined Parris's local reputation and further alienated members of his congregation. Attempting to restore order, he apologized for his role in the episode, but opposition was intent upon his removal. In 1697, Parris's wife, Elizabeth, died, and the distraught minister finally agreed to vacate the village pulpit, being quickly replaced by Reverend Joseph Green. The remainder of Parris's career involved preaching at several other Massachusetts churches including Stowe and Sudbury, where he died in 1720.

THE MAGISTRATES

Hon. John Hathorne (1641–1717)

John Hathorne, the great-great grandfather of writer Nathaniel Hawthorne, was born in Salem, Massachusetts, on August 5, 1641. He was the son of local magistrate, William Hathorne, and his wife, Anne Smith Hathorne. Although not college educated, he quickly rose to become not only a successful West Indies merchant but a political leader of the Salem community.

By the 1680s, Hathorne had been elected to several important offices including justice of the peace and Essex County magistrate. On several occasions, he was asked to resolve problems which arose in the nearby farming community of Salem Village. In 1686, he served as a member of the Salem Village committee to find a successor to their previous minister, Reverend George Burroughs.

In February 1692, he was called again by the people of Salem Village to conduct pre-trial examinations of Tituba, Sarah Good, and Sarah Osborne. From this point onward he, and his fellow magistrate Jonathan Corwin, played a significant role in the witchcraft trial events, conducting many of the pre-trial examinations to discover those suspects which should then be sent to trial before the Governor's Court of Oyer and Terminer in Salem.

Despite his direct responsibility for sending so many innocent persons to the gallows and placing so many others in danger of their lives, Hathorne never expressed regret concerning his activities during the trials. He died on May 10, 1717, and lies buried in Salem's Charter Street Burying Ground.

Hon. Samuel Sewell (1652–1730)

Samuel Sewell was born at Bishop Stoke in Hampshire, England, on March 28, 1652. He came with his family to Newbury, Massachusetts, in 1661, most likely to flee the restoration of the Stuart monarchy. In 1671, he graduated from Harvard College with a bachelor's degree and received his master's degree in 1674. On February 28, 1676, he married Hannah Hull, only daughter of Boston merchant John Hull, one of the wealthiest men in the colony, receiving a dowry of five hundred pounds.

By 1676 he was engaged in international maritime trade and enjoyed success as a Boston merchant working with his wealthy father-in-law. In May 1678, he became a freeman of Boston, a position which provided him with the right to vote for candidates to the House of Deputies. Successful in business and public life, Sewell purchased a printing press in 1681 and was soon appointed by the Massachusetts Bay Colony to serve as the colony's official publisher. Following his father-in-law's death in 1683, Samuel took over all of the extensive Hull business interests and numerous civic duties, including a position with the House of Deputies for the town of Westfield, Massachusetts; a seat on the Board of Overseers of Harvard College; and captain of the South Company of Boston militia. He was almost unique among Puritans in that he firmly believed that the establishment of the New Jerusalem in America was predicated upon the conversion of the Native Americans: "I put up a Note [posted in his meetinghouse] to pray for the Indians that Light might be communicated to the by Candlestick, but my Note was the latest, and so not professedly prayed for at all." To this goal, he welcomed the publication of John Eliot's Indian Bible in Algonquian.

Upon the arrival of the new governor, William Phips, in May 1692, Sewell was asked to serve as a justice on the newly created Court of Oyer and Terminer to try cases of witchcraft in Salem. Throughout the duration of this appointment, Sewell kept a diary of his observations and impressions of the court proceedings. When the episode was ended in May 1693, public opinion had turned against the Court and its justices, and Sewell himself suffered from pangs of guilt for his involvement. On January 14, 1696, he stood in the South Church meetinghouse while the minister, Reverend Willard, read Sewell's apology: "Samuel Sewell, sensible of the reiterated strokes of God upon himself and his family, and being sensible that as to the guilt contracted upon the opening of the late commission of Oyer and Terminer at Salem & he is, on many accounts, more concerned than any that he knows of, desires to take the blame and shame of it, asking pardon of men and especially desiring prayers that God ... would pardon that sin and all other [of] his sins ..." Each year for the remainder of his life he set aside a day of fasting, prayer, and humiliation for the role he had played in the Salem episode. He died at his home in Boston on January 1, 1730.

Hon. William Stoughton (1631–1701)

William Stoughton was born in England on September 30, 1631. He was the son of Israel and Elizabeth Stoughton who relocated to a sizeable tract of land in Massachusetts Bay Colony during the height of the Great Migration.

While growing up under prosperous circumstances in New England, William decided that he would prepare himself for the Puritan ministry. In 1650, he completed his formal theological training with a bachelor's degree from Harvard College. Desiring an advanced degree, he left Massachusetts for England and continued his studies at Oxford University. Here he received an M.A. degree in 1652. From that year until he lost his fellowship in 1660, Stoughton pursued the life and career of a professional scholar. Two years following his dismissal from Oxford, he decided to return to Massachusetts, and was soon serving as a preacher at the First Congregational Church of Dorchester.

Within a few years, his ability as a preacher was widely recognized and his parishioners offered him the position of pastor. By the 1670s Stoughton's reputation as a community leader had grown significantly and he was drawn into the political arena of colonial life. Within a short time he served as the deputy president of the royalist colonial government of New England, first from 1674 to 1676 and later from 1680 to 1686. Between these two terms of office in America, Stoughton served as agent of Massachusetts affairs in London at the Court of King Charles II.

After his return from England, Stoughton was also appointed to the office of Chief Justice of the Massachusetts Great and General Court—a position he would hold until shortly before his death. For this reason, it is not surprising to discover that Hon. William Stoughton was chosen by royal Governor Sir William Phips to serve as Chief Justice of the newly created Court of Oyer and Terminer at the start of the Salem witchcraft episode in 1692.

Throughout the trials, Stoughton distinguished himself as a close-minded, harsh, and unrelenting persecutor of the victims of the afflicted children, to such an extent that he became known for his zeal in securing as many executions as possible. To this end, he repeatedly allowed many violations of correct English court procedure, including the admission of spectral evidence and the illegal seizure of private property by the Commonwealth. In October 1692, Thomas Brattle, Boston merchant and observer of the events in Salem, described Stoughton's biased role thus: "The chief Judge is very zealous in these proceedings, and says, he is very clear as to all that hath as yet been acted by this court, and as far as ever I could perceive, is very impatient in hearing anything that looks another way."

By the fall of 1692, Stoughton and Governor Phips were on opposite ends of the witchcraft trial issue, with Governor Phips wishing to bring the trials to a speedy conclusion with minimum further bloodshed, and Stoughton intent upon condemning and executing as many of the convicted as possible. The issue reached a head when, in October, the governor finally closed the

Salem Court of Oyer and Terminer, and moved proceedings to Boston, disallowing spectral evidence and, finally, declaring that all persons then in custody awaiting trial or execution were to be set free.

Ironically, when in 1694 Governor William Phips was recalled to London to answer scandalous charges of corruption and mismanagement of colonial affairs, Stoughton stepped into the role as acting governor. He died in Boston on July 7, 1701.

POLITICAL LEADERS

Governor Sir William Phips (1651–1695)

Born on February 2, 1651, near the present-day town of Woolrich, Maine, Sir William Phips began life as the humble son of a farmer who traded with the local Wabanaki Indians. In his late teens, he walked to Boston and became apprenticed as a ship's carpenter, ultimately marrying the widow of a prosperous merchant. Rising quickly through skill and good fortune, Phips became a sea captain, who in the 1680s sought the patronage of wealthy British investors to back treasure-seeking expeditions to the Caribbean.

In 1687, Phips succeeded in locating the wreck of a Spanish treasure galleon and later shared his newfound wealth with the recently crowned monarchs, King William and Queen Mary. In response, the royal couple made him a knight and royal official in New England. By 1690, he had undergone a profound religious conversion and later became involved in the re-issuance of the new charter for Massachusetts colony. By early 1692, he was appointed as royal governor of Massachusetts and returned there from England in May, in time to witness the start of the witchcraft trials episode.

During the trial period (1692–1693), Phips established the initial Court of Oyer and Terminer that tried cases at Salem from May through September, and then moved the trials to Boston. He was closely associated with both Cotton and Increase Mather, who he frequently consulted concerning the trials proceedings, and was later praised by Cotton Mather in his 1697 biography of Phips.

During this period, Phips was also involved in waging a war against the Wabanaki on the Maine frontier, finally negotiating a treaty with them in 1693. In May of that same year, he also declared a general manumission of all those still imprisoned awaiting trial or punishment for witchcraft—effectively bringing that episode to a close. At this point, Governor Phips began to suffer from severe criticism which called into question his management of colonial affairs, including the possible misuse of colonial funds. Recalled to London to answer his critics, he died suddenly in early 1695.

Primary Documents

ARREST WARRANTS

Arrest warrants were issued throughout the Salem episode when evidence was presented to a magistrate sufficient to convince him of the likelihood of criminal behavior on the part of an individual. The arrest warrant authorized a court-appointed law enforcement official—usually a marshall or sheriff—to locate, apprehend, and bring the suspected witch to the Court for further questioning. The next step would be a pre-trial examination to determine if sufficient evidence of wrongdoing existed to warrant a trial of the suspected witch.

Document 1   (Warrant for Arrest of George Burroughs)

To Jno Partredg field Marshal

You are Required in their Maj'sts names to aprehend the body of mr George Buroughs at present preacher at Wells in the provence of Maine, & Convay him with all Speed to Salem before the Magestrates there, to be Examened, he being Suspected for a Confederacy with the devil in opressing of Sundry about Salem as they relate. I having Receved perticuler Order from the Govern'r & Council of their Maj'sts Colony of the Masathusets, for the Same, you may not faile herein,

Dated in portsmouth in the provenc of Hamshire. April 30'th 1692

Elisha Hutchinson Maj'r

By Virtue of this warrant I Apprehended s'd George Burroughs and have Brought him to Salem and Delievered him to the Authority there this fourth day of May 1692

*John Partridge field marshall of the
Provence of newhansher and maine

(*Massachusetts Historical Society*)

Document 2   (Warrant for Arrest of Giles Corey, Mary Warren, Abigail Hobbs, and Bridget Bishop)

Salem. April the 18'th 1692
    There being Complaint this day made (Before us) by Ezekiell Chevers and John putnam Jun'r both of Salem Village Yeomen: in Behalfe of theire Majesties, for themselfes and also for theire Neighbours Against Giles Cory, and Mary Waren both of Salem farmes
    And Abigaile Hobbs the daughter of Wm Hobs of the Towne of Tops-feild and Bridgett Bushop the wife of Edw'd Bishop of Salem Sawyer for high Suspition of Sundry acts of Witchcraft donne or Committed by them, upon the Bodys of: Ann putnam.Marcy Lewis, and Abig'l Williams and Mary Walcot and Eliz. Hubert—of Salem village—whereby great hurt and damage hath benne donne to the Bodys of Said persons above named.therefore craved Justice—
    You are therefore in their Majest's names hereby required to apprehend and bring before us Giles Cory & Mary Waren of Salem farmes, and Abigail Hobs the daugter of Wm Hobs of the Towne of Topsfeild and Bridget Bushop the wife of Edward Bushop of Salem To Morrow about Eight of the Clock in the forenoone, at the house of Lt Nathaniell Ingersalls in Salem Village in order to theire Examination Relateing to the premises aboves'd and here of you are not to faile Dated Salem April 18'th 1692

To George Herrick Marshall
of the County of Essex—
*John Hathorne
*Jonathan.Corwin Esq'rs
Assis'ts

(*Peabody Essex Museum, Salem, MA*)

Document 3   (Warrant for Arrest of Rebecca Nurse)

To: To the Marshall of Essex or his deputie
    There Being Complaint this day made (before us by Edward putnam and Jonathan putnam Yeomen both of Salem Village, Against Rebeca Nurce the

wife of franc's Nurce of Salem Village for vehement Suspition, of haveing Committed Sundry acts of Witchcraft and thereby haveing donne Much hurt and Injury to the Bodys of Ann putnam the wife of Thomas putnam of Salem Village Anna puttnam the dauter of Said Thomas putnam and Abigail Williams &c

You are therefore in theire Majesties names hereby required to apprehend and bring before us Rebeca Nurce the wife of franc's Nurce of Salem Village, to Morrow aboute Eight of the Clock in the forenoon at the house of Lt Nathaniell Ingersoll in Salem Village in order to her Examination Relateing to the aboves'd premises and hereof you are not to faile Salem March the 23'd 1691/2

p us *John. Hathorne [unclear:] Assists

*Jonathan Corwin

March 24'th 1691/2 I have apprehended the body of Rebeca Nurse and brought her to the house of Le't Nath. Ingersal where shee is in Costody

p'r *George Herrick Marshall of Essex

(Reverse) in the meeting house (be) Mary Walkott Marcy Lewis Eliz: Hubberd

all these accused goody Nurce then to her face that she then hurt them &c and they saw besides the others on Contra Side

(*Peabody Essex Museum, Salem, MA*)

CONFESSIONS

Nearly fifty individuals confessed to the crime of witchcraft after being accused. The Salem Court followed the policy of allowing self-confessed witches to live, but they were expected to cooperate with the Court in providing evidence to identify other witches. Confessions were written and submitted to the Court often implicating others while expressing remorse.

Document 4   (Confession of Sarah Churchill)

Sarah Churchwell confesseth that Goody pudeator brought the book to this Examin't and she signed it, but did not know her at that tyme but when she saw her she knew her to be the same and that Goody Bishop als Olliver appeared to this Examinant & told her she had killed John Trask's Child, (whose Child dyed about that tyme) & said Bishop als Olliver afflicted her as alsoe did old George Jacobs, and before that time this Examin't being afflicted could not doe her service as formerly and her s'd Master Jacobs called her bitch witch & ill names & then afflicted her as #[before] above and that pudEater brought 3: Images like Mercy Lewis, Ann putnam, Eliza' Hubbard & they brought her thornes & she stuck them in the Images & told her the persons whose likeness they were, would be afflicted & the other day saw Goody Olliver [sitt] sate upon her knee,

Jurat in Curia by
Sarah Churchill
This Confession was taken before John Hathorne and Jonathan
Corwin Esq'rs l'o Juny 1692, as attests
*Tho Newton

(Essex County Court Archives, Salem Witchcraft Papers, Vol. 1, p. 110)

DEATH WARRANTS

Death warrants were handed down by the Salem Court of Oyer and Terminer on nineteen occasions. These documents were issued by Chief Justice
William Stoughton to George Corwin, High Sheriff of Essex County. They
explain the details surrounding the indictment, conviction, and execution of
the condemned criminal including details concerning those who claimed to
be victims of his/her acts of witchcraft. Each warrant provides exact instructions as to where the criminal is being imprisoned, as well as how, when,
and where they are to be executed. In all cases, the law enforcement official
in charge of the execution is required to report back to the Court when the
orders of the death warrant have been successfully carried out.

Document 5   (Death Warrant for Bridget Bishop)

To George Corwin Gent'm high Sherriffe of the County of
    Essex Greeting
    Whereas Bridgett Bishop als Olliver the wife of Edward Bishop of [Salem]
in the County of Essex Sawyer at a speciall Court of Oyer and Termin[er held
at] Salem the second Day of this instant month of June for the Countyes of
Esse[x] Middlesex and Suffolk before William Stoughton Esq'r and his Associates J[ustices] of the said Court was Indicted and arraigned upon five severall [Seal]I[ndictments] for useing practiseing and exercisein[g] [on the
Nyneteenth day of April] last past and divers other dayes and times [before
and after certain acts of] Witchcraft in and upon the bodyes of Abigial Williams, Ann puttnam J[un'r] Mercy Lewis, Mary Walcott and Elizabeth Hubbard of Salem village singlewomen, whereby their bodyes were hurt,
afflicted pined, consu[med] Wasted and tormented contrary to the forme of
the Statute in that Case [made and] provided To which Indictm'ts the said
Bridgett Bishop pleaded no[t guilty] and for Tryall thereof put her selfe upon
God and her Country, where[upon] she was found guilty of the felonyes and
Witchcrafts whereof she stood Indicted and sentence of Death accordingly
passed ag't her as the Law directs, Execution whereof yet remaines to be
done These are theref[ore] in the Name of their Maj'ties William and Mary
now King & Queen [over] England &c to will and Comand you That upon
fryday next being the Tenth day of this instant month of June between the
houres of Eight and twelve in the afternoon of the same day You safely conduct the s'd Bridgett Bishop als Olliver from their Maj'ties Gaol in Salem

afores'd to the place of Execution and there cause her to be hanged by the neck untill she be de[ad] and of your doings herein make returne to the Clerk of the s'd Court and pr'cept And here of you are not to faile at your peril And this shall be [your] Sufficient Warrant Given under my hand & Seal at Boston. the Eig[hth day] of June in the fourth Year of the Reigne of our Sovereigne Lord and [Lady] William & mary now King & Queen over England &c Annoq'e Dm 1692;

*Wm Stoughton
June 10th—1692

According to the Within Written precept I have taken the body of the within named Brigett Bishop of their Majes'ts Goale in Salem and Safely Conveighd her to the place provided for her Execution and Caused the s'd Brigett to be hanged by the neck untill Shee was dead [and buried in the place] all which was according to the time within Required and So I make Returne by me

George Corwin Sheriff

(*Peabody Essex Museum, Salem, MA*)

Document 6   (Death Warrant for Sarah Good, Rebecca Nurse, Susannah Martin, Elizabeth Howe, and Sarah Wildes)

To: To Georg: Corwine Gent'n High Sheriff of the County of Essex Greeting

Whereas Sarah Good Wife of William Good of Salem Village Rebecka Nurse wife of Francis Nurse of Salem Villiage Susanna Martin of Amesbury Widow Elizabeth How wife of James How of Ipswich Sarah Wild Wife of John Wild of Topsfield all of the County of Essex in their Maj'ts Province of the Massachusetts Bay in New England Att A Court of Oyer & Terminer held by Adjournment for Our Soveraign Lord & Lady King William & Queen Mary for the said County of Essex at Salem in the s'd County on the 29th day of June [torn] were Severaly arraigned on Several Indictments for the horrible Crime of Witchcraft by them practised & Committed On Severall persons and pleading not guilty did for their Tryall put themselves on God & Thier Countrey whereupon they were Each of them found & brought in Guilty by the Jury that passed On them according to their respective Indictments and Sentence of death did then pass upon them as the Law directs Execution whereof yet remains to be done:

Those are Therefore in thier Maj'ties name William & Mary now King & Queen over England &ca: to will & Comand you that upon Tuesday next being the 19th day of [torn] Instant July between the houres of Eight & [torn] in [torn] forenoon the same day you Elizabeth How & Sarah Wild From their Maj'ties Goal in Salem afores'd to the place of Execution & there Cause them & Every of them to be hanged by the Neck untill they be dead and of the doings herein make return to the Clerke of the said Court & this precept and hereof you are not to fail at your perill and this Shall be your Sufficient

Warrant Given under my hand & seale at Boston the 12'th day of July in the
fourth year of the Reign of our Soveraigne Lord & Lady Wm & Mary King
and Queen &ca:

*Wm Stoughton
Annoq Dom. 1692—
(Reverse)
Salem July 19th 1692
I caused the within mentioned persons to be Executed according to the Ten-
our of the with [in] warrant
*George Corwin Sherif

(*Manuscript Collection; Rare Books and Manuscripts Department of the Boston
Public Library*)

DEPOSITIONS

A deposition is a verbatim statement of a witness—called a deponent—made
under oath and recorded by the Court Clerk. Each of the following depositions provides testimony against a suspected witch in the Salem episode.
After a sufficient number of such documents were gathered, Court officials
would issue an arrest warrant to have the suspect brought to the Court for
further questioning and held for possible trial. If a trial is determined by the
Court, deposition statements may be used as evidence if the deponent is not
available to serve as a live witness. Witnesses during the witchcraft trials
were usually brought back into Court to provide verbal testimony confirming their deposition statement.

Document 7   (John Bly, Sr. and Rebecca Bly v. Bridget Bishop)

John Bly sen'r and Rebecka Bly his wife of Salem, both Testifie and say that
s'd Jno Bly Bought a Sow of Edw'd Bushop of Salem Sawyer and by agreement with s'd Bushop was to pay the price agreed upon, unto Lt Jeremiah
Neale of Salem, and Bridgett the wife of Said Edward Bushop because she
could not have the mony or vallue agreed for, payd unto her, she [came] to
the house of the deponents in Salem and Quarrelled w'th them aboute it
soon after which the sow haveing piged, she was taken with strange fitts
Jumping up and knocking hir head against the fence and seemed blind and
deafe and would not Eat neither Lett her pigs suck but foamed at the mouth,
which goody hinderson heareing of sayd she beleived she was over-looked,
and that thay had theire cattle ill in suck a manner at the Eastward when she
lived there, and used to cure them by giveing of them Red Okar & Milk.
which wee also gave the sow. Quickly after eating of which she grew Better.-
and then for the space of neere two howres togather she getting into the
street did sett of Jumping & running betweene the house of s'd deponents
and s'd Bushops as if she ware stark mad; and after that was well againe

and wee did then Apprehend or Judge & doe still that s'd Bishop had bewitched s'd sow

Jurat in Curia
(Reverse) John Bly and wife

(Essex County Court Archives, Salem Witchcraft Papers. Vol. 1, p. 43)

Document 8   (John Bly, Sr. and William Bly v. Bridget Bishop)

June 2'th 1692 Jno Blye Senior aged about 57 years & William Blye aged about 15 years both of Salem Testifieth and sayth that being Imployed by Bridgitt Bushup Alies Oliver of Salem to help take downe the Cellar wall of The owld house she formerly Lived in wee the s'd Deponants in holes of the s'd owld wall Belonging to the s'd sellar found Severall popitts made up of Raggs And hoggs Brusells w'th headles pins in Them. w'th the points out ward & this was about Seaven years Last past

Jurat Curia
(Reverse) papers ag't B: B: no. 16 John Bly and Wm Bly Court Oy'r & Term'r held at Salem 2'd June. 92 poppets Oliver

(Essex County Court Archives, Salem Witchcraft Papers. Vol. 1, p. 42)

Document 9   (Richard Coman v. Bridget Bishop)

Richard Coman aged aboute 32 years Testifieth that sometime aboute Eight yeares since: I then being in bed with my wife at Salem. one fift day of the Weeke at night Either in the Latter end of May the Begining of June. and alight burning in our Roome I being awake, did then see Bridget Bishop of Salem Alias Olliver come into the Roome wee lay in and two Women more with her. w'ch two Women ware Strangers to mee I knew them not but s'd Bishop came in her Red paragon Bodys and the rest of her cloathing that she then usually did ware, and I knowing of her well also the garb she did use to goe in did clearely & plainely know her, and testifieth that as he locked the dore of the house when he went to bed soe he found it after wards w'n he did Rise; and quickly after they appeared the light was out, and the Curtaines at the foote of the bed opened where I did see her and presently came And lay upon my Brest or body and soe oppressed him that he could not speake nor stur noe not soe much as to awake his wife althow he Endeavered much soe to do itt; the next night thay all appeared againe in like manner and she s'd Bishop Alias Oliver tooke hold of him by the throate and almost haled him out of the bed the Satterday night followeing; I haveing benne that day telling of what I had seene and how I suffered the two nights before, my Kinsman Wm Coman

told mee he would stay with mee & Lodg with mee and see if thay would
come againe and advised mee to lay my sword on thurt my body.quickly after
Wee Went to bed that s'd night and both well awake and discoursing togather
in came all the three women againe and s'd Bishop was the first as she had
benne the Other two nights, soe I told him; Wm heer thay be all Come againe
& he was Immediatly strook speechless & could not move hand or foote and
Immediatly they gott hold of my sword & strived to take it from mee but I
held soe fast as thay did not gett it away; and I had then Liberty of speech
and called Wm also my wife & Sarah phillips that [lay with] my wife. who all
told me [afterwards they heard] mee, but had not power to speak [or stur]
afterwards An the first that spake was Sarah phillips and said in the name of
god Goodm Coman w't is the Matter with you, soe thay all vanished away

Sworne Salem June 2'd 1692.
Jurat in Curia
Before mee
*John Hathorne

(Essex County Court Archives, Salem Witchcraft Papers. Vol. 1, p. 42)

Document 10   (John Cook v. Bridget Bishop)

John Cooke aged about 18 years Testifieth that about five or six yeares agoe
One Morning about Sun rising as I was in bed before I rose I saw goodwife
Bishop alias Oliver Stand in the Chamber by the window and she looked On
me & Grinn'd on me & presently struck me on the Side of the head w'ch did
very much hurt me & then I Saw her goe Out under the End window at a little Creviss about So bigg as I Could thrust my hand into I Saw her again the
Same day w'ch was the Sabath Day about noon walke & Cross the roome &
having at the time an apple in my hand it flew Out of my hand into my
mothers lapp who State Six or Eight foot distance from me & then She disap-
eared & though my mother & Severall others were in the Same room yet they
afirmed [they afirmed] they Saw her not
    John Cooke apearid before us the Jarris of inqwest and did owne this to be
his testimony one the oath that he hath taken: this 2: dy of June. 92

Jurat in Curia
(Reverse) John Cooke Witnis

(Essex County Court Archives, Salem Witchcraft Papers. Vol. 1, p. 43)

Document 11   (The Reverend John Hale et al. v. Bridget Bishop)

John Hale of Beverly aged about 56 yeares [torn] & saith that about 5 or 6
years ago e Christian the wife of John Trask (living in Salem bounds

bordering on the abovesaid Beverly) beeing in full comunion in o'r Church came to me to [de] sier that Goodwife Bishop her Neighb'r wife of Edw: Bishop Jun'r might not be permitted to receive the Lords Supper in our church till she had given her the said Trask satisfaction for some offences that were against her.viz because the said Bishop did entertaine people in her house at unseasonable houres in the night to keep drinking and playing at shovel-board whereby discord did arise in other families & young people were in danger to bee corrupted & that the s'd Trask knew these things & had once gon into the house & fynding some at shovel-board had taken the peices thay played with & thrown them into the fyre & had reprooved the said Bishop for promoting such disorders, But received no satisfaction from her about it.

I gave s'd Christian Trask direction how to proceed farther in this matter if it were clearly prooved And indeed by the information I have had otherwise I doe fear that if a stop had not been putt to those disorders s'd Edw. Bishop's house would have been a house of great prophainness & iniquity.

But as to Christian Trask the next news I heard of her was that she was distracted & asking her husband Trask when she was so taken [he told] mee shee was taken distracted that night after shee [came from] my house when shee complained against Goody Bishop.

She continueing some time Distracted wee sought the Lord by fasting & prayer & the Lord was pleased to restore the s'd [Trask] to the use of her reason agen. I was s'th her often in [her] distraction (& took it then to bee only distraction, yet fearing sometimes somw't worse) but since I have seen the fitts of those bewitched at Salem Village I call to mind some of hers to be much like some of theirs.

he said Trask when recovered as I understood it did manifest strong suspicion that shee had been bewitched by the s'd Bishop's wife & showed so much aversness from having any conversation that I was then troubled at it hopeing better of s'd Goody Bishop at that time for wee have since [torn] At length s'd Christian Trask [was] agen in a distracted fit on a Sabboth day in the forenoon at the publ [i]ck meeting to o'r public desturbance & so continued sometimes better sometimes worse unto her death, manifesting that shee under temptation to kill her selfe or somebody else.

I enquired of Marg'rt Ring who kept at or nigh the house, what shee had observed of s'd Trask before this last distraction shee told [mee.] Goody Trask was much given to reading & search the prophecys of scrip[ture].

he day before shee made that disturbance in the meeting [house] she[e] came home & said shee had been w'th Goody Bishop & that they two were now friend or to that effect.

I was oft praying w'th & councelling of Goody Trask before her death and not many days before her end being there shee seemed more rationall & earnestly desired Edw: Bishop might be sent for that shee might make friends with him, I asked her if shee had wronged Edw. Bishop shee said not that shee knew of unless it were in taking his shovel-board pieces when people were at play w'th them & throwing them into the fyre & if she did evill in it she was very sorry for it & desiered he would be friends with her or forgive her, this was the very day before she dyed, or a few days before.

Her distraction (or bewitching) continued about a month and in those intervalls wherein shee was better shee earnestly desired prayers & the Sabboth befere she dyed I received a note for prayers on her behalf w'ch her husband said was written by her selfe & I judge was her owne hand writing beeing well acquainted with her hand.

As to the wounds she dyed of I observed 3 deadly ones; apeice of her wind pipe cutt out. & another wound above that threww the windpipe & Gullet & the veine they call jugular. So that I then judge & still doe apprehend it impossible for her w'th so short a pair of cissars to mangle her selfe so without some extraordinary work of the devill or witchcraft

signed. 20. may 1692 by
*John Hale.
To severall parts of this testimony can wittness Maj'r Gidney.
Mr Paris Joseph Hirrek Ju'r & his wife Thomas Raiment & his wife
John Traske Marget King, Hanah wife of Cornell Baker, []
Miles & others.
As also about the s'd Goody Bishop Capt W'm Raiment, his son W'm Raiment about creatures strangely dying. James Kettle, & the abovs'd Jos: Hirreck & Tho: Raiment about sundry actions that [have] the apearance of witchcraft.
(Reverse) Deposition 16 John Hale

(Essex County Court Archives, Salem Witchcraft Papers. Vol. 1, p. 39)

Document 12   (Deliverance Hobbs v. Bridget Bishop et al.)

Deliverance-Hobbs . Exam'ed May. 3. 1692 . Salem prison

Q. w't have you done since whereby there is further trouble in your appearance?
An. nothing at all.
Q. but have you nott since bin tempted?
An. yes S'r, but I have nott done itt, nor will nott doe itt
Q. here is a great change since we last spake to you, for now you Afflict & torment againe; now tell us the truth whoe tempted you to sighne againe?
An. itt was Goody Olliver; shee would have mee to sett my hand to the book, butt I would nott neither have I. neither did consent to hurt them againe.
Q. was that true that Goody Wilds appeared to you & tempted you?
An. yes, that was true.
Q. have you been tempted since?
An. yes, about fryday or Saturday night last
Q. did they bid you that you should nott tell?
An. yes they tould me soe.
Q. but how farr did thay draw you or tempt you, & how farr did you yeild to the temptation? but doe not you acknowledge that [that] was true that you tould us formerly?

An.   Yes.

Q.   and you did sighne then att the first, did you Nott?

An.   Yes, I did itt is true.

Q.   did you promiss then to deny att last what you said before?

An.   yes, I did & itt was Goody Oliver Alias Bishop that tempted me to deny all that I had confessed before.

Q.   doe you nott know the man w'th the Wenne?

An.   noe I doe nott know whoe itt is; all that I confessed before is true.

Q.   Whoe were they you named formerly?

An.   Osburne, Good, Burroughs, Olliver, Wiles, Cory & his Wife, Nurse, procter & his Wife.

Q.   who were w'th you in the chamber? (itt being informed that some were talking w'th hir there.)

An.   Wilds and Bushop or Olliver, Good & Osburne, & they had a feast both of Roast & Boyled meat & did eat & drink & would have had me to have eat and drunk w'th them but I would not; & they would have had me sighned, but I would nott then not when Goody.Olliver came to me.

Q.   Nor did nott you con [torn] children in your likeness?

An.   I doe nott know that I did.

Q.   What is that you have to tell, w'ch you canotttell yett you say?

(Reverse) Delive' Hobs her Examination & testimony ag't procter & wife & others. Bridget Bishop

(Essex County Court Archives, Salem Witchcraft Papers. Vol. 1, p. 37)

Document 13   (John Louder v. Bridget Bishop)

John Louder of Salem Aged aboute thurtey two Yeares Testifieth and sayth that aboute seaven or Eight years since I then Liveing w'th Mr John Gedney in Salem and haveing had some Controversy with Bridgett Bushop the wife of Edw'd Bushop of Salem Sawyer aboate her fowles that used to Come into our orchard or garden. Some little tyme after which, I goeing well to bed; aboute the dead of the night felt a great weight upon my Breast and awakening looked and it being bright moon; light did clearly see s'd Bridget Bushop—or her likeness sitting upon my stomake and puting my Armes of of the bed to free myselfe from that great oppression she presently layd hold of my throat and allmost Choked mee and I had noe strenth or power in my hands to resist or help my selfe; and in this Condition she held mee to almost day, some tyme after this, my Mistress Susannah Gedney was in our orchard and I was then with her. and said Bridget Bushop being then in her Orchard w'ch was next adjoyneing to ours my Mistress told s'd Bridget that I said or afirmed that she came one night & satt upon my brest as afores'd which she denyed and I afirmed to her face to be true and that I did plainely see her. upon w'ch discourse with her she Threatened mee. And some tyme after that I being not very well stayed at home on a Lords day and on the afternoon of s'd day the dores being shutt I did see a black pig in the Roome Coming towards mee soe I went towards itt to kick it and it vanished away

Immediately after I satt down in an Narrow Bar and did see a black thing Jump into the window and came & stood Just before my face, upon the bar the body of itt looked like a Munky only the feete ware like a Cocks feete w'th Claws and the face somewhat more like a mans than a Munkiey and I being greatly affrighted not being able to speake or help my selfe by Reason of fear I suppose, soe the thing spake to mee and said I am a Messenger sent to you for I understand you are trobled in mind, and if you will be Ruled by mee you shall want for Nothing in this world upon which I endeavered to clap my hands upon itt, and sayd You devill I will Kill you. but could feale noe substance and itt Jumped out of the window againe.and Imediatly Came in by the porch althow the dores ware shutt. and sayd you had Better take my Councill, where upon I strook at it with a stick butt strook the Groundsill and broak the stick, but felt noe substance, and that arme with which I strook was presently disenabled, then it vanished away and I opened the back dore and Went out and goeing towards the house End I Espied s'd Bridget Bushop in her orchard goeing to wards her house, and seing her had no power to set one foot forward but returned in againe and goeing to shutt the dore. I Againe did see that or the like creture that I before did see within dores, in such a posture as it seemed to be agoeing to fly at mee, upon which I cryed.out; the whole armor of god be between mee and you. soe itt sprang back and flew over the apple tree flinging the dust w'th its feet against my stomake, upon which I was struck dumb and soe Continued for aboute three days tyme—and also shook many of the apples of, from the tree w'ch it flu over:

(Reverse) John louder apearid before me this 2. dy of June 1692 and one the oath that he had taken did owen this testimony to be the truth before us the Jarris of Inquest

Jurat in Curia

On her tryall Bridget Bishop alias Oliver denied that she knew this deponent though the orchard of this depon't & the orchard of said Bishop Joined & they often had difference for some yeares together
(Reverse) Evidence ag't Br. Bishop. Jno Loader

(Essex County Court Archives, Salem Witchcraft Papers. Vol. 1, p. 41)

Document 14   (Samuel and Sarah Shattuck v. Bridget Bishop)

Sam'll Shattock aged 41 years testifieth that in the year 1680.

Bridged Oliver formerly wife to old Goodman Oliver: now wife to Edward Bishop did Come to my hous pretending to buy an old hh'd wc'h tho I asked verry little for: & for all her pretended want She went away w'th out it: & Sundry other tymes she came in a Smooth flattering maner in very Slighty Errants: we have thought Since on purpos to work mischief: at or very near this tyme o'r Eldest Child who promised as much health & understanding both by Countenance and actions as any other Children of his years: was taken in a very drooping Condition and as She Came oftener to the hous he grew wors & wors: as he would be standing at the door would fall out & bruis his face upon a great Step Stone as if he had been thrust out bye an invisible hand: often tymes falling & hitting his face in a very miserable maner: after this the abovesaid Oliver brought me apair of sleeves to dye & after that Sundry peeces of lace Some of w'ch were Soe Short that I could not judge them fit for any uce: she p'd me 2 d for dying them w'ch 2 d I gave to Henery Willms w'ch lived w'th me he told me put it in a purse among som other money w'ch he locked up in a box & that the purs & money was gon out of the Box he Could not tell how: & never found it after just after the dying of these things this child taken in a terrible fit; his mouth & Eyes drawne aside and gasped in Such a maner as if he was upon the point of death; after this he grew wors in his fits; and out of them would be allmost allways crying that for many months he would be crying till natures strenght was spent & then would fall a sleep and then awake & fall to crying & moaning: that his very Countenance did bespeak Compassion; and at length wee p'rceived his understanding decayed Soe that wee feared (as it has Since proved) that he would be quite bereaft of his witts; for Ever Since he has bin Stupified and voide of reason his fitts still following of him; after he had bin in this kind of Sickness Som tyme he has gon into the garden & has got upon a board of an inch thick w'ch lay flat upon the ground & wee have Called him; he would Com to the Edge of the board & hold out his hand & make as if he would Com but Could not till he was helped of the board; other tymes when he has got upon a board as aforesaide my wife has Said She has ofered him a Cake & mony to Com to her and he has held out his hand & reach't after it but Could not Com till he has bin help't of the board; by w'ch I judge som inchantm't kept him on about 17 or 18 months after, the first of this Ilnes there Came a Stranger to my hous & pittyed this Child and Said among other words wee are all borne Some to one thing & Som to another; I asked him & w't doe you Say this Child is borne too he replyed he is born to be bewitched and is bewitched I told him he did not know; he said he did know & Said to me you have a neighbor that lives not far of that is a witch: I told him wee had noe neighb'r but w't was honest folke; he replyed you have a neighb'r that is a witch & She has had a falling out w'th yo'r wife & Said in her hart your wife is a proud woman & She would bring downe her pride in this Childe: I paused in my selfe & did remember that mye [mye] wife had told me that goodwife Oliver had bin at the hous & spoke to her to beat Henry Willms, that lived w'th us & that she went away muttering & She thought threatning: but little before o'r child was taken ill; I told the aforesaid Stranger that there was Such a woman as spoke of; he asked where she lived for he would goe & see her if he knew how: I gave him money & bid him ask her for a pot of Syd'r away he went & I Sent my boy w'th him who after a short tyme: both returned; the boys face bleeding & I asked w't the matter they told me the man knock't at the door & goody Oliver Came to the door & asked the Stranger w't he would have he told her a pot of Cyd'r she saide he sheuld have none & bid him get out & took up a Spade & made him goe out She followed him & when She came w'th out the poarch She saw mye boy & ran to him & scratched his face & made it bleed: Saying to him thou roague w't dost thou bring this fellow here to plague me; now this man did say before he went: 't he would fetch blood of her And Ever Since this Child hath bin followed w'th grevious fitts as if he would never recover moor: his hed & Eyes drawne aside Soe as if they would never Come to rights moor lying as if he were in a maner dead falling any where Either into fier or water if he be not Constantly looked too, and generally in Such an uneasie and restles frame allmost allways runing too & fro acting soe Strange that I cannot judge otherwise but that he is bewitched and by these circumstances doe beleive that the aforesaid Bridged Oliver now Called Bishop is the Caus of it and it has bin the Judgem't of Docters Such as lived here & forreigners: that he is under an Evill hand of witchcraft

Sam'll Shattock & Sarah Shattock
affirmeth upon the oath they have taken
to the truth of w't is above written
Jurat in Curia June 2'd 92
*Attest *Steph: Sewall Cler*
(Reverse) Eved. Against Bridget Bishop p Sam'l Shadock & wife

(Essex County Court Archives, Salem Witchcraft Papers. Vol. 1, p. 40)

Document 15   (Susannah Sheldon v. Bridget Bishop)

The Deposistion of susannah shelldin aged about 18 years who testifieth and said that on this 2 June 1692 I saw the Apperishtion of Bridgit Bishop.and Immediatly appeared to little children and said that they ware Thomas Greens two twins and tould Bridget Bishop to hir face that she had murthered them in setting them into fits wher of they dyed

(Reverse) Susanna Sheldon Evid ag't Bridgett Bishop

(Essex County Court Archives, Salem Witchcraft Papers. Vol. 1, p. 43)

Document 16   (William Stacy v. Bridget Bishop)

William Stacy of the Towne of Salem aged, Thirty Six years or thereaboutes Deposeth and Saith: /
    That about fourteene years agone this Deponant was visited with the Small Pox, then Bridget Bishop did give him a visitt, and withall Professed a great Love for this Deponant in his affliction. more than ordinary, at which this Deponant admired, some time after this Deponant was well, the said Bishop

got him to do some work for her. for which she gave him three pense, which seemed to this Depo't as if it had been good money: but he had not gone out above 3 or 4 Rods before he Looked in his Pockett where he put it, for it, but could not find any sometime after this deponent met the said [] Bishop in the Street a goeing to Mill; she askeing this Deponent whether his father would grind her grist: he put it to the said Bishop why she Asked: she answered because folks counted her a witch this Depo't made answer: he did not Question but that his father would grind it: but being gone about 6 Rod from her the said Bishop; with a small Load in his Cart: suddenly the off Wheels Slumped or Sunk downe into a hole upon Plain ground, that this Depon't was forced to gett one to help him gett the wheele out afterwards this Depon't went Back to look for said hole where his wheele sunk in but could not find any hole some time after in the winter about midnight this Deponent felt something between his lips Pressing hard ag't his teeth: and withall was very Cold in somuch that it did awake him so that he gott up and sat upon his beed: he at the same time seeing the said Bridgett Bishop sitting at the foot of his bed: being to his seeming, it was then as light as if it had been day: or one in the said Bishops shape: she having then a black cap & a black hat, and a Red Coat with two [Eakes] of two Coulers: then she the said Bishop or her shape clapt her coate close to her Leggs & hopt upon the bed and about the Roome and then went out: and then it was Dark: againe: some time after the s'd Bishop went to this Depon't and asked him whither that which he had reported was true. that he had told to severall: he answered that was true & that it was she, and bid her denigh it if she dare, the said Bishop did not denigh it and went away very angry and said that this Dep't did her more Mischief: than any other body he asked Why: she answered because folks would believe him before any body Elce: some time after the said Bishop thretned this Deponent: and told him he was the occasion of bringing her out about the brass she stole: Some time after this Dep't in a dark night was goeing to the Barn who was suddenly taken or hoisted from the Ground & threw ag't a stone wall after that taken up againe a throwed Down a bank at the End of his house: some time after this Deponent mett the said Bishop by Issaac Sternes Brick Kill: after he had Passed buy her: this Deponents Horse stood still with a small load goeing up the hill so that the Horse striveing to draw all his Gears & tackeing flew in Peices and the Cart fell downe.

afterwward this Deponent went to lift a Bagg of Corne of about 2 bushells: but could not budge it with all his might:

This Deponent hath mett with severall other of her Pranks at severall times: which would take up a great time to tell of

This Deponent doth veryly beleive that the said Bridget Bishop was Instrumentall to his Daughter Prisillas Death: about two years agoe, the Child was alikely Thriveing Child. And suddenly Screaked out and soe continued in an unsuall Manner for about. a fortnight & soe dyed in that lamentable manner

Sworne Salem May the 30'th 1692 before us.

*John Hathorne
Assis'ts
*Jonathan. Corwin)

Jurat in Curia June. 2'd 1692
(Written on side of
paper) William Stacey

(Essex County Court Archives, Salem Witchcraft Papers. Vol. 1, p. 37)

Document 17   (Mary Warren v. Bridget Bishop and Nathaniel Cary [?])

Mary Warren aged 20: yeares or thereabouts testifyeth & saith That severall
times after the Nyneteenth day of April last when Bridgett Bishop als Olliver
who was in the Gaol at Salem she did appear to this depon't tempting her to
signe the book & oft times during her being there as afores'd the s'd Bridgett
did torture & afflict this depon't & being in Chanies said tho: she could not
do it, she would bring one that should doe it which now she knowes to be
Mr [Cary] that then came & afflicted her,
    Sworne before us the 1. day of June 1692

*John Hathorne
*Jonathan Corwin {
Assists

(Essex County Court Archives, Salem Witchcraft Papers. Vol. 1, p. 110)

Document 18   (Susannah Sheldon v. Bridget Bishop, Mary English, Phillip
             English, Giles Corey, and Martha Corey)

---

on the foarth day at night Came goody olliver and mrs English and good
man Core and ablak man with a hi crouned hatt with books in their hands
goody olliver bad mee touch her booke i would not i did not know her name
shee told mee her name was goody Olliver and bid me touch her booke now
I bid her tel mee how long shee had been a witch shee told me #[shee told
mee] S had been a witch above twenti years then their Came a streked snake
creeping over her shoulder and crep into her bosom mrs. English had a yelo
bird in her bosom and good man Core had two tircels hang to his Coat and
he opened his bosom and put his turcls to his brest and gave them suck then
good man Core and Goody oliver kneeled doune beefour the blak man and
went to prayer and then the blak man told mee goody olliver had been a
witch twenti years and an half then they all set to biteing mee and so went
away the next day Came good man Core mrs english in the morning and
told mee i should not eat no vittals i took a spoon and put on spoonful in
my mouth and good man Core gave me a blow on the ear and all most
choaked mee then he laughed at mee and told mee i would eat when he told
mee I should not then he Clenched my hands that they could not be opened

for more then a quarter of an our then cam phillip english and [and] told mee if i would touch his booke hee would not hit mee but i refused then he did bite mee and went away

the sixth day at night Came goody olliver and mrs english good man Core and his wife goodwy Core S profired mee a booke i refused it and asked her whear she lived shee told mee she lived in boston prisson then shee puled out her brest and the blak man gave her a thing like a blake pig it had no haire on it and shee put it to her brest and gave it suck and when it had sucked on brest shee put it the other and gave it suck their then she gave it to the blak man then went to praier to the blak man then goody olliver told mee that shee had kiled foar women two of them wear the fosters wifes and john trasks wife and did not name the other then they did all bitt mee and went away then the next day Came goody Core choaked mee and told mee i would not eat when my dame bid mee but now I should eat none

(Reverse) susanna sheldon ag't oliver English & his wife Core & his wife good—bucklie & her daughter & boston woman

(Essex County Court Archives, Salem Witchcraft Papers. Vol. 1, p. 45)

Document 19   (Elizabeth Hubbard v. Bridget Bishop and Mary Warren)

now whilest i was righting thes lines thar came in mary waring and another woman with hur whch woman mary waring shap said was goodey oliver and that woman came in hur sheft

(Reverse) Elizab Hubbard ag'st Mary Warrin

(Essex County Court Archives, Salem Witchcraft Papers. Vol. 1, Page 44)

Document 20   (Ann Putnam, Jr. v. George Burroughs)

The Deposition of Ann putnam : who testifieth and saith that on 20'th of April 1692 :at evening she saw the Apperishtion of a Minister at which she was greviously affrighted and cried out oh dreadfull: dreadfull here is a minister com:what are Ministers wicthes to: whence com you and What is your name for I will complaine of:you tho you be A minister: if you be a wizzard; and Immediatly I was tortored by him being Racked and all most choaked by him: and he tempted me to write in his book which I Refused with loud out cries and said I would not writ in his book tho he tore me al to peaces but tould him that it was a dreadfull thing: that he which was a Minister that should teach children to feare God should com to perswad poor creatures to give their souls to the divill: oh. dreadfull tell me your name that I may know who you are: then againe he tortored me & urged me to writ in his book: which I Refused: and then presently he tould me that his name was George Burroughs and that he had had three wives: and that he had bewitched the Two first of them to death: and that he kiled Mist. Lawson because she was so unwilling to goe from the village and also killed Mr Lawsons child because he went to the eastward with Sir Edmon and preached soe; to the souldiers and that he had bewicthed a grate many souldiers to death at the eastword, when Sir Edmon was their. and that he had made Abigail Hobbs a wicth and: severall wicthes more: and he has continewed ever sence; by times tempting me to write in his book and greviously tortoring me by beating pinching and almost choaking me severall times a day and he also tould me that he was above wicth for he was a cunjurer

Jurat in Curia
(Reverse) Ann putnam ag'st Burroughs

(Essex County Court Archives, Salem Witchcraft Papers. Vol. 2, p. 10)

Document 21   (Mercy Lewis v. Giles Corey)

The Deposistion of Mercy lewes agged about 19 years who testifieth and saith that on the 14'th April 1692 I saw the Apperishtion of Giles Cory com and afflect me urging me to writ in his book and so he contineued most dreadfully to hurt me by times beating me & almost braking my back tell the day of his examination being the 19th April and then allso dureing the time of his examination he did afflect and tortor me most greviously: and also several times sence urging me vehemently to writ in his book and I veryly beleve in my heart that Giles Cory is a dreadfull wizzard for sence he had ben in prison he or his Apperance has com and most greviously tormented me.

   Mercy Lewis: affirmd to the Jury of Inquest. that the above written evidence: is the truth upon the oath: she has formerly taken in the Court of Oyer & terminer: Sept'r 9: 1692

(Reverse) Mercy Lewis again't Geoyles Cory

(Essex County Court Archives, Salem Witchcraft Papers. Vol. 2, p. 41)

Document 22   (Ann Putnam, Jr. v. Giles Corey)

The Deposistion of Ann putnam who testifieth and saith that on 13'th of April 1692, I saw the Apperishtion of Gilles Cory com and afflect me urging me to writ in his book and so he continewed hurting me by times tell the 19'th April being the day of his examination : and dureing the time of his examination Giles Cory did tortor me a grat many times.and allso severall times sence Giles Cory or his Apperance has most greviously afflected me by beating pinching and almost Choaking me to death urging me to writ in his book also on the day of his examination I saw Giles Cory or his Apperance most greviously afflect and torment mary walcott mercy lewes and sarah vibber and I veryly beleveue that Giles Cory is [is] a dreadfull wizzard for sence he has ben in prison he or his Apperance has come to me a grat many tims and afflected me.

An Putnam owned upon her oath that the above written evidence is the truth to the Jury of inquest Sept 9: 92

(Reverse) Ann puttnam agst Giles Cory

(Essex County Court Archives, Salem Witchcraft Papers. Vol. 2, p. 41)

Document 23   (Elizabeth Hubbard v. Tituba)

The Deposistion of Elizabeth Hubbard agged about 17 years who testifieth that on the 25'th february 1691/92 I saw the Apperishtion of Tituba Indian which did Immediatly most greviously torment me by pricking pinching and almost choaking me: and so continewed hurting me most greviously by times tell the day of hir examination being the first of march and then also at the beginning of hir examination but as soon as she began to confess she left ofc hurting me and has hurt me but litle sence

(Reverse) Eliz: Hubbard contra Titaba

(Peabody Essex Museum, Salem, MA)

Document 24   (Samuel Parris v. Tituba)

The Deposition of Sam: Parris aged about thirty & nine years testifyeth & saith that Eliz: Hubbard were most grevously & severall times tortured during the examination of Sarah Good, Sarah Osburne & Tituba Indian before the Magistrates at Salem village I. March. 1691/2 And the said Tituba being the last of the abovesaid that was examined they the aboves'd afflicted persons were grievously distressed until the said Indian began to confess & then they were immediately all quiet the rest of the said Indian womans examination.

(Peabody Essex Museum, Salem, MA)

Document 25   (Ann Putnam, Jr. v. Tituba)

The deposition of Ann putnam who testifieth and saith that on the 25'th of february 1691/92 I saw the Apperishtion of Tituba Mr. parishes Indian woman which did tortor me most greviously by pricking and pinching me most dreadfully tell the first day of march being the day of hir examination and then also most greviously allso at the beginning of hir examination: but senc she confessed she has hurt me but little

(Reverse) Ann putnam ag'st Tittuba Indian

(*Peabody Essex Museum, Salem, MA*)

Document 26   (Thomas Putnam and Ezekiel Cheever v. Tituba)

Also Tho: Putman aged about fourty years & Ezek: Cheevers aged about thirty & six years testify to the whole of the aboves'd & all the three depo-nents aforesaid farther testify that after the said Indian began to confess she was her self very much afflicted & in the face of authority at the same time & openly charged the abovesaid Good & Osburne as the persons that afflicted her the aforesaid Indian

Sworne Salem May the 23'd 1692 Before us * John Hathorne
*Jonathan. Corwin
P ord'r of the Govern'r & Councill
mr paris on his oath owned this to be the truth before the Juryars for inquest this 28 of Jun: 1692
Jurat in Curia
(Reverse) The depion of S. Parris Tho putnam & Ezek Cheevers
ag't [*unclear*:] Sarah Good
Sarah Osburne
Tituba Indian

(*Peabody Essex Museum, Salem, MA)*

EXAMINATIONS

Examinations were conducted for each individual accused of witchcraft. The purpose of such direct questioning was to ascertain the response of the alleged witch to the accusations of the victims, witnesses, and deponents.

In all cases, the questions and responses, as well as the occasional interrup-tion by persons in the Court, were recorded by the Court Clerk. (The role of Court Clerk was usually assumed by either Reverend Samuel Parris or Eze-kiel Cheever.) This verbatim record of courtroom testimony is critical evi-dence in understanding the trial process as well as the positions taken by the accused when faced directly by their accusers.

Document 27   (Examination of Bridget Bishop, First Version)

The Examination of Bridget Byshop at Salem Village 19. Apr. 1692
   By John Hathorn & Jonathan Corwin Esquiers

As soon as she came near all fell into fits

H. Bridget Bishop, You are now brought before Authority to Give account. of what witchcrafts you are conversant in
B. I take all these people (turning her head & eyes about) to witness that I am clear.
H. Hath this woman hurt you speaking to the afflicted.

Eliz: Hubbard Ann Putman, Abigail Williams & Mercy Lewes affirmed she had hurt them.

H. You are here accused by 4.or.5. for hurting them, what do you say to it,
B. I never saw these persons before, nor I never was in this place before.

Mary Walcot said that her brother Jonathan stroke her appearance & she saw that he had tore her coat in striking, & she heard it tare.
Upon some search in the Court, a rent that seems to answer what was alleged was found.

H. They say you bewitched your first husband to death.
B. If it please your worship I know nothing of it.

She shook her head & the afflicted were tortured.
The like again upon the motion of her head.
Sam: Braybrook affirmed that she told him to day that she had been accounted a Witch these 10 years, but she was no Witch, the Devil cannot hurt her.

B. I am no witch
H. Why if you have not wrote in the book, yet tell me how far you have gone? Have you not to do with familiar Spirits?
B. I have no familiarity with the devil.
H. How is it then, that your appearance doth hurt these?
B. I am innocent.
H. Why you seem to act witchcraft before us, by the motion of your body, which seems to have influence upon the afflicted.
B. I know nothing of it. I am innocent to a Witch. I know not what a Witch is.
H. How do you know then that you are not a witch
B. I do not know what you say.
H. How can you know, you are no Witch, & yet not know what a Witch is?
B. I am clear: if I were any such person you should know it.
H. You may threaten, but you can do no more than you are permitted .
B. I am innocent of a witch.
H. What do you say of those murders you are charged with?
B. I hope, I am not guilty of Murder

Then she turned up her eyes, the eyes of the afflicted were turned up

H. It may be you do not know, that any have confessed to day, who have been examined before you, that they are Witches.
B. No. I know nothing of it.

John Hutchinson & John Lewis in open Court affirmed that they had told her

    H.   Why look you, you are taken now in a flat lie.
    B.   I did not hear them.

Note: Samuel Goldsmith [said] that after this examination he asked Bridget Bishop if she were not troubled to see the afflicted persons so tormented, said Bishop answered no, she was not Troubled for them: Then he asked her whether she thought they were bewitched, she said she could not tell what to think about them. Will Good, & John Buxton, junior was by, & he supposeth they heard her also.

Salem Village April the.19th 1692 Mr. Samuel Parris being desired to take into writing the Examination of Bridget Bishop, hath delivered it as aforesaid. And upon hearing the same, and seeing what we did then see, together with the Charge of the afflicted persons then present: We Committed said Bridget Oliver –[to jail].

*John Hathorne.
(Peabody Essex Museum, Salem, MA)*

Document 28   (Examination of Bridget Bishop, Second Version)

The examination of Bridget Bishop before the Worshipful John Hathorne and Jonathan Corwen esq'rs

Bridget Bishop being now coming in to be examined relating to her accusation of Suspicon of sundry acts of witchcrafts the afflicted persons are now dreadfully afflicted by her as they doe say.

(Mr Harthon)	Bishop what doe you say you here stand charged with sundry acts of witchcraft by you done or committed upon the bodyes of mercy Lews and An Putnam and others.
(Bishop)	I am innocent I know nothing of it I have done no witchcraft
(Mr Har)	Looke upon this woman and see if this be the woman that you have seen hurting you. Mercy Lewes and An Putnam and others doe [doe] now charge her to her face with hurting of them.
(Mr Harthon)	What doe you say now you see they charge you to your face
(Bish)	I never did hurt them in my life I did never see these persons before I am as innocent as the child unborn
(Mr Harth)	is not your coate cut
(Bish)	answers no but her garment being Looked upon they find it cut or toren two wayes Jonathan walcoate saith that the sword that he strucke at goode Bishup with was not naked but was within the scabbord so that the rent may very probablie be the very same that mary walcoate did tell that she had in her coate by Jonathans stricking at her apperance

The afflicted persons charge her, with having hurt them many wayes and by tempting them to sine to the devils Booke at which charge she seemed to be very angrie and shaking her head at them saying it was false they are all greatly tormented (as I conceive) by the shaking of her head

(Mr Har)	good Bishop what contract have you made with the devill
(Bish)	I have made no contract with the devill I never saw him in my life. An Putnam sayeth that shee calls the devill her God
(Mr Har)	what say you to all this that you are charged with can you not find in your heart to tell the truth
(Bish)	I doe tell the truth I never hurt these persons in my life I never saw them before.
(Mercy Lewes)	oh goode Bishop did you not come to our house the Last night and did you not tell me that your master made you tell more than you were willing to tell
(Mr Har)	tell us the truth in this matter how comes these persons to be thus tormented and to charge you with doing
(Bish)	I am not come here to say I am a witch to take away my life
(Mr H)	who is it that doth it if you doe not they say it is your likenes that comes and torments them and tempts them to write in the booke what Booke is that you tempt them with.
(Bish)	I know nothing of it I am innocent.
(Mr Harth)	doe you not see how they are tormented you are acting witchcraft before us what doe you say to this why have you not an heart to confese the truth
(Bish)	I am innocent I know nothing of it I am no witch I know not what a witch is.
(Mr H)	have you not given consent that some evill spirit should doe this in your likenes.
(B)	no I am innocent of being a witch I know no man woman or child here
(Marshall Herrik)	how came you into my bed chamber one morning then and asked me whether I had any curtains to sell shee is by some of the afflicted persons charged with murder
(Mr Harth)	what doe you say to these murders you are charged with
(B)	I am innocent I know nothing of it
	now shee lifts up her eyes and they are greatly tormented again
(Mr Har)	what doe you say to these things here horrible acts of witch craft.
(Bish)	I know nothing of it I doe not know whither be any witches or no
(Mr Har)	no have you not heard that some have confessed.
(Bish)	no I did not. two men told her to her face that they had told her here shee is taken in a plain lie now shee is going away they are dreadfully afflicted 5 afflicted persons doe charge this woman to be the very woman that hurts them

This is a true account of what I have taken down at her examination according to best understanding and observation I have also in her examination taken notice that all her actions have great influence upon the afflicted persons and that have been tortored by her

Ezekiel Cheever.

(Reverse) Examination ag't Bishop

(*Peabody Essex Museum, Salem, MA*)

Document 29   (Examination of Rebecca Nurse)

(See also: Bridget Bishop—Physical Examination; Sarah Good—Death Warrant.)
   The examination of Rebekah Nurse at Salem Village
   24. mar. 1691/2
   Mr. Hathorne: What do you say (speaking to one afflicted) have you seen this Woman hurt you?
   Yes, she beat me this morning
   Abigail, Have you been hurt by this Woman?
   Abigail:Yes.
   Ann Putman in a grievous fit cried out that she hurt her.

   H.   Goody Nurse, here are two An: Putman the child & Abigail Williams complains of your hurting them What do you say to it?
   N.   I can say before my Eternal father I am innocent, & God will clear my innocency.
   H.   Here is never a one in the Assembly but desires it, but if you be guilty Pray God discover you.
        Then Hen: Kenny rose up to speak.
   H.   Goodman Kenny, what do you say ?

   Then he entered his complaint & farther said that since this Nurse came into the house he was seized twice with an amazed condition

   H.   Here are not only these but, here is the wife of Mr. Thomas Putman who accuseth you by credible information & that both of tempting her to iniquity, & of greatly hurting her.
   N.   I am innocent & clear & have not been able to get out of doors these 8. or 9. days.
   H.   Mr. Putman: give in what you have to say
        Then Mr. Edward Putman gave in his relate
   H.   Is this true Goody Nurse
   N.   I never afflicted no child never in my life
   H.   You see these accuse you, is it true?
   N.   No.
   H.   Are you an innocent person relating to this Witchcraft?

Here Thomas Putman's wife cried out, Did you not bring the Black man with you, did you not bid me tempt God & dye How oft have you eat and drunk your own damnation. What do you say to them?

N. Oh Lord help me, & spread out her hands, & the afflicted were greviously vexed

H. Do you not see what a solemn condition these are in? When your hands are loose the persons are afflicted.

Then Mary Walcott (who often heretofore said she had seen her, but never could say or did say that she either bit or pinched her, or hurt her) & also Eliz: Hubbard under the like circumstances both openly accused her of hurting them

H. Here are these 2 grown persons now accuse you, what say you? Do not you see these afflicted persons, & hear them accuse you?

N. The Lord knows I have not hurt them: I am an innocent person

H. It is very awful to all to see these agonies & you an old Professor thus charged with contracting with the Devil by the [a] effects of it & yet to see you stand with dry eyes when there are so many whet—

N. You do not know my heart

H. You would do well if you are guilty to confess & give Glory to God

N. I am as clear as the child unborn

H. What uncertainty there may be in apparitions I know not, yet this with me strikes hard upon you that you are at this very present charged with familiar spirits: this is your bodily person they speak to: they say now they see these familiar spirits com to your bodily person, now what do you say to that?

N. I have none, Sir:

H. If you have confess & give glory to God I pray God clear you if you be innocent, & if you are guilty discover you And therefore give me an upright answer: have you any familiarity with these spirits?

N. No, I have none but with God alone.

H. How came you sick for there is an odd discourse of that in the mouths of many—

N. I am sick at my stomach—

H. Have you no wounds

N. I have none but old age

H. You do Know whither you are guilty, & have familiarity with the Devil, & now when you are here present to see such a thing as these testify a black man whispering in your ear, & birds about you what do you say to it

N. It is all false. I am clear.

H. Possibly you may apprehend you are no witch, but have you not been led aside by temptations that way

N. I have not

H. What a sad thing it is that a church member here & now another of Salem, should be thus accused and charged.

Mrs. Pope fell into a grievous fit, & cried out a sad thing sure enough: And then many more fell into lamentable fits.

H. Tell us have not you had visible appearances more than what is common in nature?

    N.   I have none nor never had in my life.

    H.   Do you think these suffer voluntary or involuntary.

    N.   I cannot tell.

    H.   That is strange every one can judge.

    N.   I must be silent.

    H.   They accuse you of hurting them, & if you think it is not unwillingly but by design, you must look upon them as murderers.

    N.   I cannot tell what to think of it

Afterwards when this was, some what insisted on she said, "I do not think so". She did not understand aright what was said.

    H.   Well then give an answer now, do you think these suffer against their wills or not

    N.   I do not think these suffer against their wills

    H.   Why did you never visit these afflicted persons

    N.   Because I was afraid I should have fits too

Note Upon the motion of her body fits followed upon the complainants abundantly & very frequently

    H.   Is it not an unaccountable case that when you are examined these persons are afflicted?

    N.   I have got no body to look to but God

Again upon stirring her hands the afflicted persons were seized with violent fits of torture

    H.   Do you believe these afflicted persons are bewitched?

    N.   I do think they are.

    H.   When this Witchcraft came upon the stage there was no suspicion of Tituba (Mr Paris's Indian woman) she professed much love to that child Betty Paris, but it was her apparition did the mischief, & why should not you also be guilty, for your apparition doth hurt also?

    N.   Would you have me belie my self?—

She held her Neck on one side, & accordingly so were the afflicted taken

Then Authority requiring it Sam: Paris read what he had in characters taken from Mr. Thomas Putman's wife in her fits

    H.   What do you think of this?

    N.   I cannot help it, the Devil may appear in my shape.

This is a true account of the sum of her examination but by reason of great noises by the afflicted & many speakers, many things are pre-termitted [omitted]

Memorandum

Nurse held her neck on one side & Eliz: Hubbard (one of the sufferers) had her neck set in that posture whereupon another Patient Abigail Williams cried out set up Goody Nurses head the maid's neck will be broke & when come set up Nurses head Aaron Wey observed that Betty Hubbard's was immediately righted.

Salem Village March. 24'th 1691/2

The Reverend Mr Samuel Parris being desired to take in writing the Examination of Rebekah Nurse hath Returned itt as aforesaid

Upon heareing the afores'd and seeing what wee then did see together with the Charge of the persons then present—wee Committed Rebekah Nurse the wife of fran's Nurce of Salem village unto their Majestys Goale in Salem as p a Mittimus then given out, in order to farther Examination

*John Hathorne [unclear:] Assis'ts
*Jonathan. Corwin

(Peabody Essex Museum, Salem, MA)

Document 30   (Summary of Examinations of Tituba)

Salem Village March 1'st 1691

Titiba an Indian Woman brought before us by Const' Jos Hertick of Salem upon Suspition of Witchcraft by her Commited according to the Compl't of Jos. Hutcheson & Thomas putnam &c of Salem Village as appeares p Warrant granted Salem 29 febr'y 1691/2 Titiba upon Examination and after some denyall acknowledged the matter of fact according to her Examination given in more fully will appeare and who also charged Sarah Good and Sarah Osburne with the same Salem Village March the 1'th 1691/2

Sarah Good Sarah Osborne and Titiba an Indian Woman all of Salem Village Being this day brought before us upon Suspition of Witchcraft &c by them and Every one of them Committed. titiba an Indian Woman acknowledging the matter of fact. and Sarah Osburne and Sarah Good denying the same before us: but there appeareing in all theire Examinations sufficient Ground to secure them all. And in order to further Examination they Ware all p mittimus sent to the Goales in the County of Essex.

Salem March 2'd Sarah Osburne againe Examined and also titiba as will appear in their Examinations given in

titiba againe acknowledged the fact & also accuse the other two. Salem March 3'd Sarah Osburn and titiba Indian againe Examined the Examination now Given in

titiba againe s'd the same

Salem March 5'th Sarah Good and titiba againe Examined. & in theire Examination titiba acknowledg the same she did formerly and accused the other two-aboves'd—

titiba againe s'd the same

p. us. *John Hathorne [unclear:] Assis'ts
*Jonathan. Corwin

(Peabody Essex Museum, Salem, MA)

Document 31   (Examination of Tituba)

The Examination of Titibe

(H) Titibe what evil spirit have you familiarity with
(T) none
(H) why do you hurt these children
(T) I do not hurt them
(H) who is it then
(T) the devil for ought I know
(H) did you never see the devil.
(T) the devil came to me and bid me serve him
(H) who have you seen
(T) 4 women sometimes hurt the children
(H) who were they?
(T) goode Osburn and Sarah good and I doe not know who the other were
     Sarah good and Osburne would have me hurt the children but I would
     not shee furder saith there was a tale man of Boston that shee did see
(H) when did you see them
(T) Last night at Boston
(H) what did they say to you they said hurt the children
(H) and did you hurt them
(T) no there is 4 women and one man they hurt the children and then lay all
     upon me and they tell me if I will not hurt the children they will hurt me
(H) but did you not hurt them
(T) yes, but I will hurt them no more
(H) are you not sorry you did hurt them.
(T) yes.
(H) and why then doe you hurt them
(T) they say hurt children or wee will doe worse to you
(H) what have you seen a man come to me and say serve me
(H) what service
(T) hurt the children and last night there was an appearance that said Kill
     the children and if I would no go on hurting the children they would do
     worse to me
(H) what is this appearance you see
(T) sometimes it is like a hog and some times like a great dog this appear-
     ance shee saith shee did see 4 times
(H) what did it say to you
(T) the black dog said serve me but I said I am a fraid he said if I did not he
     would doe worse to me
(H) what did you say to it
(T) I will serve you no longer then he said he would hurt me and then he
     lookes like a man and threatens to hurt me shee said that this man had a
     yellow bird that keept with him and he told me he had more pretty
     things that he would give me if I would serve him
(H) what were these pretty things
(T) he did not show me them
(H) what else have you seen
(T) two rats, a red rat and a black rat
(H) what did they say to you

(T)   they said serve me
(H)   when did you see them
(T)   Last night and they said serve me but shee said I would not
(H)   what service
(T)   shee said hurt the children
(H)   did you not pinch Elizabeth Hubbard this morning
(T)   the man brought her to me and made me pinch her
(H)   why did you goe to thomas putnams Last night and hurt his child
(T)   they pull and hall me and make goe
(H)   and what would have you doe Kill her with a knif Left. fuller and others
      said at this time when the child saw these persons and was tormented by
      them that she did complain of a knif that they would have her cut her
      head off with a knife
(H)   how did you go
(T)   we ride upon stickes and are there presently
(H)   doe you goe through the trees or over them
(T)   we see no thing but are there presently
(H)   why did you not tell your master
(T)   I was a fraid they said they would cut off my head if I told
(H)   would not you have hurt others if you could
(T)   they said they would hurt others but they could not
(H)   what attendants hath Sarah good
(T)   a yellow bird and shee would have given me one
(H)   what meate did she give it
(T)   it did suck her between her fingers
(H)   Did not you hurt mr Currins child
(T)   goode good and goode Osburn told that they did hurt mr Currens child
      and would have had me hurt him two but I did not
(H)   what hath Sarah Osburn
(T)   yesterday shee had a thing with a head like a woman with 2 leggs and
      wings Abigail williams that lives with her uncle mr Parris said that shee
      did see this same creature and it turned into the shape of goode osburn
(H)   what else have you seen with goode osburn
(T)   an other thing hairy it goes upright like a man it hath only 2 leggs
(H)   did you not see Sarah good upon elisebeth Hubbar last Saturday
(T)   I did see her set a wolfe upon her to afflict her the persons with this maid
      did say that shee did complain of a wolf
(T)   shee furder said that shee saw a cat with good at another time
(H)   what cloathes doth the man go in
(T)   he goes in black clouthes a tal man with white hair I thinke
(H)   how doth the woman go
(T)   in a white whood and a black whood with a tup knot
(H)   doe you see who it is that torments these children now
(T)   yes it is goode good she hurts them in her own shape
(H)   & who is it that hurts them now
(T)   I am blind noe I cannot see

Salem Village
March the 1st 1691/2
written by
Ezekiell Chevers
Salem Village March the 1't 1691/2

(*Peabody Essex Museum, Salem, MA*)

Document 32   (Examination of Tituba—A Second Version)

Tittuba the Ind'n Woem'ns Examn March. 1. 1691/2

Q. why doe you hurt these poor Children? whatt harme have thay done unto you?

A. thay doe noe harme to me I noe hurt them att all.

Q. why have you done itt?

A. I have done nothing; I Can't tell when the Devill works

Q. what doth the Devill tell you that he hurts them

A. noe he tells me nothing.

Q. doe you never see Something appeare in Some shape?

A. noe never See any thing.

Q. whatt familiarity have you w'th the devill, or w't is itt if you Converse w'th all? tell the truth whoe itt is that hurts them

A. the Devill for ought I know.

Q. w't appearanc or how doth he appeare when he hurts them, w'th w't shape or what is he like that hurts them

A. like a man I think yesterday I being in the Lentoe Chamber I saw a thing like a man, that tould me Searve him & I tould him noe I would nott doe Such thing. she charges Goody Osburne & Sarah Good as those that hurt the Children, and would have had hir done itt, she sayth she Seen foure two of w'ch she knew nott she saw them last night as she was washing the Roome, thay tould me hurt the Children & would have had me gone to Boston, ther was.5. of them w'th the man, they tould me if I would nott goe & hurt them they would doe soe to mee att first I did agree w'th them butt afterward I tould them I doe soe noe more.

Q. would they have had you hurt the Children the Last Night

A. yes, butt I was Sorry & I sayd, I would doe Soe noe more, but tould I would feare God.

Q. butt why did nott you doe Soe before?

A. why they tell mee I had done Soe before & therefore I must goe on, these were the.4.woemen & the man, butt she knew none butt Osburne & Good only, the others were of Boston.

Q. att first begining w'th them, w't then appeared to you w't was itt like that Got you to doe itt

A. one like a man Just as I was goeing to sleep Came to me this was when the Children was first hurt he sayd he would kill the Children & she would never be well, and he Sayd if I would nott Serve him he would do soe to mee

Q. is that the Same man that appeared before to you that appeared the last night & tould you this?

A. yes.

Q. w't Other likenesses besides a man hath appeared to you?

A. Sometimes like a hogge Sometimes like a great black dogge, foure tymes.

Q. but w't did they Say unto you?

A. they tould me Serve him & that was a good way; that was the black dogge I tould him I was afrayd, he tould me he would be worse then to me.

Q. w't did you say to him after that?

A. I answer I will Serve you noe Longer he tould me he would doe me hurt then.

Q. w't other Creatures have you seene

A. a bird

Q. w't bird?

A. a little yellow Bird.

Q. where doth itt keep?

A. w'th the man whoe hath pretty things there besides.

Q. what other pretty things?

A. he hath nott showed them [yet] unto me, butt he s'd he would show them me tomorrow, and he tould me if I would Serve him I should have the Bird.

Q. w't other Creatures did you see?

A. I saw 2 Catts, one Red, another black as bigge as a little dogge.

Q. w't did these Catts doe?

A. I dont know; I have seen them two tymes.

Q. w't did they say?

A. thay say serve them.

Q. when did you see them?

A. I saw them last night.

Q. did they doe any hurt to you or threaten you?

A. they did scratch me.

Q. when?

A. after prayer; and scratched mee, because I would not serve them and when they went away I could nott see but thay stood before the fire.

Q. what Service doe thay Expect fro you?

A. they Say more hurt to the Children.

Q. how did you pinch them when you hurt them?

A. the other pull mee & hall me to the pinch the Childr, & I am very sorry for itt,

Q. What made you hould yo'r arme when you were Searched? w't had you there?

A. I had nothing

Q. doe nott those Catts suck you?

A. noe never yett I would nott lett them but they had almost thrust me into the fire.

Q. how doe you hurt those that you pinch? doe you gett those Catts? or other thing to doe it for you? tell us, how is it done?

A. the man sends the Catts to me & bids me pinch them, & I think I went over to mr Grigg's & have pinched hir this day in the morning. the man brought mr Grigg's mayd to me & made me pinch hir.

Q. did you ever goe w'th these woemen?

A. they are very strong & pull me & make me goe w'th them.

Q. where did you goe?

A. up to mr putnams & make me hurt the Child.

Q. whoe did make you goe?

A. man that is very strong & these two woeman, Good & Osburne but I am Sorry.

Q. how did you goe? Whatt doe you Ride upon?

A. I Rid upon a stick or poale & Good & Osburne behind me we Ride takeing hold of one another don't know how we goe for I Saw noe trees nor path, but was presently there. when wee were up.

Q. how long Since you began to pinch mr parriss Children?

A. I did nott pinch them att the first, butt he make me afterward.

Q. have you Seen Good and osburne Ride upon a poule?

A. yes & have held fast by mee: I was nott att mr Grigg's but once, butt it may be Send Something like mee, with or would I have gone, butt that they tell me, they will hurt me; last night they Tell me I must kill Some body w'th the knife.

Q. who were they that told you Soe

A. Sarah Good & Osburne & they would have had me killed Thomas putnam's Child last night. the Child alsoe affirmed that att the Same tyme thay would have had hir Cutt #[hir own throat] of hir own head for if she would nott then tould hir Tittubee would Cutt itt off & then she Complayned att the Same Time of a knife Cutting of hir when hir master hath asked hir about these things she sayth thay will nott lett hir tell, butt Tell hir if she Tells hir head shall be Cutt off.

Q. whoe Tells you Soe?

A. the man, Good & Osburnes Wife. Goody Goody Came to hir last night w'n hir master was att prayr & would not lett hir hear & she Could not hear a good whyle. Good hath one of these birds the yellow bird & would have given mee itt, but I would not have itt & prayer tyme she stoped my eares & would nott lett me hear.

Q. w't should you have done with itt

A. give itt to the Children. w'ch yellow bird hath bin severall tymes Seen by the Children I saw Sarah Good have itt on hir hand when she Came to hir when mr parris was att prayr: I saw the bird suck Good betwene the fore finger & Long finger upon the Right hand.

Q. did you never practise witch-craft in your owne Country?

A. Noe Never before now.

Q. did you #[ever] See them doe itt now?

A. yes. to day, butt that was in the morneing.

Q. butt did you see them doe itt now while you are Examining.

A. noe I did nott See them butt I Saw them hurt att other tymes. I saw Good have a Catt beside the yellow bird w'ch was with hir

Q. what hath Osburne gott to goe w'th hir?

A. Some thing I dont know what itt is. I can't name itt, I don't know how itt looks she hath two of them one of them hath wings & two Leggs & a head like a woeman the Children Saw the Same butt yesterday w'ch afterward turned into a woeman.

Q. What is the other Thing that Goody Osburne hath?

A. a thing all over hairy, all the face hayry & a long nose & I don't know how to tell how the face looks w'th two Leggs, itt goeth upright & is about two or three foot high & goeth upright like a man & last night itt stood before the fire In mr parris's hall.

Q. Whoe was that appeared like a Wolfe to Hubberd as she was goeing fro proctures?

A. itt was Sarah Good & I saw hir Send the Wolfe to hir.

Q. what Cloathes doth the man appeare unto you in?

A. black Cloaths Some times, Some times Searge Coat of other Couler, a Tall man w'th white hayr, I think.

Q. What apparrell doe the woeman ware?

A. I don't know w't couller.

Q. What Kind of Cloathes hath she?

A. I don't know w't couller.

Q. What kind of Cloathes hath she?

A. a black Silk hood w'th a White Silk hood under itt, w'th top knotts, w'ch woeman I know not but have Seen hir in boston when I lived there.

Q. what Cloathes the little woeman?

A. A Searge Coat w'th a White Cap as I think. the Children having fits att this Very time she was asked whoe hurt them, she Ans'r Goody Good & the Children affirmed the same butt Hubbard being taken in an extreame fit after she was asked whoe hurt hir & she Sayd she Could nott tell, but sayd they blinded hir, & would nott lett hir see and after that was once or twice taken dumb hirself.

Document 33   (Second Examination of Tituba. March 2, 1691/2)

Q. What Covenant did you make w'th that man that Came to you? What did he tell you.

A. he Tell me he god, & I must beleive him & Serve him Six yeares & he would give me many fine things.

Q. how long a gone was this?

A. about Six weeks & a little more fryday night before Abigall was Ill.

Q. w't did he Say you must doe more? did he Say you must write anything? did he offer you any paper?

A. yes, the Next time he Come to me & showed me some fine things, Some thing like Creatures, a little bird something like green & white.

Q. did you promiss him then when he spake to you then what did you answer him

A. I then sayd this I tould him I Could nott believe him God, I tould him I ask my maister & would have gone up but he stopt mee & would nott lett me

Q. whatt did you promiss him?

A. the first tyme I beleive him God & then he was Glad.

Q. what did he Say to you then? what did he Say you must doe?

A. then he tell me they must meet together.

Q. w'n did he Say you must meet together.

A. he tell me wednesday next att my m'rs house, & then they all meet together & thatt night I saw them all stand in the Corner, all four of them, & the man stand behind mee & take hold of mee to make mee stand still in the hall.

Q. where was your master then?

A. in the other Room.

Q. What time of Night?

A. a little before prayr time.

Q. What did this man Say to you when he took hold of you?

A. he Say goe & doe hurt to them and pinch them & then I went in, & would nott hurt them a good while, I would nott hurt Betty, I loved Betty, but they hall me & make me pinch Betty & the next Abigall & then quickly went away altogether & I pinched them.

Q. did they pinch

A. Noe, but they all lookt on & See mee pinch them.

Q. did you goe into that Room in your own person & all the rest?

A. yes, and my master did nott See us, for they would nott lett my Master See.

Q. did you goe w'th the Company?

A. Noe I stayd & the Man stayd w'th mee.

Q. whatt did he then to you?

A. he tell me my master goe to prayer & he read in book & he ask me what I remember, but don't you remember anything.

Q. did he ask you noe more but the first time to Serve him or the secon time?

A. yes, he ask me againe, & that I Serve him, Six yeares & he Come the Next time & show me a book.

Q. and when would he come then?

A. the next fryday & showed me a book in the day time betimes in the morneing.

Q. and what Booke did he Bring a great or little booke?

A. he did nott show it me, nor would nott, but had itt in his pockett.

Q. did nott he make you write yo'r Name?

A. noe nott yett for mistris Called me into the other roome.

Q. whatt did he say you must doe in that book?

A. he Sayd write & sett my name to itt.

Q. did you write?

A. yes once I made a marke in the Booke & made itt with red Bloud.

Q. did he gett itt out of your Body?

A. he Said he must gett itt out the Next time he Come againe, he give me a pin tyed in a stick to doe itt w'th, butt he noe Lett me bloud w'th itt as yett butt Intended another time when he Come againe.

Q. did you See any other marks in his book?

A. yes a great many Some marks red, Some yellow, he opened his booke a great many marks in itt.

Q. did he tell you the Names of them?

A. yes of two note more Good & Osburne & he Say thay make them marks in that book & he showed them mee.

Q. how many marks doe you think there was?

A. Nine.

Q. did they write there Names?

A. thay made marks Goody Good Sayd she made hir mark, butt Goody Osburne would nott tell she was Cross to mee.

Q. when did Good tell you, She Sett hir hand to the Book?

A. the same day I Came hither to prison.

Q. did you See the man thatt morneing?

A. yes a litle in the morneing & he tell me the Magistrates Come up to Exa in mee.

Q. w't did he Say you must Say?

A. he tell me, tell nothing, if I did he would Cutt my head off.

Q. tell us [tru] how many woemen doe use to Come when you Rid abroad?

A. foure of them these two Osburne & Good & those two strangers.

Q. you Say that there was Nine did he tell you whoe they were?

A. noe he noe lett me See but he tell me I should See them the next tyme

Q. what sights did you see

A. I see a man, a dogge, a hogge, & two Catts a black and Red & the strange monster was Osburne that I mentioned before this was was the hayry Imp. the man would give itt to mee, but I would nott have itt.

Q. did he show you in the Book w'ch was Osburne & w'ch was Goods mark?

A. yes I see there marks.

Q. butt did he tell the Names of the other?

A. noe s'r

Q. & what did he say to you when you made your Mark?

A. he sayd Serve mee & always Serve mee the man w'th the two women Came fro Boston.

Q. how many times did you goe to Boston?

A. I was goeing & then Came back againe I was never att Boston.

Q. whoe Came back w'th you againe?

A. the man Came back w'th mee & the woemen goe away, I was nott willing to goe?

Q. how farr did you goe, to what Towne?

A. I never went to any Towne I see noe trees, noe Towne.

Q. did he tell you where the Nine Lived?

A. yes, Some in Boston & Some herein this Towne, but he would nott tell mee wher thay were, X

(Examination of Tituba (Mass.-Essex Co. Box); Manuscripts and Archives Division; The New York Public Library; Astor, Lenox, and Tilden Foundations)

Document 34   (Examination of Mary Warren, April 19, 1692)

(See also Giles Corey – Warrant)

The Examination of Mary Warren At a Court held at Salem Village by

John Hauthorne [*unclear*:] Esq'rs

Jonath: Corwin

As soon as she was coming towards the Bar the afflicted fell into fits.

Mary Warren, You stand here charged with sundry acts of Witchcraft, what do you say for yourself, are you guilty, or not?

M. I am innocent.

Hath she hurt you (speaking to the sufferers) some were Dumb.

Betty Hubbard testified against her, & then said Hubbard fell into a violent fit.

You were a little while ago an Afflicted person, now you are an Afflicter: How comes this to pass?

M. I looked up to God, & take it to be a great Mercy of God.

What do you take it to be a great mercy to afflict others?

Betty Hubbard testified that a little after this Mary was well, she the said Mary, said that the afflicted persons did but dissemble [pretend].

Now they were all but John Indian grievously afflicted, & Mrs. Pope also, who was not afflicted before hitherto this day: & after a few moments John Indian fell into a violent fit also.

Well here was one just now that was a Tormentor in her apparition & she owns that she had made a league with the Devil.

Now Mary Warren fell into a fit, & some of the afflicted cried out that she was going to confess, but Goody Corey, & Procter, & his wife came in, in their apparition, & struck her down, & said she should tell nothing.

Mary Warren continued a good space in a fit, that she did neither see, nor hear, nor speak.

Afterwards she started up, & said I will speak & cried out, "Oh! I am sorry for it, I am sorry for it." & wringed her hands, & fell a little while into a fit again & then came to speak, but immediately her Teeth were set, & then she fell into a violent fit, & cried out, "Oh Lord help me, Oh good Lord save me!"

And then afterwards cried again, "I will tell, I will tell", & then fell into a dead fit again.

And afterwards cried, "I will tell, they did, they did, they did", & then fell into a violent fit again.

After a little recovery she cried, "I will tell, I will tell, they brought me to it"; & then fell into a fit again: which fits continuing, she was ordered to be had out, & the next to be brought in, viz: Bridget Bishop

Some time afterwards she was called in again, but immediately taken with fits, for a while.

Have you signed the Devils book?

M.   No.

Have you not touch it?

M.   No.

Then she fell into fits again, & was sent forth for air.

After a considerable space of time she was brought in again, but could [not] give account of things, by reason of fits, & so sent forth.

Mary Warren called in, afterwards in private, before magistrates & Ministers.

M.   She said, I shall not speak a word: but I will speak Satan—She saith she will kill me: Oh! 'she saith, she owes me a spite, & will claw me off—

Avoid Satan, for the name of God avoid.

And then fell into fits again: & cried will ye I will prevent ye in the Name of God,—

Tell us, how far have you yielded?

A fit interrupts her again.

What did they say you should do, & you should be well?

Then her lips were bit so that she could not speak. so she was sent away

Note That not one of the sufferers was afflicted during her examination after once she began to confess, though they were tormented before.

Salem Village Aprill 19'th 1692.

Mr Samuell Parris being desired to take in writing the Examination of Mary Warren hath delivered it as aforesaid And upon hearing the same and seeing what wee did then see; together with the Charge of the afflicted persons then present. We Committed said Mary Warren

*John Hathorne [unclear:] Assis'ts
*Jonathan. Corwin
(Reverse) (3) The examination of Mary Warren 19. Apr. 1692

(Peabody Essex Museum, Salem, MA)

Document 35   (Examination of Mary Warren in Prison)

Mary Warren's Examination in Salem Prison
  She Testifies that Her master Proctor was always very averse to the putting up Bills for public prayer.

Q: Did you not know it was the Devils book when you Signed?
A: No. But I thought it was no good book.
Q: after you had a Mark in the Book what did you think then?
A: Then I thought it was the Devil's book.
Q. How did you come to know your Master and Mistress were Witches?
A. The Sabbath Eve after I had put up my note for thanks in public, my Mistress appeared to me, and pulled me out of the Bed, and told me that She was a witch, and had put her hand to the Book, She told me this in her Bodily person, and that This Examination might have known she was a Witch, if She had but minded what Books she read in.
Q. What did she say to you before you tormented the Children?
A. The night after she told me she was a Witch, she in son told me this Examinant, that my self and her son John would quickly be brought out for witches.

This Examinant saith that Giles Cory in apparition told her, the night before that the Magistrates were going up to the farms, to bring down more witches to torment her. Moreover being in a dreadful fit in the prison she Charged it on Giles Cory, who was then in Close prison, affirming that he came into the Room where she was, and afflicting her, Charged her not to Come into the Other Room while he was Examining, But being sent for and he Commanded to look upon her, He no sooner turned his face to her but she fell into a dreadful fit again, and upon her recovery, charged him to his face with being the procurer of it. Moreover the said Cory in prison formerly threatened her that he would fight her for it, because he told her she had Caused her Master to ask more for a piece of Meadow than he was willing to give she likewise in her fit in the Other Room before she had seen Giles Cory in person, Charging him with afflicting off her, described him in all his garments, both of hat Coat and Colour of them, with a Cord about his wast, and a white Cap on his head and in Chains, as several then in Company Can affirm.

(Peabody Essex Museum, Salem, MA)

Document 36   (Examination of Mary Warren, April 21, 1692)

Mary Warren's examination of April 21: 1692

Being Asked by the Honored Magistrates:	whether the Bible that then was Showed her: was the book: that was brought: to her to touch: & that she saw the flourish and answered, no: she saw she was deceived

Being asked:	whether she had not told Mercy Lewis that she had signed to a book.
Answered:	no
She was Asked:	whether her Mistress had brought a book to her to sign
Answered:	her mistress brought none. but her Master brought one.
Being Asked:	whether she signed to it.
Answered:	not unless putting her finger to it was signing.
Being asked:	whether she did not see a spot where she had put her finger
Answered:	there was a spot.
She was Asked:	what colour the spot was:
Answered:	black
She was Asked:	whether her Master did not threaten her to run the hot tongs down her throat if she did not sign.
Answered:	that her Master threatened her to burn her out of her fit.
Being Asked:	whether she had made a mark in the book
Answered:	she made no mark but with her top of her finger
She was asked:	what she dipped her finger in when it made the mark:
Answered:	in nothing but her mouth.
She was Asked:	whether her finger was wet when she touched the book with it
Answered:	she knew not that it was wet: or whether it was wet with sweat or with cider: that she had bin drinking of she knew not: but her finger did make a mark and the mark was black
She was asked:	whether any but her Master and Mistress was with her when she was threatened with the hot tongs:
Answered:	none but them
	She said her Master put her hand to the book and her finger made a black spot which made her tremble: then she said she was undone body and soul and cried out grievously. She was told that it was he[r] own Voluntary act: she would have denied it: but she was told the devil could have done nothing: if she had not yielded and that she for ease to her body: not for any good of her soul: had done it. With this she much grieved and cried out: she said her Master & mistress threatened to drown her: & to make her run through the hedges.
She was asked:	whether she had not seen her Master & mistress since she came to prison?
Answered:	she thought she saw her Master and dare say it was he.
She was Asked:	what he said to her:
Answered:	nothing
	After a fit she cried out "I will tell: I will tell: thou wicked Creature it is you stopped my mouth: but I will confess the little that I have to confess."
Being asked:	who she would tell off whether Goodwife Proctor or no.
Answered:	"O Betty Procter it is she: it is she I lived with last".
	She then cried out: "it shall be known: thou wretch; hast thou undone me body and soul."
She said also:	"She wishes she had made me make a thorough league."
She was again asked:	what her finger was blacked with when she touched the book?

Answered:	she knew not that her finger was black 'til she saw it black[en] the book and after she had put her finger to the book: she ate: bread and butter and her finger blacked the bred and butter also.
Being asked:	what her mistress now said to her when she complained of her mistress?
She said:	her mistress bid her not tell that her mistress was a witch. Coming out of another fit said she would tell she would tell: she said her Master now bid her not tell that he had sometimes gone to make away with himself.
	For her Master had told her that he had been sometimes about to make away with himself because of his wife's quarreling with him.
Being Asked:	how she knew Goodwife Procter was a witch?
	She coming out of a fit said: "she would tell she would tell".
And she said:	her Mistress Procter said she might know she was a witch if she hearkened to what she used to read. She said her Mistress had many books and her mistress carried one book with her to Reading when she went to see her sister.
Being Asked:	whether she knew her Mistress to be a witch before she touched the book, and how she knew it?
She said:	her mistress told her she had set her hand to the devil's book "that same night that I was thrown out of bed". said she "which was the same night after she had a note of thanksgiving put up at the meeting house".
	She said her mistress came to her in her body not her [spectral] shape as far as she knew. She affirmed her mistress was a witch.
Being Asked:	whether she had seen any of the witches since she came to prison?
She said:	Said she had seen Goodman Cory & Sarah Good. They brought the book to her to sign. but she would not own that she knew her master to be a witch or wizard. Being asked whether she did not know her finger would make a mark if she touched the book with it: she answered, no but her master and mistress asked her to read and she said the first word she read was Moses: the next word she could not tell what it was but her Master and Mistress bid her: if she could not pronounce the word she should touch the book.
Being asked:	why she would not tell the whole truth?
She said:	she had formerly not told all the truth. because she was threatened to be torn in pieces: if she did but now she would and had told the truth
Being asked:	whether she did not suspect it was the devil's book that she touched
Answered:	she did not suspect it before. She said her finger blacked it.
She was Asked:	why: she yielded to do as she did?
Answered:	that her master said if she would not, when she was in her fit she should run into the fire or water if he would and destroy herself.
Being Asked:	whether she had not been instrumental to afflict the afflicted persons?

Answered:	no but when she heard: they were afflicted in her shape she began to fear it was the devil [that hurt in her shape].
Being Asked:	whether she had images to stick pins or thorns into to hurt people with:
Answered:	no
She was asked:	whether the devil never asked her consent to hurt in her shape
Answered:	no: she had heard her master and mistress tell of images and of sticking of thorns in them to hurt people with.
She was asked:	whether she knew of any images in the house:
Said:	no.
Being asked:	if she knew of any ointment they had in the house?
She said:	her Mistress ointed her once for some ail she had: but it was with ointment that came from Mrs. Bassit's of Lynn the colour of it was greenish.
She was asked:	how it smelt:
Said:	very ugly to her.
	She said when she touched the book she went to put her finger to another line buther finger went to the same place: where her finger had blacked it.
	Mr. Noyce told her she had then touched the book twice: and asked her whether she did not suspect it to be the devils book before she touched it the second time: she said she feared it was no good book: being asked what she meant by no good book: she said a book to deceive

(On Reverse) Mary Warrens Examination

(*Peabody Essex Museum, Salem, MA*)

Document 37   (Examination of Mary Warren, May 12, 1692)

Mary Warrens Examination May 12'th 1692

Q. Whether you did not know that itt was the Devills book when you signed?

A. I did nott know itt then but I know itt now, to be sure itt was the Devills book, in the first place to be sure I did sett my hand to the Devills book; I have considered of itt, since you were here last & itt was the Devills book that my Master procter brought to me, & he tould me if I would sett my hand to that book I should be well; & I did sett my hand to itt, butt that w'ch I did itt was done w'th my finger, he brought the Book & he tould me if I would take the book & touch itt that I should be well & I thought then that itt was the Devills book.

Q. Was there nott your consent to hurt the children, when you were hurt?

A. Noe sir, but when I was afflicted my master Procter was in the Roome & said if ye are Afflicted I wish ye were more Afflicted & you and all: I said Master, w't make you say soe he Answered because you goe to bring out Innocent persons. I tould him that could nott bee & whether the Devill took advantage att that I know not to afflict them and one Night talking about them I said I did nott care though ye were tormented if ye charged mee:

Q. Did you ever see any poppetts?

An. yes once I saw one made of cloth in Mistris procters hand.

Q. whoe was itt like or w'ch of the Children was itt for?

An. I cannot tell, whether for Ann putnam or Abigail Williams, for one of them itt was I am sure, itt was in my mistri's hand.

Q. What did you stick into the poppitt?

An. I did stick in a pin about the Neck of itt as itt was in proctors hand.

Q. How many more did you see afterwards?

An. I doe nott remember that ever I saw any more. yes I remember one and that Goody parker brought a poppitt unto me of Mercy. Lewis & she gave me another & I stook itt some where about the wasts; & she appeared once more to me in the prison, & she said to me what are you gott here? & she tould me that she was comeing here hirself. I had another person that appeared to me, itt was Goody. Pudeator & said she was sorry to se me there, itt was in apparition & she brought me a pop-pitt, itt was like to Mary Walcott & itt was a peice of stick that she brought me to stick into itt & somewhare about hir armes I stook itt in.

Q. Where did she bring itt to you?

An. up att procters. Goody parker tould me she had bin a Witch these. 12 years & more; & pudeator tould me that she had done damage, & tould me that she had hurt James Coyes child takeing itt out of the mothers hand.

Q. whoe brought the last to you?—

An. my mistris & when she brought itt, she brought itt in hir owne person & hir husband w'th his owne hands brought me the Book to Sighne, & he brought me an Image w'ch looked yellow & I beleive itt was for Abigall Williams being like hir & I putt a thing like a thorne into itt, this was done by his bodily person after I had sighned the

night after I had sighned the book: while she was thus confessiong parker appeared & bitt her extreamly on hir armes as she affirmed unto us.

Q. Whoe have you sene more?

An. Nurse & Cloys and Goods Child after I had sighned.

Q. What sayd [th'y] to you?

An. They sayd that I should never Tell of them nor anything about them, & I have seen Goody Good hirself.

Q. Was that true of Giles Cory that you saw him & that he Afflicted you the other day?

An. yes I have sene him often & he hurts me very much & Goody Oliver hath appeared to me & Afflicted me & brought the Book to tempt mee, & I have seen Goody Cory. the first night I was taken, I saw as I thought the Apparition of Goody Cory & catched att itt as I thought & caught my master in my lap tho I did nott see my master in that place att that time, upon w'ch my master said itt is noe body but I itt is my shaddow that you see, but my master was nott before mee as I could descerne, but Catching att the Apparition that looked like Goody Cory I caught hold of my master & pulled him downe into my Lap; upon w'ch he said I see ther is noe heed to any of your talkings, for you are all possest with the Devill for itt is nothing butt my shape, I have sene Goody Cory att my masters house in person, and she tould mee that I should be condemned for a Witch as well as she hirself, itt was att my masters house, & she said that the children would cry out & bring out all.

Q. was this before you had signned?

An. yes, before I had any fitts.

Q. Now tell the truth about the Moutebank what writeing was that?

An. I don't know. I asked hir what itt was about but she would not tell mee saying she had promised nott to Lett any body see itt.

Q. Well, but whoe did you see more?

An. I don't know any more.

Q. how long hath your Mast'r & Mistris bin Witches?

An. I don't know, they never tould me.

Q. What likeness or appearance have you had to bew'ch you?

An. they never gave me any thing. while I was reading this over upon the comeing in of mr Higginson & mr Hale as soon as I read the name parker, she imediately fell into dreadfull fitts as she affirmed

after hir fitt was over by the appearance of Goody parker, & mr Hathorne presently but Naming Goody pudeator she alsoe appeared & tormented hir very much. and Goody parker in the time of hir examination in one of Warrens fitts tould this examinant that she had bewitched the examinants sister & was the cause of hir dumbness as alsoe that she had lately killed a man aboard a vessell & tould me that his name was Michaell Chapleman aboard the vessell in the harbour after they ware come to Anchor & that he dyed with a paine in his side & that she had done itt by striking something into his side & that she had strook this examinants sister dumb that she should never speak more. and Goody pudeater att the same tyme appeared & tould this examinant that she had throwne John Turner off of a chery tree & almost killed him & Goody parker s'd that she had cast away Capt prices ketch Thomas Westgate master, & Venus Colefox in itt & presently tould her that Jno Lapshorne was lost in itt and that they were foundred in the sea and she saith that Goody pudeator tould hir that she went up to mr Corwins house to bewitch his mare that he should nott goe up to the farmes to examine the witches, also mr Burroughs appearing at the same tyme and Afflicting her tould hir that he went to tye mr Hathornes horses leggs when he went last to Boston & that he tryed to bewitch him 'tho he could not his horse. Goody pudeator tould hir that she killed hir husband by giving him something whereby he fell sick and dyed, itt was she tould hir about 7 or 10 years since and Goody parker tould her that she was Instrumentall to drowne Orne's son in the harbour also shee s'd she did bewitch Jno Searles's boy to death as his master was carrying him out to sea soe that he was forced to bring him back againe, alsoe Burroughs tould her that he killed his wife off of Cape Ann parker tould hir alsoe that Margarett Jacobs was a wittness against hir and did charge hir yesterday upon hir (that is Jacobs's) examination.

(Peabody Essex Museum, Salem, MA)

INDICTMENTS

An indictment is a court document prepared by the state prosecutor—or in the case of Salem, the Court of Oyer and Terminer—where the criminal defendant is formally charged with a criminal complaint or charged with a crime. The purpose of this statement is to provide the defendant with a clear description of the alleged crime of which he/she is being charged. It usually contains the names of the victims, a brief description of the offense, as well as information as to when and where the crime occurred. In the Salem episode, indictments were not issued until depositions were gathered, a pre-trial hearing was held, and evidence was deemed sufficient to formally charge the alleged witch with the crime of witchcraft.

Document 38   (Indictment v. Bridget Bishop, No. 1)

Anno Regni Regis et Reginae W[illm et]
   Mariae nunc Angliae &c Quarto:
   Essex Ss
The Jurors for our Sovereigne Lord & lady the King & Queen p'esents that Bridgett Bishop als Olliver the wife of Edward Bishop of Salem in the County of Essex Sawyer the Nyneteenth Day of April in the fourth Year of the Reigne of our Sovereigne Lord and Lady William and Mary by the Grace of God of England Scottland France & Ireland King & Queen Deffenders of the faith &c and Divers other Dayes & times awell before as after. certaine Detestable Arts called Witchcraft & Sorceries.wickedly.and felloniously hath used Practised & Exercised, at and within the Towneship of Salem in the County of Essex afores'd in upon.and ag't one: Mercy Lewis of Salem Village in the County afors'd singlewoman by which said wicked Arts the said Mercy Lewis—the s'd Nyneteenth Day of April in the fourth Year aboves'd and divers other Dayes and times as well before as after, was & is hurt Tortured Afflicted Pined, Consumed, wasted: & tormented ag't the Peace of our said Sovereigne Lord And Lady the King & Queen and ag't the forme of the Statute in that Case made & provided

Wittnesses
Mercy Lewis
Nathan'll Ingersoll
Mr Sam'll paris
Thomas puttnam Jun'r
Mary Walcott
Ann puttnam Jun'r
Elizabeth Hubbard
Abigal Williams
(Reverse) Billa vera
*John Rucke foreman in the name of the Rest

of the Grand Jurie

(Reverse) Bills ag't Bishop No (1)

(*Peabody Essex Museum, Salem, MA*)

Document 39   (Indictment v. Bridget Bishop, No. 2)

Anno Regni Regis et Reginae Willim et
  Mariae nunc Angliae &c Quarto
  Essex Ss

The Jurors for our Sovereigne Lord & Lady the King & Queen pr'sent that Bridgett Bishop als Olliver the wife of Edward Bishop of Salem in the County of Essex Sawyer—the Nyneteenth day of April in the fourth year of the Reigne of our Sovereigne Lord & Lady William & Mary by the Grace of God of England Scottland France & Ireland King & Queen Defend'rs of the faith &c and Divers other dayes & times as well before as after, certaine Detestable Arts Called Witchcrafts & Sorceries. wickedly and felloniously hath used Practised & Exercised at and within the Towneship of Salem in the County of Essex afores'd in upon and ag't one Abigail Williams of Salem Village in the County of Essex afores'd singlewoman.. by which said wicked Arts the said Abigail Williams the Nyneteenth Day of April afores'd in the fourth Year aboves'd and divers other Dayes and times as well before as after, was, and is tortured Afflicted Pined Consumed wasted & tormented ag't the Peace of our Said Sovereigne Lord & Lady the King & Queen and ag't the forme of the Statute in that Case made and Provided

Wittnesses
Abigail Williams
Mr Sam'll paris sworne
Nathan'll Ingersoll sworne
Thomas puttnam sworne
Mercy Lewis
Ann Puttnam Jun'r Sworne
Mary Walcott sworne
Elizabeth Hubbard sworne
Jno Bligh & Rebecka
his wife sworn
Samuel Shattock and Sarah his
wife sworne
William Bligh sworne
William Stacey sworne
John Loader sworne
(Reverse) Billa vera *John Ruck foreman in the name of the Rest
(2)

(*Peabody Essex Museum, Salem, MA*)

Document 40   (Indictment v. Bridget Bishop, No. 3)

Anno Regni Regis et Reginae Willim et
    Mariae nunc Angliae &c Quarto
    Essex Ss
    The Jurors for our Sovereigne Lord & Lady the King & Queen pr'sent that
Bridgett Bishop als Olliver the wife of Edward Bishop of Salem in the County
of Essex Sawyer—the Nyneteenth Day of April—in the fourth year of the
Reigne of our Sovereigne Lord & Lady William & Mary by the Grace of God
of England Scottland France & Ireland King and Queen Defend'rs of the faith
&c and Divers other Dayes & times as well before as after, certaine Detestable Arts, called Witchcraft & Sorceries, Wickedly and feloniously hath used
Practised & Exercised, at and within the Towneship of Salem in the County
of Essex afores'd in an upon and ag't one Elizabeth Hubbard of Salem Village in the County afores'd singlewoman—by which said wicked arts the
said Elizabeth Hubbard the s'd Nyneteenth Day of April—in the fourth year
aboves'd and divers other dayes, and times as well before as after was & is
hurt tortured Afflicted Pine Consumed, wasted, and tormented ag't the
Peace of our s'd Sovereigne Lord & Lady the King and Queen, and ag't the
forme of the Statute in that Case made and Provided.

Wittnesses
Elizabeth Hubbard
Mercy Lewis
Mr Sam'll paris
Nathan'll Ingersoll
Thomas puttnam
Ann puttnam Jun'r
Mary Walcott
Abigail Williams,
(Reverse) Billa vera *John Rucke formane in the name of the Rest
(4)

(*Peabody Essex Museum, Salem, MA*)

Document 41   (Indictment v. Bridget Bishop, No. 4)

Anno Regni Regis et Reginae Willim et
    Mariae nunc Angliae &c Quarto:
    Essex Ss
    The Jurors for our Sovereigne Lord & Lady the King & Queen pr'sent that
Bridgett Bishop als Olliver the wife of Edward Bishop of Salem in the County
of Essex Sawyer the Nyneteenth Day of April—in the fourth year of the

Reigne of our Sovereigne Lord & Lady William & Mary By the Grace of God of England Scottland France & Ireland King & Queen Defend'rs of the faith &c and divers other Dayes & times as well before as after.certaine Detestable Artes called Witchcraft & Sorceries, Wickedly and felloniously hath used Practised & Excercised at and within the Towneship of Salem, afores'd in upon ag't one Ann puttnam of Salem Village in the County afores'd single-woman by which said wicked arts the said Ann puttnam the s'd Nyneteenth Day of April in the fourth Year aboves'd and divers other Dayes & times as well before as after was & is hurt, tortured. Afflicted Pined Consumed wasted & Tormented ag't the Peace of our said Sovereigne Lord & Lady the King and Queen and against the forme of the Statute in that Case made & Provided

Wittnesses
Ann Puttnam Jun'r
Mr Sam'll paris
Nathan'll Ingersoll
Thomas puttnam
Mercy Lewis
Mary Walcott
Abigail Williams
Elizabeth Hubbard
(Reverse) Billa vera *John Rucke foreman in the name of the Rest
(Reverse) (5) Bills ag't Brid't Bishop alias Olliver Found by the Grand Inquest Folio 966

(*Peabody Essex Museum, Salem, MA*)

LETTERS

Letters were customarily and regularly sent by royal governors to report on developments in their respective colonies to the King's Privy Council in London, England. Sir William Phips was a newly appointed colonial governor with a unique problem, a colony in crisis resulting from an outbreak of witchcraft. His official letters attempt to explain to the members of the Privy Council the essential nature of the problem and seek official advice as to how best to proceed.

Document 42   Two Letters of Governor William Phips (1692–1693)
(Letter No. 1)

When I first arrived I found this Province miserably harrassed with a most Horrible witchcraft or Possession of Devills which had broke in upon severall Townes, some scores of poor people were taken with preternaturall torments some scalded with brimstone some had pins stuck in their flesh others hurried into the fire and water and some dragged out of their houses and carried over the tops of trees and hills for many Miles together; it hath been represented to mee much like that of Sweden about thirty years agoe, and there were many committed to prison upon suspicion of Witchcraft before my arrivall. The loud cries and clamours of the friends of the afflicted people with the advice of the Deputy Governor and many others prevailed with mee to give a Commission of Oyer and Terminer for discovering what witchcraft might be at the bottome or whether it were not a possession. The chief Judge in this Commission was the Deputy Governour and the rest were persons of the best prudence and figure that could then be pitched upon. When the Court came to sitt at Salem in the County of Essex they convicted more than twenty persons of being guilty of witchcraft, some of the convicted were such as confessed their Guilt, the Court as I understand began their proceedings with the accusations of the afflicted and then went upon other humane evidences to strengthen that. I was almost the whole time of the proceeding abroad in the service of Their Majesties in the Eastern part of the County and depended upon the Judgment of the Court as to a right method of proceeding in cases of Witchcraft but when I came home I found many persons in a strange ferment of dissatisfaction which was increased by some hott Spiritts that blew up the flame, but on enquiring into the matter I found that the Devill had taken upon him the name and shape of severall persons who were doubtless inocent and to my certain knowledge of good reputation for which cause I have now forbidden the committing of any more that shall be accused without unavoydable necessity, and those that have been committed I would shelter from any Proceedings against them wherein there may be the least suspition of any wrong to be done unto the Innocent. I would also wait for any particular directions or commands if their Majesties please to give mee any for the fuller ordering this perplexed affair. I have also put a stop to the printing of any discourses one way or other, that may increase the needless disputes of people upon this occasion, because I saw a likelyhood of kindling an inextinguishable flame if I should admitt any publique and open Contests and I have grieved to see that some who should have done their Majesties and this Province better service have so far taken Councill of Passion as to desire the precipitancy of these matters, these things have been improved by some to give me many interuptions in their Majesties service and in truth none of my vexations have been greater than this, than that their majesties service has been hereby unhappily clogged, and the Persons who have made soe ill improvement of these matters here are seeking to turne it all upon mee, but I hereby declare that as soon as I came from fighting against their Majesties Enemyes and understood what danger some of their innocent subjects might be exposed to, if the evidence of the afflicted persons only did prevaile either to the committing or trying any of them, I did before any application was made unto me about it put a stop to the proceedings of the Court and they are now stopt till their Majesties pleasure be known. Sir I beg pardon for giving you all this trouble, the reason is because I know my enemies are seeking to turn it all upon me and I take this liberty because I depend upon your friendship, and desire you will please to give a true understanding of the matter if any thing of this kind be urged or made use of against mee. Because the justnesse of my proceeding herein will bee a sufficient defence. Sir

I am with all imaginable respect Your most humble Servt

*William Phips.

Dated at Boston the 12'th of october 1692.

Mem'dm

That my Lord President be pleased to acquaint his Ma'ty in Councill with the account received from New England from Sir Wm. Phips the Governor there touching Proceedings against severall persons for Witchcraft as appears by the Governor's letter concerning those matters.

(George Lincoln Burr, ed., *Narratives of the Witchcraft Cases, 1648–1706* [New York, Charles Scribner's Sons, 1914], 196–198. The letter was addressed to William Blathwayt, clerk of the Privy Council, and it is he who added the memorandum.)

Document 43   (Letter No. 2)

Boston in New England Febry 21st, 1692/3.

May it please yor. Lordshp.

By the Capn. of the Samuell and Henry I gave an account that att my arrival here I found the Prisons full of people committed upon suspition of witchcraft and that continuall complaints were made to me that many persons were grievously tormented by witches and that they cryed out upon severall persons by name, as the cause of their torments. The number of these complaints increasing every day, by advice of the Lieut Govr. and the Councill I gave a Commission of Oyer and Terminer to try the suspected witches and at that time the generality of the people represented to me as reall witchcraft and gave very strange instances of the same. The first in Commission was the Lieut. Govr. and the rest persons of the best prudence and figure that could then be pitched upon and I depended upon the Court for a right method of proceeding in cases of witchcraft. At that time I went to command the army at the Eastern part of the Province, for the French and Indians had made an attack upon some of our Fronteer Towns. I continued there for some time but when I returned I found people much disatisfied at the proceedings of the Court, for about Twenty persons were condemned and executed of which number some were thought by many persons to be innocent. The Court still proceeded in the same method of trying them, which was by the evidence of the afflicted persons who when they were brought into the Court as soon as the suspected witches looked upon them instantly fell to the ground in strange agonies and grievous torments, but when touched by them upon the arme or some other part of their flesh they immediately revived and came to themselves, upon [which] they made oath

that the Prisoner at the Bar did afflict them and that they saw their shape or
spectre come from their bodies which put them to such paines and torments:
When I enquired into the matter I was enformed by the Judges that they
begun with this, but had humane testimony against such as were condemned
and undoubted proof of their being witches, but at length I found that the
Devill did take upon him the shape of Innocent persons and some were
accused of whose innocency I was well assured and many considerable persons of unblameable life and conversation were cried out upon as witches
and wizards. The Deputy Govr. notwithstanding persisted vigorously in the
same method, to the great disatisfaction and disturbance of the people, untill
I put an end to the Court and stopped the proceedings, which I did because
I saw many innocent persons might otherwise perish and at that time I
thought it my duty to give an account thereof that their Ma'ties pleasure
might be signifyed, hoping that for the better ordering thereof the Judges
learned in the law in England might give such rules and directions as have
been practized in England for proceedings in so difficult and so nice a point;
When I put an end to the Court there ware at least fifty persons in prison in
great misery by reason of the extream cold and their poverty, most of them
having only spectre evidence against them, and their mittimusses being
defective, I caused some of them to be lett out upon bayle and put the Judges
upon considering of a way to reliefe others and prevent them from perishing
in prison, upon which some of them were convinced and acknowledged that
their former proceedings were too violent and not grounded upon a right
foundation but that if they might sit againe, they would proceed after
another method, and whereas Mr. Increase Mather and severall other
Divines did give it as their Judgment that the Devill might afflict in the shape
of an innocent person and that the look and touch of the suspected persons
was not sufficient proofe against them, these things had not the same stress
layd upon them as before, and upon this consideration I permitted a spetiall
Superior Court to be held at Salem in the County of Essex on the third day
of January, the Lieut Govr. being Chief Judge. Their method of proceeding
being altered, all that were brought to tryall to the number of fifty two, were
cleared saving three, and I was enformed by the Kings Attorny Generall that
some of the cleared and the condemned were under the same circumstances
or that there was the same reason to clear the three condemned as the rest
according to his Judgment. The Deputy Govr. signed a Warrant for their
speedy execution and also of five others who were condemned at the former
Court of Oyer and terminer, but considering how the matter had been managed I sent a reprieve whereby the execucion was stopped untill their Maj.
pleasure be signified and declared. The Lieut. Gov. upon this occasion was
inraged and filled with passionate anger and refused to sitt upon the bench
in a Superior Court then held at Charles Towne, and indeed hath from the
beginning hurried on these matters with great precipitancy and by his warrant hath caused the estates, goods and chattles of the executed to be seized
and disposed of without my knowledge or consent. The stop put to the first
method of proceedings hath dissipated the blak cloud that threatened this
Province with destruccion; for whereas this delusion of the Devill did spread
and its dismall effects touched the lives and estates of many of their Ma'ties

Subjects and the reputation of some of the principall persons here, and indeed unhappily clogged and interrupted their Ma'ties affaires which hath been a great vexation to me, I have no new complaints but peoples minds before divided and distracted by differing opinions concerning this matter are now well composed.

I am Yor. Lordships most faithfull humble Servant
*William Phips
To the Rt. Honble
The Earle of Nottingham att Whitehall London
R[i. e., received] May 24, 93 abt. Witches

(*George L. Burr, ed.*, Narratives of the Witchcraft Cases, *pp. 198–202.*)

PETITIONS

Petitions were formal requests made to the court, executive body, or official asking for an order, ruling, or determination on a particular matter of concern. Several petitions were produced during the Salem witchcraft episode. The most famous was the request to the Court to order the acquittal and release of Rebecca Nurse signed and submitted by twenty neighbors in the Salem Village community. Petitions are not meant to override the formal decision of the Court, but to appeal to the Court's sense of justice to address a matter of special concern to the petitioner.

Document 44   (Petition of Mary Eastey)

The humbl petition of mary Eastick unto his Excellencyes S'r W'm Phipps to the honour'd Judge and Bench now Sitting In Judicature in Salem and the Reverend ministers humbly sheweth

That whereas your poor and humble Petition being condemned to die Doe humbly begg of you to take it into your Judicious and pious considerations that your Poor and humble petitioner knowing my own Innocencye Blised be the Lord for it and seeing plainly the wiles and subtility of my accusers by my Selfe can not but Judg charitably of others that are going the same way of my selfe if the Lord stepps not mightily in i was confined a whole month upon the same account that I am condemed now for and then cleared by the afflicted persons as some of your honours know and in two dayes time I was cryed out upon by them and have been confined and now am condemned to die the Lord above knows my Innocencye then and Likewise does now as att the great day will be known to men and Angells—I Petition to your honours not for my own life for I know I must die and my appointed time is sett but the Lord he knowes it is that if it be possible no more Innocentt blood may be shed which undoubtidly cannot be Avoydd In the way and course you goe in I question not but your honours does to the uttmost of your Powers in the discovery and detecting of witchcraft and witches and would not be gulty of Innocent blood for the world but by my own Innocencye I know you are in the wrong way the Lord in his infinite mercye direct you in this great work if it be his blessed will that no more Innocent blood be shed I would humbly begg of you that your honors would be plesed to examine theis Aflicted Persons strictly and keepe them apart some time and Likewise to try some of these confesing wichis I being confident there is severall of them has belyed themselves and others as will appeare if not in this wor[l]d I am sure in the world to come whither I am now agoing and I Question not but youle see an alteration of thes things they say my selfe and others having made a League with the Divel we cannot confesse I know and the Lord knowes as will shortly appeare they belye me and so I Question not but they doe others the Lord above who is the Searcher of all hearts knowes that as I shall answer it att the Tribunall seat that I know not the least thinge of witchcraft therfore I cannot I dare not belye my own soule I beg your honers not to deny this my humble petition from a poor dy ing Innocent person and I Question not but the Lord will give a blesing to yor endevers

(Reverse) To his Excellencye S'r W'm Phipps: Govern'r and to the honoured Judge and Magistrates now setting in Judicature in Salem.
(Reverse) Mary Easty Petition

(Essex County Court Archives, Salem Witchcraft Papers. Vol. 1, p. 127)

Document 45   (Petition of Abigail Faulkner)

The humblee Petition of Abigall: Falkner unto his Excellencye S'r W'm Phipps knight and Govern'r of their Majestyes Dominions in America: humbly sheweth

That your poor and humble Petitioner having been this four monthes in Salem Prison and condemned to die having had no other evidences against me but the Spectre Evidences and the Confessors w'ch Confessors have lately since I was condemned owned to my selfe and others and doe still own that they wronged me and what they had said against me was false: and that they would not that I should have been put to death for a thousand worldes for they never should have enjoyed themselves againe in this world; w'ch undoubtedly I shouled have been put to death had it not pleased the Lord I had been with child. Thankes be to the Lord I know my selfe altogether Innocent & Ignorant of the crime of witchcraft w'ch is layd to my charge: as will appeare at the great day of Judgment (May it please yo'r Excellencye) my husband about five yeares a goe was taken w'th fitts w'ch did very much impaire his memory and understanding but w'th the blessing of the Lord upon my Endeavors did recover of them againe but now through greife and sorrow they are returned to him againe as bad as Ever they were: I having six children and having little or nothing to subsist on being in a manner without a head to doe any thinge for my selfe or them and being closely confined can see no otherwayes but we shall all perish Therfore may it please your Excellencye your poor and humble petition'r doe humbly begge and Implore of yo'r Excellencye to take it into yo'r pious and Judicious consideration that some speedy Course may be taken w'th me for my releasement that I and my children perish not through meanes of my close confinement here w'ch undoubtedly we shall if the Lord does not mightily prevent and yo'r poor petitioner shall for ever pray for your health and happinesse in this life and eternall felicity in the world to come so prayes

Your poor afflicted humble sevants Petition'r
Abigall: Falkner
from
Salem Prison
Decem
the 3d: 1692
(Reverse) These:
To his Excellencye
S'r W'm Phipps knight and Govern'r of their Majestyes Dominions in America
p-sent

(Thomas J. Madigan Collection; Manuscripts and Archives Division; The New York Public Library; Astor, Lenox, and Tilden Foundations)

Document 46   (Petition of Rebecca Nurse to the Court)

To: To the Honour'd Court of Oryr and Terminer now Sitting In Salem, this 28 of June An'o 1692

The humble petission of Rebecca Nurse of Salem Village Humbley Sheweth

That whareas sum Women did sarch your Petissioner At salem, as I did then Conceive for Sum Supernaturall Marke, and then one of the s'd women which is known to be, the Moaste Antient Skillfull prudent person of them all as to Any such Concernd: Did Express hirselfe to be: of A contrary opinion from the Rest And Did then Declare, that shee saw nothing In or Aboute yo'r Honors poare pettissioner but what Might Arise from A naturall Cause: And I then Rendered the said persons asuficient knowne Reason as to My selfe of the Moveing Cause thereof: which was by Exceeding weaknesses: decending partly from an overture of Nature and difficult Exigences that hath Befallen me In the times of my Travells: And therefore Yo'r pettissioner Humbley prayes That you Honours would be pleased to Admitt of sum other women to Enquire Into this Great: Concerne, those that are Moast Grand wise and Skillfull: Namely Ms: Higginson sen'r Ms Buckstone: Ms: Woodbery two of them being Midwives: Ms: Porter Together with such others, as may be Choasen, on that Account: Before I am Brought to my triall: All which I hoape yo'r Honours: will take Into yo'r prudent Consideration, And find it requisite soe to doe: for my Lyfe Lyes Now In yo'r Hands under God: And Being Conscious of My owne Innocency—I Humbley Begg that I may have Liberty to Manifest it to the would partly by the Meanes Abovesaid. And yo'r Poare pettissioner shall Evermore pray as In duty Bound &c//

Rebecca Nurse
hir marke

(*Peabody Essex Museum, Salem, MA*)

PHYSICAL EXAMINATIONS

Accused female witches were frequently physically examined by a court-appointed committee of women. Male victims would be examined by men. The purpose of these examinations was to discover the presence of possible witch's unnatural marks or teats on the body of the suspected witch. There was a traditional belief held that witches were provided with a demonic imp or "familiar" by Satan. Such supernatural beings were thought to sustain themselves by sucking blood from the body of the witch to whom it was assigned. The following are reports of examinations made upon suspected witches in search of such suspicious marks.

Document 47 **(Physical Examination of Bridget Bishop, Rebecca Nurse, Elizabeth Proctor, Alice Parker, Susannah Martin, and Sarah Good, No. 1)**

1692 Salem June 2'd aboute 10 in Morning
  Wee whose names are under written being Comanded by Capt George Corwine Esq'r Sherriffe of the County of Essex this 2'd day of June 1692 for to vew the bodyes of

Bridgett Bishop alias Oliver
Rebecah Nurse
Elizabeth procter
Alice parker
Susanna Martine
  Sara Good
  The first three, Namely: Bishop: Nurse: procter, by dilligent search have discovered apreternathurall Excresence of flesh between the pudendum and Anus much like to Tetts & not usuall in women & much unlike to the other three that hath been searched by us & that they were in all the three women neer the same place

*J Barton Chyrurgen
Alice

pickering
her marke
Jane
Woolings
her marke
Marjery
Williams
her marke
Anna
Stephens
her marke
Elizabeth
Hill
her marke
Elanor
Henderson
her marke
Rebecah
Sharpe
her marke
Lydia Pickman
*Hannah
Kezer
Sworne in Court June 2'd 1692

*Attest * Step: Sewall Cle*

Document 48   (Physical Examination, No. 2)

(Reverse) Salem aboute 4 afternoon June 2'd 1692 .

We whose names are Subscribed to the w'th in mentioned, upon a second search about 3 or 4 houres distance, did find the said Brigett Bishop alias Oliver, in a clear & free state from any p'eternaturall Excresence, as formerly seen by us alsoe Rebecah Nurse in stead of that Excresence w'thin Mentioned it appears only as a dry skin without sense, & as for Elizabeth procter which Excresence like a tett red & fresh, not any thing appears, but only a proper [procedeulia Ani,] & as for Susanna Martine whose breast in the Morning search appeared to us very full; the Nibbs fresh & starting, now at this searching all lancke & pendant which is all at pr'sent from the w'th in Memtioned subscribers and that that piece of flesh of Goodwife Nursess' formerly seen is gone & only a dry skin nearer to the anus in another place

Rebecah
Sharpe
marke
the marke of

Elizabeth Hill
Lidia
pickman
Elanor
Henderson
her marke
*J Barton Chyrurgen
Alice
pickring
marke
*Hannah Kezer
Marjery
Williams
marke
Anna
Stephens
Jane
Wollings
marke
Sworne in Court June 2'd 1692
(Reverse) Jury of Womens Return

(Essex County Court Archives, Salem Witchcraft Papers. Vol. 1, p. 35)

Document 49   (Physical Examinations of George Burroughs and George Jacobs, Jr.)

Wee whoes names are under written having r'ceived an order from the sreife for to search the bodyes of George Burroughs and George Jacobs. wee find nothing upon the body of the above sayd burroughs but w't is naturall: but upon the body of George Jacobs wee find 3. tetts w'ch according to the best of our Judgements wee think is not naturall for wee run a pinn through 2 of them and he was not sinceible of it: one of them being within his mouth upon the Inside of his right shoulder balde an a 3'rd upon his right hipp

Ed. Weld swone
Will Gill sworne
Tom flint Jurat
Tom West sworne
Zeb Hill Jurat
Sam Morgan sworne
John Bare Jurat.
(Reverse) Jury men Return about Jacobs & Burroughs

(Essex County Court Archives, Salem Witchcraft Papers. Vol. 2, p. 10)

RECOGNIZANCE

A note of recognizance is essentially a note of acknowledged state of indebtedness posted by the accused person or members of his/her family guaranteeing their attendance at a future court date. If the accused fulfills the demand of the court and attends their hearing date, the note of indebtedness is cancelled. If the accused fails to attend their hearing, the note becomes due and the required amount of land or money is collected by the court. It was a means of guaranteeing an accused person's cooperation with the court.

Document 50   **(Recognizance for Mary Bridges, Sr.)**

Memorandum
   That on the Twelfth Day of January 1692 In the fourth year of the Reigne of o'r Soveraigne Lord and Lady William and Mary by the Grace of God of England &c King and Queen Defenders of the faith &c Personally appeared before William Stoughton Esq'r Chief Justice of their Maj'ties Province of the Massachusets Bay in New England Jno Bridges of Andover in the County of Essex Blacksmith and Jno Osgood of the same Towne Husbandman and acknowledged themselves to be joyntly and Severally Indebted unto o'r said Soveraigne Lord and Lady and the Survivor of them Their Heires and Successors in the Sume of One hundred pounds to be levied on their or Either of their Lands and Tenem'ts Goods and Chatles for the use of our said Soverainge Lord and Lady the King and Queen or Survivor of them On Condition that Mary Bridges haveing Stood Comitted for Suspition of Witchcraft shall make her personall apperance Before the Justices of o'r s'd Lord and Lady the King and Queen at the next Court of Assizes and Gen'll Goal Delivery to be held for the County of Essex Then & There to answer to all such matters and things as shall in their Maj'ties Behalfe be aledged against her and to doe and receive that w'ch by the said Court shall be then and there enjoyned her and thence not to depart without lycence

Attest.
*Jon Elatson Cler
(Reverse) Recognizance of John Bridges & John Osgood for Mary Bridges May 10th Apears

(*Mass. Archives Vol. 135*)

SUMMONS

A summons is a statement issued by a court requiring the accused to appear before the court to answer questions relating to a charge against them or another person.

Document 51   (Summons for Mary Towne and Rebecca Towne)

W'm & Mary by the Grace of God of England Scotland france & Ireland King & Queen defend'rs of the faith

To Mary Towne widow & Rebecka Towne her Daughter

Greeting.

Wee Comand you all Excuses Set apart to be & appear at the Court of Oyer & Terminer holden at Salem to morrow morning at Eight of the Clock precisely there to Testify the truth to the best of your knowledge on Sever'll Indictments Exhibited against Mary Easty hereof fail not at your utmost perill

Dated in Salem Sep'r. 8th. 1692 & in the fourth yeare of Our Reign

Stephen Sewall Cler

To the Constable of Topsfield hereof Make return fail not

(Reverse) I have Warned the Widow town and hare dauter to apere at the corte.acording to time spoken of in the warant as atested.

by me *Ephraim Wildes*

contabl of Topsfeld

(Essex County Court Archives, Salem Witchcraft Papers. Vol. 1, p. 123)

VERDICTS

A verdict is a concluding statement issued by a court concerning the guilt or innocence of an accused person. If the verdict is guilty, it also usually includes the approved penalty or punishment to be suffered by the accused. If the verdict is not guilty, no further statement is required.

Document 52   (Verdict and Death Sentence v. Abigail Faulkner)

Att a Court of Oyer and Terminer

holden att Salem by adjournment

Septem'r: 1692—

Abigall Faulkner of Andover Indeated and arraigned for the Crime of fellony by Witchcraft Comited on the bodyes of Martha Sprague Evidences being Called and sworne in open Court Matter of fact Comitted the Jury

The Jury find Abigall Faulkner wife of Francis Faulkner of Andover guilty of the fellony by Witchcraft Comited on the body of Marthah Sprague allsoe on the body of Sarrah Phelps—

Sentence of Death pased on Abigall Faulkner

Copia Vera

(Mass. Archives, Vol. 135, No. 49)

Glossary

afflicted children—a group of females ranging in age from nine to thirty-six who were regularly involved in providing testimony and accusations against individuals for acts of witchcraft allegedly directed against themselves. Beginning with the daughter of Reverend Samuel Parris, Betty Parris (9), and her cousin, Abigail Williams (12), the group ultimately included Ann Putnam, Jr. (12), Ann Putnam, Sr., Elizabeth Hubbard (18), Mary Warren (17), Mercy Lewis (19), Mary Walcott (16), Sarah Bibber (36), Elizabeth Booth (16), Elizabeth Churchill (20), and Susannah Sheldon (18).

amnesty (or manumission)—the general liberation of prisoners without charge or penalty from imprisonment. During the Salem episode, Governor William Phips declared a general amnesty in May 1693, allowing all those still in jail to go free pending the payment of the cost of their room and board to their jailer.

Court of Oyer and Terminer—A specialized court established by a commission to investigate and render a judgment on serious criminal cases such as treason and felonies; from the Anglo-Norman: "to hear and determine." Such courts were permitted to travel to a particular district or county, as needed, to conduct trials that otherwise would be handled by Quarterly Courts or Courts of Assizes. Courts of Oyer and Terminer were allowed the authority to confine alleged criminals in a jail and, if necessary, authorize executions for those found guilty of capital crimes. In the Salem episode, Governor William Phips established a Court of Oyer and Terminer in May 1692 to handle the growing backlog of witchcraft cases then pending. This special court included Deputy Governor William Stoughton and Chief Justice and Associate Justices: Captain Samuel Sewell, William Sargent, Wait Winthrop, Bartholomew Gedney, John Richards, Major Nathaniel Saltonstall, and (upon Saltonstall's resignation) Jonathan Corwin. (Leo Bonfanti, *The Witchcraft Hysteria of 1692*, Vol. 1).

coven—a group or gathering of witches who are associated and work together in the casting of spells and for mutual support.

covenant—a mutual agreement or promise between two or more persons. In Puritan congregations all members were required to agree to a covenant mutually binding themselves together as a body of believers to further the work of Christ and his church and to follow the principles of the Christian faith and Calvinist doctrine.

crying out against—a public accusation of a crime usually made by the victim against the accused during a pre-trial examination as a part of the evidence-gathering process. Such public statements were customarily written down in a formal deposition against the alleged perpetrator of the crime and used as justification for their arrest and trial.

deposition—a formal statement under oath and submitted in writing to the court testifying to the witness of a crime, and used as evidence against an accused person.

Devil's Book—the superstitious counterpart to the biblical *Book of Life* which, according to the book of Revelations, holds the names of all Christian believers. In the Salem episode, numerous testimonies were given by afflicted persons that they had been tempted by alleged witches to sign the *Devil's Book*—an act which would confirm their pact with Satan to serve him and give to him their soul. This tradition often requires that such a signature be made in the blood of the newly converted witch.

familiar or familiar spirit—an imp or demonic being assigned by Satan to serve as an intermediary and assistant to a witch. Familiars are frequently mentioned in Salem witchcraft testimony and described in considerable detail sometimes bearing both human and animal characteristics. Familiars were expected to be sustained by feeding off the blood of the witch to whom it was assigned by means of sucking at a "witch's mark" or "witch's teat." (See: *witch's mark*.)

"Great Migration"—the migratory movement of Puritans to New England involving over 30,000 people between 1630 and 1640.

maleficarum—the practice of using magic to harm individuals, their health, property, children, or livestock. It was believed that this was the primary way that witches were able to hurt a community, but such acts were not considered their most serious offense. Their real crime was rejecting their faith and embracing Satan in place of God.

poppet—an archaic term meaning small person or doll. When Reverend Cotton Mather visited accused witch Mary Glover in Boston in 1688, she showed him how she made "poppets" to harm her victims. In the Salem episode, testimony was given to the Court by John Bly, Sr. that he and his son had found "several small poppets made of rags and hog bristles" embedded in the cellar wall of Bridget Bishop's house. Traditionally such small images were known to have been used by persons attempting to use magic to harm another by harming a doll made in the victim's likeness.

pre-trial examination—This was the third stage of the procedure used to conduct a trial against persons accused of witchcraft. Following the accusation of a suspected witch, and the issuance of a warrant for that person's arrest, the alleged witch underwent a pre-trial interview or examination. During this, two or more Magistrates of the Court of Oyer and Terminer would ask questions of the accused, and they would examine the collected body of evidence against the alleged witch to determine if likelihood of guilt warranted a hearing before the Grand Jury. If, after a Grand Jury hearing, the subject was formally indicted of the crime of witchcraft, he or she would be tried before the Court of Oyer and Terminer.

Salem Village—a rural, farming area located about two miles northwest of the seaport of Salem Town. It was separated from Salem Town not only by distance but also by several broad rivers, making church attendance in Salem Town a hardship for village residents. It was in Salem Village that Reverend Parris served as pastor from 1689 until his resignation in 1697, and where the Salem witchcraft episode had its start.

specter—the spirit or spiritual likeness of a human being which may be visible to an observer and not visible to others present.

spectral evidence—evidence presented to the Salem Court by witnesses who claimed to see the spiritual likeness of an accused person committing acts of witchcraft. Often this evidence was corroborated by more than one witness, but never confirmed by all those persons in attendance. Spectral evidence was, by 1692, no longer allowed in British courts, but considered admissible under the ruling of Chief Justice William Stoughton. Stoughton allowed spectral evidence to serve as the basis for most convictions, ignoring the advice of the committee of Boston ministers who, in "The Return of Several Boston Ministers," warned against making use of such unreliable proof.

touch test—the superstitious belief that if a victim of witchcraft were touched by the person guilty of afflicting them, their malady would be returned to the offending witch, and normalcy be restored. This practice was followed by the Salem Court, and criticized by several clergy as using magic to discover magic.

warrant—an official document issued by the justice of a court requiring the apprehension and arrest of an accused person. It authorizes the sheriff bearing the warrant to take the alleged criminal into custody, and bring him or her to a place of confinement until a court appearance may be arranged.

water test or swimming test—a test used extensively in England during the Protectorate era whereby an individual is bound hands-to-feet and thrown into a body of water. If the individual floated they were deemed guilty, if they sank, they were declared innocent of witchcraft.

witch or witchcraft—In the seventeenth century, a witch was considered to be any person who willingly and deliberately had made a pact with Satan exchanging their soul for certain supernatural abilities or powers. Such an act was considered a capital offense against the state as well as a heretical act against the Church, and when discovered, was punishable by death in every European nation.

witch's cake—During the Salem episode, Reverend John Hale recorded that "In the latter end of the year 1691, Mr. Samuel Parris ... had also an Indian manservant (John Indian), and his wife [Tituba] who afterwards confessed, that without the knowledge of their master or mistress, they had taken some of the afflicted persons' urine, and mixing it with meal had made a cake, and baked it, to find out the witch, as they said. After this the afflicted persons cried out of the Indian woman, named Tituba. ..." (John Hale, *A Modest Inquiry into the Nature of Witchcraft*, Ch. 2) This practice was suggested to Tituba and John Indian by a neighbor, Mary Sibley, who recommended that the cake be fed to the Parris family dog. It was an old superstitious practice for witch-finding and was angrily interpreted by Reverend Parris as an attempt to "go to the Devil for help against the Devil." Parris's denouncement of this act is recorded in the church records wherein he states clearly that, until the witch's cake was made, no thought of witchcraft or report of afflicting specters had been considered.

witch's mark or witch's teat—As one means of determining possible guilt or innocence, the bodies of alleged witches were carefully searched for "witch's
marks" or "witch's teats." These abnormalities of the skin were thought to be
places where a witch's demonic familiar would suck blood from the body of
their host. If such a mark or abnormality was discovered by the court-
appointed, examining committee of midwives, it would be tested by having a
pin or needle passed through it. This was done to determine if it were a natural imperfection of the skin, or of supernatural origin. If pain were felt or blood
drawn, the mark was assumed to be normal. If otherwise, it was suspected to
be a "witch's mark," and an affidavit to that effect would be provided to the
court by the examiners.

witch's Sabbath (or, Black Sabbath)—a ceremony allegedly observed and described
by some of the afflicted children and several confessed witches, consisting of a
perverse, satanic version of the Christian practice of the sacrament of Holy
Communion.

Annotated Bibliography

PRINT SOURCES

Primary Sources

Calef, Robert. *More Wonders of the Invisible World; also called The Wonders of the Invisible World Displayed in Five Parts*. Printed for Nath. Hillar at the Princess–Arms in Leaden-Hall-Street over against Mary-Ax, and Joseph Collier at the Golden Bible on London Bridge, London, 1700.

Robert Calef, a merchant of seventeenth-century Boston, was also the most outspoken critic of the Salem trials, the actions of the Court of Oyer and Terminer, and especially Reverend Cotton Mather. Even the title of Calef's book is a satirical parody of Mather's well-known, *Wonders of the Invisible World*. The Mathers prevented this book from being printed in Boston, and Calef was compelled to seek a publisher in London. It provides an excellent counterpoint to other more sympathetic contemporary sources.

Hale, Reverend John. *A Modest Inquiry into the Nature of Witchcraft*. Boston, 1702.

Reverend Hale, the pastor of the Beverly congregation, uses this book to explain the genuine fear of witchcraft experienced by the Salem community together with a description of the historic precedents for witchcraft commonly known by the local populace. Far from denying the existence of witchcraft, Hale explains why it poses a threat. His greatest objection to the trials is that the methods of evidence gathering, especially the use of spectral evidence, were ill conceived and misdirected, resulting in a number of innocent deaths.

Hobbes, Thomas. *Leviathan*. Richard Tuck, ed. Cambridge: Cambridge University Press, 1991.

Written by English political philosopher Thomas Hobbes in 1660, this work attempts to describe the means by which a state or commonwealth functions. In the latter chapters of *Leviathan* he deals with spiritual matters and the importance of religion to the political state as a means of ensuring stability and morality. Although incredulous about the reality of witchcraft per se, Hobbes condemns witchcraft because of its inherently anarchistic and antisocial character, advocating that those claiming to be witches should be executed because of the potential threat they pose to the stability of the state.

Kramer, Henrich and Jacob Sprenger. *Malleus Maleficarum*. Translated by Montague Summers. Dover Publications, 1971.

This work was sponsored by the papacy and produced by two German monks who wished to provide all future witch-finders with a basic guide to identifying and condemning witches. It provides historic examples of actual cases of witchcraft, how witches may be correctly identified from those who are innocent, types of evidence which are reliable in witchcraft cases, and how best to proceed when an outbreak of witchcraft occurs in a particular community or region. Puritan religious leaders, such as Reverend Cotton Mather, were well versed in this publication and gave it credence in the process of dealing with the supernatural.

Lawson, Deodat. *A Brief and True Narrative of Some Remarkable Passages Relating to Sundry Persons Afflicted by Witchcraft, at Salem Village Which Happened from the Nineteenth of March to the Fifth of April, 1692*. Boston, 1692.

Reverend Deodat Lawson had formerly served as pastor to the Salem Village congregation. He traveled to Salem Village from Boston in March 1692, and remained there through April observing the activities of the afflicted children and especially the actions of the Putnam family. The result of these observations was this ten-page booklet which provides the reader with a firsthand account describing some of the most unusual activities to take place in the village at the very start of the outbreak of witchcraft.

Mather, Reverend Cotton. *Memorable Providences*. Boston, 1689.

A best-selling book in Boston during the years 1689–90, this provides a firsthand account of Reverend Cotton Mather's experiences in Boston during the previous year dealing with an outbreak of witchcraft involving the children of John Goodwin and an Irish washerwoman, Goody Glover. The behavior of the afflicted Goodwin children is described in detail by Mather and mirrors closely the behavior of the "afflicted children" of Salem Village three years later. Glover finally confesses to witchcraft and demonstrates her magical abilities to Mather in her prison cell, claiming that other witches will carry on her work after she was gone.

Mather, Reverend Cotton. As reprinted in *The Wonders of the Invisible World: Being an Account of the Tryals of Several Witches Lately Executed in New England*. Printed first at Boston in New England and reprinted at London for John Dunton at the Raven in the Poultry, 1693.

Commissioned by Governor Sir William Phips, this volume provides Reverend Cotton Mather's personal assessment of the Salem witchcraft episode. In his writing of the narrative of the trials, Mather was instructed by Phips to provide a text placing the Salem episode in a reasonable light. As a result, the book focuses upon those witchcraft cases which, in Mather's opinion, made the episode appear most rational to the general public both in New England and in old England. This approach was an attempt to make both Mather and the governor appear less controversial and to divert attention away from some of the harsh criticism raised by people like Thomas Brattle and Robert Calef.

The Holy Bible, New King James Version. Nashville, TN: Thomas Nelson Publishers, 1990.

Secondary Sources

Barry, Mary Ann Hester and Gareth Roberts, eds., *Witchcraft in Early Modern Europe: Studies in Culture and Belief*. Cambridge: Cambridge University Press, 1996.

This exhaustively researched academic work provides much evidence of cases of witchcraft during the period from the 1400s to the 1700s drawn from court records across Europe. It underscores the longstanding cultural traditions of European common people whose beliefs in witchcraft extend far back into pre-Christian times, yet prevailed until the early modern era.

Bonfanti, Leo. *The Witchcraft Hysteria of 1692*. Burlington, MA: Pride Publications, 1979, New England Historical Series.

This two-volume series of booklets summarizes the Salem witchcraft episode and provides a selection of primary source materials.

Boyer, Paul and Stephen Nissenbaum, eds. *The Salem Witchcraft Papers: Verbatim Transcripts of the Legal Documents of the Salem Witchcraft Outbreak of 1692*, 3 vols. New York: DaCapo Press, 1977.

The most complete collection of legal documents relating to the Salem witchcraft episode currently available; for persons interested in researching the testimony and court proceedings it is essential reading.

Boyer, Paul and Stephen Nissenbaum. *Salem Possessed: The Social Origins of Witchcraft*. Cambridge: Harvard University Press, 1974.

This excellent study of the demographic details of Salem Village suggests the strong possibility that there was political, religious, and economic motivation underlying the conflict between bitter factions in the village community.

Burr, George Lincoln. *Narratives of the Witchcraft Cases, 1648–1706*. Barnes & Noble, 1914.

This is a collection of many primary source materials drawn from witchcraft cases in Anglo-American history.

Caporeal, Linnda R. "Ergotism: The Satan Loosed in Salem?" *Science*, April 2, 1976.

This controversial article discusses the possibility that ergot mold may have been responsible for producing hallucinogenic and physiological symptoms in the afflicted girls of Salem Village in 1692.

Carlson, Laurie Winn. *A Fever in Salem: A New Interpretation of the New England Witchcraft Trials*. Chicago: Ivan R. Dee, 1999.

This work attempts to attribute the symptoms of the "afflicted children" to encephalitis lethargica, a disease which produces many similar characteristics such as hallucinations, seizures, fever, and sometimes coma. Generally regarded as very controversial, this theory exhibits some serious problems in analysis, but provides an even-handed treatment of the Puritan leadership. It is similar to the ergot mold theory in that it identifies a possible physiological rationale for the Salem episode.

Demos, John Putnam. *Entertaining Satan: Witchcraft and the Culture of Early New England*. London: Oxford University Press, 1982.

Demos attempts to find certain common characteristics among the many episodes of witchcraft accusations that happened in seventeenth-century New England. He focuses upon what types of individuals might be accused, what personality traits were exhibited by victims, and what social circumstances were frequently present in communities beset by witchcraft outbreaks. This book combines an excellent interpretive narrative and biographical details with understandable demographic data.

Godbeer, Richard. *The Devil's Dominion: Magic and Religion in Early New England*. New York, Cambridge University Press, 1992.

Godbeer examines the dichotomy in New England Puritan society: While practices of English folk magic were embraced at the popular level, these were condemned at the theological level from the pulpits of New England's ministers. The Salem episode is mentioned as an example of how certain practices (such as the making of a "witch's cake") were viewed by some Salem Village parishioners as acceptable options to cure the afflicted children, although the same practices were condemned by Reverend Parris. This volume examines what the author calls the tension between the "elite doctrine" and "folk tradition" of early New England culture.

Goss, K. David, Richard Trask, Bryant F. Tolles, Joseph Flibbert, and James McAllister. *Salem: Cornerstones of a Historic City*. Beverly, MA: Commonwealth Editions, 1999.

This compilation of five essays focuses on key themes relating to Salem history: maritime history, the Salem witchcraft trials, Nathaniel Hawthorne, architecture, and industrial history.

Hall, David D. *Witch-Hunting in Seventeenth-Century New England: A Documentary History 1638–1693*. Boston: Northeastern University Press, 1991.

Hall examines all known outbreaks of witchcraft in seventeenth-century New England, other than those at Salem. What distinguishes this work from all others is its attention to primary sources, court records, and verbatim transcripts of testimony from a wide range of trials. Through these documents, the reader receives a vivid picture of seventeenth-century daily life and the role of witchcraft in it.

Hansen, Chadwick. *Witchcraft at Salem*. New York: George Braziller, 1969.

This extraordinary analysis of the Salem witchcraft episode concludes that, while the majority of victims were undoubtedly innocent of any wrongdoing, there is reason to suspect that acts of witchcraft, similar to those performed by practitioners of voodoo, were taking place. Dr. Hansen takes an anthropological approach in explaining how the internalized belief in witchcraft can actually produce the expected results in victims who believe they are cursed.

Hill, Frances. *The Salem Witch Trials Reader*. New York: Da Capo Press, 1984.

This excellent and well-written sourcebook of excerpted primary source materials also contains a chronology of the Salem witchcraft episode. Beginning with the *Malleus Malificarum* (1486) by Jacob Sprenger and Heinrich Kramer and concluding with Arthur Miller's 1996 essay, "Why I Wrote the Crucible," Ms. Hill provides an impressive array of witchcraft trial–related materials, including verbatim transcripts and a selection of essays summarizing interpretations by various historians since the eighteenth century.

Hole, Christina. *A Mirror of Witchcraft*. London: Chatto and Windus, Ltd., 1957.

This is a valuable sourcebook for references to cases involving witchcraft in seventeenth- and eighteenth-century England.

Holmes, Thomas J. ed., *Cotton Mather: A Bibliography of His Works*, 3 vols. Cambridge, MA, 1940.

This is a nearly complete collection of the writings of Reverend Cotton Mather.

Johnson, Claudia Durst and Vernon E. Johnson. *Understanding the Crucible*. Westport, CT: Greenwood Press, 1998.

This student casebook examines Arthur Miller's play, *The Crucible*, and compares Miller's interpretation of the Salem witchcraft trials with the actual event.

Karlsen, Carol F. *The Devil in the Shape of a Woman: Witchcraft in Colonial New England*. New York: W. W. Norton & Co., 1987.

Feminist historian Dr. Carol F. Karlsen analyzes the underlying reasons why certain women in colonial New England were more likely than others to be accused and ultimately convicted of witchcraft. To Karlsen, women in colonial society were categorized into two distinct groups, one that conformed to the expected standards and another that stood at odds with societal expectations. The women of the latter group, identified as "handmaidens of the Devil," could expect to find themselves accused of witchcraft.

Kences, James E. "Some Unexplored Relationships of Essex County Witchcraft to the Indian Wars of 1675 and 1687." Essex Institute Historical Collections (EIHC), July 1984.

This article reflects the theory first suggested in 1984 by Professor James E. Kences that psychological pressure emanating from the frontier wars in Maine had a profound and unsettling impact upon the afflicted children and numerous members of the Salem Village community.

Kors, Alan C. and Edward Peters, eds., *Witchcraft in Europe, 1100–1700: A Documentary History*. Philadelphia: University of PA Press, 1972.

This is an important compilation of information relating to the numerous outbreaks of witchcraft in continental Europe to the end of the seventeenth century.

Levin, David. *What Happened in Salem?* 2nd edition. New York: Harcourt, Bruce and World, Inc., 1960.

In this excellent, though somewhat dated, student orientation of the Salem witchcraft trials Dr. Levin provides a good summary overview of the event combined with a selection of primary source testimonies and depositions from the trials. He follows with the evaluations of contemporary observers Deodat Lawson, Cotton Mather, Increase Mather, and Thomas Brattle. As a point of comparison, Levin concludes with two short stories that deal with the subject of New England witchcraft: Nathaniel Hawthorne's "Young Goodman Brown" and Ester Forbes' "A Mirror for Witches."

Norton, Mary Beth. *In the Devil's Snare: The Salem Witchcraft Crisis of 1692*. New York: Vintage Books, 2002.

Dr. Norton examines the Salem episode in the broader context of Essex County, Massachusetts. She asserts that previous studies have focused on a wide range of issues and possible causes, but have largely ignored the important question: Why was Salem so different from all previous witchcraft outbreaks in New England? Her answer is because of Essex County's proximity to the Maine frontier and the devastating social and psychological impact of the concurrent frontier Indian wars upon the regional population. It is for this reason, she asserts, that the Salem episode had the scope it did—focusing upon the entire community of Essex County, Massachusetts.

Roach, Marilynne K. *The Salem Witchcraft Trials: A Day-by-Day Chronicle of a Community Under Siege*. New York: Cooper Square Press, 2002.

A remarkable and exhaustive compendium of detailed Salem witchcraft trial information arranged chronologically from January 1692 to January 1697, this is the ultimate reliable source for anyone interested in what occurred on a daily basis.

Robinson, Enders A. *The Devil Discovered: Salem Witchcraft, 1692*. New York: Hippocrene Books, 1991.

Dr. Robinson explores the interrelationships between accused and accuser in Salem Village and suggests that the Salem witchcraft episode had its origins in personal animosities and envy between local residents. He goes on to outline how a conspiracy deprived members of the community of their property by means of accusations of witchcraft.

Rosenthal, Bernard. *Salem Story: Reading the Witch Trials of 1692*. Cambridge: Cambridge University Press, 1993.

Dedicated to debunking many of the myths that have sprung up surrounding the Salem witchcraft trials and their participants, Rosenthal is intrigued by questions concerning the need to create an American popular mythology about this event, and why it occupies such a disproportionately large place in our popular culture.

Starkey, Marion. *The Devil in Massachusetts: A Modern Inquiry into the Salem Witch Trials*. New York: Alfred Knopf, 1949.

This is an early and entertaining narrative study of the Salem events of 1692–93. Although lacking in the sophisticated interpretive analysis of some of the more recent works on the subject, Starkey provides the reader with a vivid account of the episode including occasional personal speculation as to the underlying motives of those involved.

Summers, Montague. *The History of Witchcraft and Demonology*. London, England: Kegan Paul, Trench, Trubner & Co. Ltd., 1926.

This work explores the cases and traditions surrounding witchcraft going back into ancient times.

Taylor, John M. *The Witchcraft Delusion in Colonial Connecticut*. New York: The Grafton Press, 1908.

Taylor examines the lesser-known cases of witchcraft which occurred in Hartford, Stamford, and Fairfield, Connecticut, between 1669 and 1693.

Trask, Richard. *"The Devil Hath Been Raised": A Documentary History of the Salem Village Witchcraft Outbreak of March 1692*. Danvers, MA: Yeoman Press, 1997.

Richard Trask, town archivist for Danvers, Massachusetts (Salem Village), has compiled a collection of primary source materials, including depositions, arrest warrants, other legal documents, and letters. These sources, when tied together with an insightful narrative, provide an easy-to-follow chronological overview of the Salem witchcraft outbreak from its inception to its end.

Upham, Charles. *Salem Witchcraft*, Vols. 1 & 2. Boston: Wiggin and Lunt, 1867.

This is one of the best known and most thorough summaries of the events of the trials ever published. Though shallow in analysis and interpretation, the Victorian antiquarian Charles Upham provides the reader with an extensive array of details in a well-written narrative that follows the trials from the beginning to the end of the episode.

Williard, Reverend Samuel. *A Brief Account of a Strange and Unusual Providence of God Befallen to Elizabeth Knapp of Groton* in Samuel A. Green's, *Groton in the Witchcraft Times*. Hartford, 1883.

This is another, somewhat obscure, work which provides information about the lesser known Connecticut witchcraft outbreaks. The story is also handled effectively in the more contemporary, *Witch-Hunting in Seventeenth-Century New England* by David D. Hall.

Woodward, William E., ed. *Records of Salem Witchcraft, Copied from the Original Documents*, 2 vols. Roxbury, MA, 1864.

Although an important compilation of witchcraft trial documents, it has been in large part superseded by Boyer and Nissenbaum's more recent three-volume collection of transcriptions.

NONPRINT SOURCES

Web sites

Sitecolopedia Network. http://salemwitchtrials.com

Developed by Tim Sutter, this site contains a broad selection of information suitable for a novice researcher of the witch trials at Salem.

University of Virginia. http://etext.lib.virginia.edu/salem/witchcraft

Developed by Professor Benjamin Ray of University of Virginia, this site is without a doubt the most comprehensive and detailed electronic source for witch trial document reproductions, texts of trial materials, maps, portraits, and illustrations relating to the event.

Films

Three Sovereigns for Sarah. 1985. Not rated. Running time: 3 hours. Featuring: Vanessa Redgrave, Phillis Thaxter, and Kim Hunter

A made-for-television film produced by Victor Pisano and Night Owl Productions and televised on PBS, it provides the viewer with a very accurate portrayal of the Salem witchcraft episode, and especially focuses on the case of the three Towne sisters, Rebecca Towne Nurse, Mary Towne Eastey, and Sarah Towne Cloyce.

Days of Judgment. 1992. Documentary.

Produced in conjunction with the "Days of Judgment Exhibition" by the Essex Institute (Peabody Essex Museum) for the Salem Witchcraft Trial Tercentenary in 1992, it is the most informative and well-researched program of its kind. Featuring such noted historians of the trials as Stephen Nissenbaum and Richard Godbeer, it provides the most authoritative and accurate interpretation of the episode currently available.

The Crucible. 1996. Directed by Nicholas Hytner, screenplay by Arthur Miller, released and distributed by Twentieth Century Fox Studios, running time: 2 hours, 4 minutes.

This film adaptation of Arthur Miller's classic 1950s play is an excellent screen representation of the author's ideas and remains true to the play's original plotline. It is not, however, an accurate representation of the historical events as they happened in Salem in 1692, and should not be viewed as such.

Index

About the Author

K. DAVID GOSS is Assistant Professor of History at Gordon College, specializing in American history and museum studies. His many published works include *Cornerstones of Salem* (2000) and *Treasures of a Seaport Town* (1998).